Mungo William MacCallum

Studies in Low German and High German Literature

Mungo William MacCallum

Studies in Low German and High German Literature

ISBN/EAN: 9783744771245

Printed in Europe, USA, Canada, Australia, Japan

Cover: Foto ©Andreas Hilbeck / pixelio.de

More available books at **www.hansebooks.com**

STUDIES IN
LOW GERMAN AND HIGH GERMAN
LITERATURE

STUDIES

IN

LOW GERMAN AND HIGH GERMAN

LITERATURE

BY

M. W. MacCALLUM

LONDON

KEGAN PAUL, TRENCH & CO., 1, PATERNOSTER SQUARE

1884

TO THE

MEMORY OF MY FATHER

THIS BOOK

IS DEDICATED.

PREFACE.

THE contents of this volume are on the surface quite miscellaneous and disjointed, and what connection they possess for me is apt to disappear when they are separated from my regular work. Perhaps they may be best described as studies on the outskirts of English Literature : first, in so far as it is English, dealing as they do with kindred or contrasted phenomena abroad ; and, again, in so far as it is Literature, for the second and third essays are almost technical in subject. But as these rambles from my ordinary route have been to me full of pleasure and suggestiveness, perhaps there are others who may find in them something of interest.

I must also say a word on my indebtedness,

which is great, to foreign scholars and critics. Their utterances on the matters that I discuss are little known in this country, and I have not scrupled to make use of them, especially in the case of those whose names I mention at the beginnings of my essays. At the same time my study of the authors generally preceded my perusal of the commentators, and I must be considered responsible for any statements that I make.

My thanks are due to Messrs. Smith and Elder for their permission to reprint the last three essays, which appeared in the *Cornhill Magazine* in the years 1879 and 1880.

ABERYSTWYTH,
December, 1883.

CONTENTS.

		PAGE
FRITZ REUTER	... ...	1
ANGLO-SAXON JOCOSERIA	... ...	56
SOLOMON IN EUROPE	... ...	87
THE THREE CYCLES OF MEDIÆVAL ROMANCE	...	131
THE MINNESONG	... ...	183
THE DON QUIXOTE OF GERMANY	... ...	223
HANS SACHS AND THE MASTERSONG	... ...	249
KLOPSTOCK	... ...	291

STUDIES IN LOW GERMAN AND HIGH GERMAN LITERATURE.

FRITZ REUTER.

[In the "Sämmtliche Werke von Fritz Reuter" are included his more important productions, but none of his dramas and not all of his miscellanies. For the development of Platt Deutsch literature and for Reuter's relations with Groth, the "Quickborn" and "Briefe über Plattdeutsch und Hochdeutsch" of the latter, and the "Abweisung der ungerechten Angriffe" of the former (not reprinted in the collected edition) should be read. Among the chief authorities for Reuter's life are his autobiographic sketches, "Meine Vaterstadt Stavenhagen" and "Ut Mine Festungstid;" his selected letters; and Adolf Wilbrandt's admirable memoir.]

THE present is the halcyon day of poets in dialect. Critics pet them and premiers pension them; and they are patronized even by their dainty brethren of the universities, who, disguising themselves as farmers and cobblers, try to shape their mouths to the rustic shibboleth. This success is due to the freshness of thought and language in the provincial poems. The experiences may be very old and elementary, yet on

B

that very account may interest a rapidly ageing society that has for long seldom heard, but never quite forgotten, the lessons of its childhood. And in the same way the words, belonging for the most part to the oldest vocabulary of the language, though since more or less dropped by our "educated" classes, have, with their strange youth-in-age, the feel and smell of the fresh-turned sod, pleasant enough after the dusty paving-stones of London journals. No doubt the study of philology has had its share in this movement. It has shown that there was a time when the Queen's English did not reign alone, or reign at all, and has pointed out that the patois of London society differs from the many patois of the country only in being somewhat staler and corrupter. The compilers of country glossaries and investigators of local grammar smile, therefore, on the local poet, and he is the rarely fortunate artist who can nowadays boast of the favours of science. Still, though such patronage has helped the growth of dialectical poetry, the origin of its influence and revival is to be sought, as we have seen, in its own nature and its relation with modern life. The simpler interests and experiences of man, if expounded with feeling, appeal to all and are necessary for all; and it is precisely these that are apt to find no utterance from the authorized mouth-pieces of an artificial age. It is characteristic that modern dialectical poetry and modern realistic poetry have almost the same point of departure, viz. the songs of Burns.

The position of this author as first in order both of time and merit among dialectical poets is instructive. *A priori* it would have seemed a hard problem to find access in the literary circles of the eighteenth century for what was considered the vulgar idiom of the rustic. The circumstances of Scotland, however, were altogether exceptional. If now something less than a kingdom, it was still more than a county; and its speech, if no longer a European language, was even less the dialect of a shire. The poet had literary traditions behind him, and around him an audience which, in character and patriotism, was still a nation. He had, therefore, the self-confidence necessary for the first step, and at the same time his art and horizon rather transcended those of the ordinary county bard. Hence the father of dialectic poets, alone among the race, has exercised a European influence, and he alone with one exception has become popular in other countries than his own. That exception is Fritz Reuter.

Now, the reasons for the pre-eminence of Burns return with but little modification to account for the pre-eminence of Reuter, the circumstances of the "Braid Scottis" of last century being strikingly analogous to those of Platt Deutsch in the present day. Both are not properly dialects, but groups of dialects; both in the past had their classical literatures, for "Reineke" is a Platt poem, and the Old Saxon of the "Heliand" may be considered the original of Platt; both, even when they lost an authoritative standard, continued to be spoken as mother speech by thousands of educated families, to whom High German and English were respectively foreign tongues, which had, as such, to be learned at school with grammars. In the Plattlands of to-day, as in the Lowlands of Burns, the idiom of ceremony, of business, and of the Church has come from without, and has to be mastered more or less completely by all the middle classes; but the language of home, of friendship, of master and servant, continues to be their own old Low German in its traditional forms. Of course the differences between Scotch and Platt are also very great. In some respects the latter is even more independent and powerful. Its area, spreading from Königsberg to the confines of Holland, includes an immensely greater population than Scotland; and though the local variations in forms, pronunciations, and even words are very great, these do not interfere with the general intelligibility of any one of its dialects. The Platt writer thus appeals to an even wider audience than Burns. Again the difference between Scotch and

English is between members of the same group; the difference between Platt and High German, in so far quite parallel with the difference of High German and English in the United States, is the difference between separate groups, and hence is much harder and faster than the other and gives more scope for free treatment. Those advantages, however, are more than counterbalanced by other differences. Even if we reckon the Old Saxon poems to the credit of the Platt Deutsch, there had been, for centuries at least, no literature to speak of in any of its dialects, and hence it had no literary tradition. And one reason for this was that there had been, since the days of the great Saxon dukes, no independent Platt Deutsch States of importance. A few Hanse towns, like Hamburg, had always been international, and had latterly sunk into political insignificance. The little free community of Ditmarch had long waged an heroic combat against its encroaching Danish and Holstein neighbours, but in the end it too had succumbed to numbers. Still it is interesting to find that precisely here the new Platt literature had its origin, and some of the Ditmarcher Groth's * stirring songs of the struggles of his

* One or two writers precede him in date, but their efforts were too sporadic or too feeble to fonnd a school. The history of modern Platt literature begins with Groth rather than with Voss, just as the history of the modern English parliament begins with Edward I. rather than with De Montfort.

ancestors breathe a patriotism as of " Scots wha hae."
But he could not get over the want of a literary
tradition. The impulse came to him, not from the
fragments of old local songs, but from Robert Burns,
whose full notes from beyond the sea almost drowned
the last echoes that lingered round Groth's own home.
In this way he stands far behind his original. He is
an imitator and a learned author. His prose theo-
rizings on his Platt Deutsch poems exceed in bulk the
poems themselves, and this is characteristic of the
man and his position. A foreigner must be careful
in his criticisms; but to me it seems that Groth in
his sentiments and measures is hardly more true to
the spirit of the dialect than Tennyson himself. A
local patriot of fine poetical feeling and wide culture,
he learned from the study of Burns that there ought
to be Platt Deutsch lyrics, and he set himself on conscious principles to produce them. But he is thus
rather a poet in Platt Deutsch than a Platt Deutsch
poet. Just as Lessing breaks ground for Goethe, so
he, introducing the popular literature in theory from
above, prepares the way for Reuter, whose stories
pulse direct from the heart of the people. It is quite
what we might expect, that there should at first be
collision between the two. Reuter, crudely natural
in his early works, seemed in Groth's eyes merely to
be degrading the infant art that he had so carefully

tended. " Reuter's muse," he wrote, " is a byre wench." This attack was promptly resented by its object, and Groth's own defects unsparingly exposed; but in the end both men recognized their mutual relations, and learned to regard each other with gratitude and admiration. Reuter fulfilled the purpose that Groth set himself, and, but for Groth, he could not have fulfilled it. It is the completeness of his success that gives his life its climax of interest; for, in view of it, his already romantic career is elevated into the region of principle as the equipment, perhaps the only possible equipment, for his work. " Each nation should be its own exponent, and the exposition should be in its own words;" and this saying, when they are important enough, is equally true of districts. But the difficulty was to find a man with the necessary qualifications of thought and culture, who should not be lost to the people, who should not devote himself to a special calling, or be charmed within the magic circle of High German letters.

There is little in Mecklenburg, the land of his birth, that could have made one prophesy it a literary leadership even in Platt Deutsch. Though the Mecklenburgers have erected a statue to their country, and flatteringly personified it as Megalopolis, in the first place it is not great, and in the second, is not, and scarcely has, a city. Wismar and Rostock were

Hanse towns, but their independence is a forgotten story; and in Rostock University, to which Wallenstein, the fool of astrology, called Keppler, there is now a professor or docent to every three students. A stirring history it no doubt had as battle-ground of Dane, Slave and German, but that history belongs to the past, and never was of immediate concern to Western Europe. For generations it has lain apart, a mine of old usages, a land hedged in, its population nearly stationary, its agricultural commerce passing circuitously through the Baltic, its towns beaten by their western neighbour, Lübeck, its political existence checked by the *enfant terrible* Prussia. The two Mecklenburgs, Schwerin and Strelitz, joined like a two-headed nightingale in legislature, have their heads in the almost absolute grand dukes, who built palaces, neglected the people, and allowed serfdom to continue even in the nineteenth century. Perhaps only two facts about them are familiar to the English reader, but these are typical. The first is that the reigning family is the only one, even in Germany, that belongs directly to an old Slavonic stock, and this shows how little Mecklenburg has latterly been a prey to change. The other is the unspeakable episode of the unspeakable duchess, narrated by Carlyle in his "Frederick the Great," which shows how little the stranger dynasty was affected by German popular opinion.

The want of commerce in Mecklenburg has repelled the commercial traveller, and its want of history has, despite its statues of Blücher and Moltke, guarded it against the sentimental tourist; while its long undulating plains and slopes of cornland, its wastes of heath or sand, its innumerable lakes and patches of woodland have not been sufficient to draw the sight-seer. It has thus been left to its own old fashions and local habits, and these have given it a distinct character that almost compensates for the absence of independent nationality. "Mecklenburg," says Reuter, "is a fair land, and a rich land, and the farmer above all has good reason to be pleased with it." Its real life is agricultural, and though that is concentrated here and there in the villages, and the village life in turn is concentrated in the towns, in winter, before the days of railroads, animation was suspended, and existence was left uneventful and undisturbed. Mecklenburg is the Sleepy Hollow of Europe, and only the trumpets of the Napoleonic wars wakened the sleepers for a time. Its grand dukes were the first to desert the confederation of the Rhine, and its sons bore their share in the expulsion of the foreigner from the fatherland.

It was in these eventful days, in the year 1810, that Fritz Reuter was born in the little town of Stavenhagen. Something he remembered of the disorderly

French retreat in 1813, partly from the vivid impressions of childhood, more perhaps from the recurring stories to which it would give rise. For the honest Stavenhagen citizens had little to interest them beyond those stories in the quiet of the next few years, when little Fritz was growing up to clearer insight and observation. What a picture he has given us of his father-town in its isolation and simplicity! It could be approached only by the two classes of roads, the mended and the unmended, and the latter were the less dangerous. Mid comments and queries, the stray traveller was accompanied by all the juvenile population to his inn, where, while refreshing himself with Dutch cheese, he was appropriated by their elders as a gift direct from heaven. When one of the Stavenhageners was going to travel to Hamburg, he took the sacrament the day before, and paid a round of farewell visits, while the admiring tribute, "There's a man for you!" in his retreating ears, rewarded the daring of his attempt. The only time of bustle was the yearly fair, to Fritz chiefly memorable for its paradise of confectioners' booths. Among these he ranged, a penny in his hand, and his hand in his pocket ("such," he says, "were my aunt's injunctions"), and unsuspicious of invisible steaks and beer, found in the rosy bulk of the chief confectioner an obvious refutation of his father's idea that sweetmeats were unwholesome. "I quite uphold," he confesses, "the opinion of the Mecklenburg peasant, who, when asked at confirmation what were the three chief Christian festivals, answered, 'Christmas, Whitsuntide, and Autumn fair.'" When that was past, the town was thrown back on itself, and on that community of interest which is only possible, or at least only tolerable, in a very small place. Reuter grew up more interested in his neighbour's dinner, at which, if he liked it, he was an imaginary guest, and in street-fights, than in political rumours and European crises. Perhaps the gossip of nations is, after all, not so much more nourishing than that of street corners, at any rate it is not so good a training for the sort of Netherlands painting in which Fritz was to excel. And this mutual concern in other people's business, if it had its lower and garrulous, had also its higher and brotherly side. Reuter's father was mayor of Stavenhagen for forty years, and during that time was unwearied in his efforts to protect and improve the place. In the famine years after the war, his prudence and care averted the danger of destitution, and what industries Stavenhagen possessed were restored and multiplied by his enterprise. From old Reuter, Fritz learned the nobility of forethought, firmness, and principle; but no artistic influence, save perhaps a certain conscientious regard for truth of fact, could work on him from that quarter. From his sickly mother, with her gentle subdued humour, and her love of poetical and religious books, he had his poet's disposition by inheritance, and there were several in his circle to develop it by their unconscious training. Such, for instance, was the Amtshauptmann Wewer who inhabited the castle that overlooked the town, the one romantic feature in the neighbourhood, and whose native overflowing kindliness led him to address every one, even his grim worship the mayor, with the endearing diminutive of " heart's childie." Sometimes, indeed, his benevolence was taken ill, or could barely counterbalance his terrible frankness ; as, for instance, in the delightful episode of the Stavenhagen Masque Ball, in which every one knew and pretended not to know everybody else, and the Herr Amtmann making wilful errors in identity, fully thought he was furthering the general satisfaction, while really he left every one indignant at being mistaken for that particular neighbour,—witness also that other scene with the dancing-master, after which even good-humoured uncle Herse is driven to declare him a " crusty old hedgehog." " My father admitted the adjectives with some modification, but warmly denied the substantive," says Fritz. It was indeed easy to offend uncle Herse's self-importance, but it was not difficult to assuage his wrath.

No one who reads the sketches of this most *un-*typical town councillor, this "genius in embryo," as his assumed nephew calls him, can mistake the influence *he* exercised on Fritz's development. An overgrown child, but a gifted one, who when he became a man did *not* put away childish things, proud of his fine figure and portly person, he has a boy's interest in birds, in gaudy paintings, in local legends; and Fritz turns unsatisfied from his father's "perhaps" and "probably," to have his dreams about the old castle certified and outdone by the unhesitating assent of his uncle. Indeed, Fritz made his first acquaintance with a work of imagination during the private writing-lessons which uncle Herse was so kind as to administer.

The solution of this paradox is simple though unexpected. The amateur pedagogue hit on the ingenious plan of dictating a romance of his own invention, and thus converted the most tedious of school hours into one of breathless suspense. Alas! from the suspense the pupil was never delivered. One among the many excellences of the hero was his capacity of becoming invisible at will, and uncle Herse had tried to check the budding scepticism of his pupil by revealing to him the secret. It was to smoke toadstools. Unhappily Fritz would have had a good flogging had he been caught with a pipe, whatever its contents, so he had to rest satisfied with a scientific experiment *in corpore vili*. In other words, he gave their old man-servant a pipe of what purported to be the mayor's tobacco, and then sat intently watching to see him vanish into thin air. But no disappearance took place; on the contrary, old Friedrich, in alarm for his life, accused Fritz of trying to poison him, and the investigator to clear himself had to tell the whole story. Old Reuter perused the copy-book with strong symptoms of disgust, and from that day uncle Herse gave no more writing-lessons.

Fritz's private lessons were, no doubt, the result of his father's well-grounded distrust of the Stavenhagen schools. Of these there were three; in the first, the severest punishment was the disgrace of the dunce's cap—a disgrace coveted like an order of merit; in the second, all were thrashed indiscriminately, or, as Reuter says, the teacher charged per week a shilling the back; in the third, the flogging was systematic, in three grades, with three rods of increasing thickness. Fritz went to none of these, but was subjected to the apparently more genial discipline of a girls' school. However, "to be the owl among crows," as he says, is unpleasant, and he was often the victim of " these accomplished little Megæras." After this, private lessons were felt to be a deliverance, even when those in geography were administered every evening by

his exacting father, still unwearied by a day of private
and public work. The record of this home instruction
in branches useful and ornamental, respectively patronized and opposed by his father and his aunt; the
list of his numerous improvised teachers, including
a tailor journeyman, a refugee from Cagliostro, a
strolling player, a theological student, and uncle
Herse for painting, is too long for quotation. The
last named might have seduced Fritz to art, but his
father had determined to make a jurist of him. So
his pleasant home lessons end when he is fourteen,
and a year later his home life ends too. In 1824 he
was sent to the gymnasium in Friedland, to study
there three years, and in 1825 he lost the mother he
so tenderly loved. This of itself would make the
time dismal, but here, and even later when he
continued his studies at Parchim, it is easy to see
that he thought the exchange unfortunate from genial
uncle Herse to school pedantry; and he had the extra
discomfort of hating his juridical studies the more,
the better he got to know them. At this stage,
indeed, it·seemed that his father's indomitable will
would only mould Fritz into one of those moderately
successful lawyers who grow everywhere luxuriantly,
and who do *not* have their lives written. Yet already
he had given evidence of literary ability, which we,
who can be wise after the event, find so striking as to

be almost incredible. At the age of twelve he had his first outing in the world, and his father, whom he accompanied, made him write an account of it for his godfather, old Amtmann Wewer. The close observation, fluent style, and, above all, racy humour which Fritz displays in this somewhat forbidding task, would be praised in one half again as old as he. A later excursion to Rügen called forth his first poem— "a very remarkable one," says he, humorously, but it was lost in the tragedy of his life, which was already fast approaching.

For now his father sent him, in his twenty-first year, to Rostock University, in the next stage apparently of an average legal career, really to unknown heights, which, if known, would have filled the youth with more horror than desire, had the depths too been known through which alone they should be gained.

In those reactionary days the aspirations of Germany for unity and freedom were almost confined to her universities, but there they were warm and eager, and the students of the great inter-university Fellowship did much to nurse and spread them. The aims of the Fellowship were poison to the petty princelings, who wished to maintain their authority uncurbed either by a national Government or by the popular voice. After the murder of Kotzebue they succeeded in suppressing its public gatherings, but it never altogether died out, and in 1827 sprang again into activity, nobly if naïvely avowing as its aim "to prepare the way by moral, scientific, and athletic education in the university, for a State ordered in freedom and righteousness, and established in the unity of the people." Could this day-dream at once be realized? No, said the moderate Arminian party in the Fellowship. Yes, answered the more enterprising Germans, who, one need hardly add, had the majority in so youthful a parliament. They carried the resolution, "That every member shall be bound to further their common aims by force, and hence to take part in any popular risings that may be of service." The Polish revolt of 1832, and the general sympathy with the Polish refugees, greatly strengthened the hands of the German faction, who again, for a time, but only for a time, drew back the seceding Arminians; and, after the second schism, carried the most violent motion in their record: "That the general German Fellowship shall strive to promote the unity and freedom of Germany by means of revolution." At this stage, the Governments of the old Bund united to suppress so frank-hearted a band of conspirators.

Fritz Reuter after one semester's initiation at quiet old Rostock, in the mysteries of student debating, student drinking and student fighting, was

C

transplanted to the University of Jena, the centre of the Fellowship and stronghold of the German party. That he, hardy, muscular, inconsiderate, always ready for a row with the constable or a bout with a rival clubsman, should not be drawn to the peaceable Arminians is very intelligible. But it is also clear that he shone more among the humorists than among the statesmen of the association. We know little of his success in debate, but we do know something of his skill in composing comic songs, one of which has survived. Reuter, too, had left the Fellowship before its dissolution, and so must be supposed but slightly tinged even with the harmless red of the youthful enthusiasts. But it soon appeared that neither youth nor innocence, neither good intentions nor high purpose could save Reuter or hundreds more from crimination on the charge of—what? . "Merciful Heaven knows!" answers Reuter, "unless that we wore the German colours in broad day-light, and spoke in whispers what is now shouted in the streets."

For meanwhile, in 1833, when Fritz was quietly enjoying the Easter holidays at his home in remote Stavenhagen, a strange event was taking place in Frankfort-on-the-Main. A handful of peasants, led by a stray student or two, and an occasional revolutionary from abroad, overpowered a few policemen and watch-

men, and paraded the streets inviting the inhabitants
to follow their unknown leadership to an unknown
political Utopia. The citizens naturally refused, but
troops had to be called in, and blows given and taken
before "the rebels were put to flight!" Such
disorders cannot of course be tolerated in any well
regulated State, and the ringleaders merited severe
castigation. But Germany was not a well-regulated
State, and this little scratch roused it to an agony
of terror and vengeance. The Bund established a
Central Board of Investigation, which proceeded to the
insanest frenzy of persecution, with the insanest arts
of inquisition and chicane. On account of the partici-
pation of a few university men, and the theoretical
revolutionism of the Fellowship, more than a thousand
students, many of them members of merely literary
clubs, were arrested and cross-examined, numbers
were declared accomplices and locked up for pro-
tracted trial and tardy sentence. The proceedings
were almost more infamous and hardly less cruel than
those of our own Bloody Assizes, if we remember that
on that occasion vengeance was exacted from actual
insurgents and their protectors, while on this the
victims were mere political dreamers, of whom few
were desirous and none were capable of endangering
the State by force. Tzchoppe, Kamptz, Kleist, and
Dambach, the four evangelists of the gospel of Judge

Jeffreys, made no allowances, but rather stooped to extort from 'the youths the avowal of their ideals, which they twisted into a confession of high treason. Sentences of imprisonment for half a year, for ten years, for thirty years, for life, fell thick ; and thirty-seven, not the most guilty, were condemned to death. Amongst these was Fritz Reuter.

When the storm broke out, he had waited quietly at home, instead of returning to the university ; but as the fury of prosecution seemed to abate, and the Mecklenburg Government did not even inquire after him, he thought he might safely, without the loss of another semester, continue his studies in Prussia, which had no legal control over him. Incautious in his innocence, he arrived at the end of October, 1833, in Berlin, and on the 31st was seized by the police. His detention was a breach of international law, and the Mecklenburg Government demanded his extradition. No notice was taken of this request in Berlin. On the contrary, Fritz, though he was a foreigner, and not yet found guilty even in the Prussian courts, was treated as a criminal of the worst class. His confinement in the Stadtvogtei was exchanged for the harsher *régime* of the Hausvogtei, where even ink and pens were refused him. He extemporized substitutes for them from a splinter torn out of the floor and a dye made with burnt walnut shells, and with these proceeded to write original Byronic poems, "which," he says, "have happily been lost," and, from memory, a copy of Byron's "Jepthah's Daughter," which is happily extant as a memento of the time.

Meanwhile the case dragged along, for to cruelty and chicane the most shameless procrastination was added. The accused were, indeed, at the mercy of the accusers. They were not so much as allowed to choose their own counsel, and the one appointed to represent Fritz, so far from doing his duty in the case, never troubled to answer his client's letters or to go near him. More than a year had elapsed without any judgment being pronounced, when Fritz was haled across the country, in bitterly cold winter, to a new imprisonment in the Silesian fortress of Silberberg. This, too, was in defiance of his rights; but he was strongly recommended by the Prussian officials, among them Dambach himself, to submit without complaint. "You'll certainly be sent home to Mecklenburg," they said. And, indeed, the demand for his extradition was thrice renewed, but as often refused. And the Prussian Government was as arbitrary in other respects. Two full years—the second and third since his arrest—passed away, and still the court pronounced no judgment on the youth whose life was withering in the shadows of Silberberg. We know little of these two years; but one fact is certain, that his nervous system was undermined and his eyesight ruined by the darkness of the casemates, before ever he was condemned; and one letter has survived that shows how the iron had entered into his soul. It is dated October 31st, exactly three years, therefore, from the time when he lost his liberty. " This day," he tells his father, "has made me unspeakably wretched. It has robbed me of health and happiness and, what is worse, of self-reliance. So I beg you from my heart try once more to have me set free, and then stop wasting your time and powers over a chimera as monstrous and incredible as any in mythology. . . . If this effort fails, let things go as they will. It would not be fair to yourself or my sisters if you were to spend your strength in a hopeless undertaking, which at the best would restore you only the shadow of your former son. A week hence is my birthday, my fourth in prison. I shall think fondly of you and of the many little tokens of love you used to give me as a child. Truly, they were more worth than all the fine promises I used to make you on that day."

It is not often that a young man has to look forward with such weariness and despair to his twenty-sixth birthday, and the tidings of the next few days might well suffice to crush a less exhausted spirit. Now at last he heard that he was sentenced to death, but that his majesty Frederick William III. was graciously pleased to commute his punishment to incarceration in a fortress for thirty years. This was bad enough; but Fritz was not even now delivered from that hope deferred that makes the heart sick. Assurances flowed in from all sides that the king would pardon him, and it was long, very long, before he learned to abandon this heartbreaking illusion. Meanwhile his rapid loss of sight could not be overlooked, and for the sake of what remained he was in February, 1837, transferred from Silberberg to Glogau, a change that introduced some variety into his monotonous existence. To us it is for another reason important. With his arrival in Glogau begin the recorded reminiscences of his imprisonment, in the charming sketch, " My Fortress Time." This is a happy compound of truth and fiction; but fortunately he has enabled us roughly to distinguish the ingredients. " After the lapse of five and twenty years," he writes, " I can regard even this period from its humorous side. But not all its moments can be made bright; some still remain clad in their horrible grey, and, if I have freshened up the bright ones a little with fictitious comedy, the grey ones I have honestly left alone in their gloomy truth."

Over these experiences we must, however, pass lightly, for in outline they are similar, and we have no time to penetrate into the tragi-comic labyrinth of detail. In Glogau his stay was, on the whole, tolerable, for here he had a human governor and gaolers; but it lasted for only six weeks. Then he had the pleasing break in his prison routine of a journey to Magdeburg, whither he was transferred, the good-natured Glogau commandant arranging that he should not reach his destination too soon. Wherever he and his guards put up, two citizens were appointed, as it were, special constables, to sleep in the same room with him, to prevent his flight. They usually, while drinking beer and smoking tobacco at his expense, catechised him as to his reasons for wishing to "kill the king;" and on the whole the population testified its loyalty by calling him names. Occasionally, however, some little kindness was done him that went to his heart. Thus at one inn he sat down to supper with the family of the landlord; at another, his host would have helped him to make off; at a third, a few schoolboys, who were drinking punch in a corner, sent one of their number to invite him to join them, and to confide to him in strict secret that they had formed a branch-fellowship at their school. "So much for Prussian repression! There's not much good in capital punishment or in the deterrent theory," is Reuter's sage remark on this occasion. If this interlude was too pleasant for a criminal guilty of high treason, the balance of justice was soon to be more than readjusted.

Arrived in Magdeburg, Reuter was quartered, not in the Citadel, but in the Inquisitoriat. "That was bad," he says. "However miserable a fortress may be, one has always room for the necessary exercise in the old casemates; now and then one sees another man; and, as a whole, it is not built with the express purpose of tying down the prisoner in all directions: but a prison, with its separate system, deprived us of the little light, air, motion, and sight-seeing that were ours by law. Confinement in a fortress was what we were condemned to; but what did the Prussian State care about that, if it served its turn to confine us in the cells of a gaol!" This bad beginning was fittingly followed up. The governor, Count Hacke, delighted to aggravate the punishment of the "regicides" by gratuitous insult and oppression. They were debarred from all religious services, the food was barely eatable, the water poisonous; even a Government commission reported and censured the almost total want of ventilation, warmth, and light. Fritz had been removed from the Silberberg on account of his eyes, but no direct sunbeam ever penetrated into his Magdeburg cell. And to these great grievances petty vexations were added; as, for example, when Hacke, regardless of their feelings and their moustaches, insisted on his prisoners being shaved twice a week at their own expense. He addressed a note to one of them, " To the Demagogue

✕," who refused the title, and, after an appeal to Government, carried his point so far that Hacke's superscription was in future, "To the Political Criminal ✕." This was felt to be a triumph for all, and with a humour only to be understood in that land of privy councillors and privy officials of all kinds, they debated together whether, since they had committed no overt treasonous act, they should not rather be styled "privy political criminals." It was possible for them to meet and converse only through Reuter's *finesse* and firmness. He defeated Hacke's efforts to enforce solitary confinement by making presents to the gaolers, and then threatening to report their receiving them unless they permitted some mutual visits among the prisoners. By-and-by, by a certain cleverness in sketching, he succeeded in conciliating some of the authorities; and, when the Government commission made its report, the worst of his imprisonment was already behind him. This report, however, and the death of Hacke, who was one of their chief enemies, and sometimes regretted he could not give them hard labour, brought for Reuter and some of his fellows removal to new prisons. On the way he and a friend, whom they nicknamed the "Captain," had to pass through Berlin, and now again had to experience the tender mercies of Dambach. They were lodged in the Hausvogtei, strangely enough in the very room which

Reuter had formerly occupied. All was the same—
the walls with the cracks, the guarded windows, the
planking from which he had torn his splinter. There
was only one change. Then there had been a bed-
stead in the corner, with a straw-sack thrown over it :
now both were away. It was freezing hard that
night, and the room was not at all warmed. Still
there was no help for it. They lay down in their
clothes on the bare boards, threw each his cloak over
him, and shivered the whole night through.

Next morning the inspector appeared, and mock-
ingly asked them how they had slept. Their only
answer was a request that they might have a bed
should they be detained there another night. The
inspector could not say, but would ask the director
Dambach. Meanwhile he told them they were credited with five groschen (sixpence) to spend on their
food for the day. Reuter was horrorstruck, and
urged that they were allowed twenty groschen when
travelling. "The director has restricted you to five,"
was the reply, as the inspector walked off. Next
came the turnkey, asking what they would have. They
were freezing to the bone, rushing up and down the
cell like wild beasts, vainly trying to get warm, so
they asked for two cups of coffee. But this cost four
groschen each, so they could get nothing else but a
penny's worth of bread for the remaining four and

twenty hours. As the evening closed a miserable day, the inspector made his rounds again, and brought with him insults, but no bed. Fritz in vain represented that, besides their allowance, they had both some private money in the care of the gensdarmes who had accompanied them; let a bed be got, then, with part of that. "No," said the inspector, "the director has fixed that you are to save your bed-money from your daily allowance." That was an impossibility, so Reuter demanded to see the director. "The director can't be spoken to at this time of night," was the answer; and the two half-famished wretches had to lie down on the boards again to freeze a second night.

The next morning the same thing happened again— a cup of coffee and a penny's-worth of bread had to last them the whole day. Fritz again demanded to see the director, whose official duty it was to hear complaints. Once for all, was the reply, the director *would not* speak to them. They sent him a note, which remained unanswered, and the third night and the third morning brought round again the same rotation of miseries.. The third day a new one was added. The Captain became ill. He would rush backwards and forwards, restless and hurried, seize the Bible which had shamelessly been left them, the only furniture in their room, read a few lines, throw it away, and pick it up again. "Let the book lie,

Captain," cried Reuter at last. "Don't make yourself an accomplice of the blasphemers who wantonly bring us to despair and then offer to console us with God's Word." He rattled at the door till it was opened, and asked one of the porters, "How long must we remain here?" The man knew they were to be removed the next day, but he answered, with a drawling laugh, "You wait here always. Do you think the King will let all these fine buildings stand empty? No, you are always to stay here, and your friends will join you." "Three days such as we had had don't screw up one's courage, and I won't deny that this news completely overcame me. I was far more terror-stricken than when I heard my sentence of death. When we were locked in again we fell into each other's arms, and remained so I know not how long. I only know that at last the Captain was walking to and fro, erect and determined, and that resistless indignation was raging in my soul: the devil must be driven out by the devil!" He wrote a formal complaint, which came to nothing. They lay down in each other's arms, and the evening and the morning were the fourth day. Their despairing waking thought was, "And we are to be here five and twenty years!" when suddenly the door opened for a gendarme. "Gentlemen, get ready; in half an hour we must be on the road."

During these very days old Reuter was in Berlin, inquiring of Dambach if anything could now be done for the liberation of his only son. Dambach never told him that only twenty paces off he might see and hear, and console that son for himself.

I have narrated in detail this, perhaps the blackest episode in Fritz Reuter's prison life, because it is important to remember that he suffered not only isolation and confinement, but bodily pain and privation enough to shatter any but the hardiest constitution. Even that of "Charles Douze," as his comrades called him, did not escape without incurable damage; but henceforward he was delivered from these extraneous miseries, and passed into the care of commandants who alleviated, so far as they could, the hard lot of a prisoner. First he was lodged in the fortress of Graudenz, where he and the other political criminals formed a little social world, which, like the great one, had its factions and its quarrels, its romances and its feasts. Fritz was its authority in matters of taste, and improvised the pleasures of both kinds of palates—most satisfied then with his pictorial but afterwards with his culinary achievements. In these little occupations, diversified by a little tutoring which he was allowed to undertake, and a little versifying which came to nothing, time slipped away, till in June, 1839, a new and greater change improved his position still further.

His extradition at last took place, and he was sent back to Mecklenburg;—not as a free man—the condition of his delivery was that the grand duke should keep him in continued confinement. Still it was something to be in the charge of a sympathetic countryman, and Reuter found in the Dömitz commandant a true friend, who strained matters to give him every allowable liberty; and in the Dömitz fortress a "nest full of the commandant's daughters." A year passed here as pleasantly as a year of confinement can, and in the following June the death of the Prussian king was followed by an amnesty for all political offenders. Fritz read this in the newspaper, and waited four weeks in daily expectation of the news of his own release. But the Prussians had quite forgotten his existence, and at last the grand duke took the matter in his own hands, and presumed on his own responsibility to set his own subject free. A week later, as Fritz and his father were at dinner, an official announcement arrived from the Prussian minister of justice, that young Reuter would soon regain his liberty.

His liberty was indeed regained, but no power could restore him the seven beautiful wasted years, perhaps the most important in a man's life. Reuter tells us that when he left his prison he had to pass through a region of sand and thorns, traversed by

many paths that might lead nowhere, and this he
found emblematic of his own condition. He felt as
though he were playing hide-and-seek with the world ;
amidst the unaccustomed life and growth, like a tree
that had been stripped of its branches. Visiting his
schoolboy friends who had now wives and children of
their own, he " seemed like one with muddy boots
intruding in a drawing-room." The delight of returning home was half sorrowful, "for over all the joy
lay, with the weight of lead, the question, ' What
now ? ' on my breast,—and on my father's too, I could
read it in his face. Long years I stumbled up and
down under the burden of this question." Truly his
position was a heartbreaking one. He was willing to
work, but there was nothing that he could do. His
attempts at painting had been clever but not pro-
gressive, for in prison he could get no instruction. His
juridical studies he had neglected, for, as he himself
says, " in confinement prisoners may acquire manual
dexterity, but never scientific training"—especially,
we may add, in a science they dislike. His father
indeed sent him, ætatis 30, to begin again his law
course in Heidelberg, but he could not catch up
younger competitors or recover the capacity and
methods of study. He returned to Mecklenburg to
become agriculturist, and in this occupation, besides in
part re-establishing his health, soon showed himself

among the shrewdest and most enterprising; but another sadder obstacle spoiled his success in this as in everything else.

It is with a surprise approaching consternation that the reader of Reuter's novels—perhaps the manliest and sanest in any literature—hears that their author was the victim of drink, and was frequently in a state of delirium. Reuter, lavish of his other experiences, maintained strict silence on this, and exacted it from his friends, so it is only since his death that the publication of Wilbrandt's memoir has in a measure explained the circumstance to the public. The privations of Reuter's prison life—of which one specimen has been given in this sketch—induced a disorder in the nerves of the stomach and alimentary canal which was never completely cured. When this neurosis became acute, Reuter found a remedy only in the excessive comsumption of spirituous liquors, till the agonies of disease and cure together culminated and abated in nausea and vomiting, which left him weak as a child. Sometimes these attacks lasted a couple of days; sometimes it was five or six before he ceased to drink, though he had arranged his potations artificially so as to be overcome as soon as possible.

It may be left to moralists with a system to estimate and apportion the exact degrees of blame in this matter. How much should be attributed to the

D

Prussian Government and how much to Fritz himself, how much was avoidable and how much came as an external fate, are questions that each censor will decide in his own way. Fritz himself wavers in his answers. Sometimes the evil is one that is to be overcome by sacred resolve, sometimes it is a mere physical disease to be treated like gout or rheumatism, and to be cured, if at all, not by himself but by the doctor. But at any rate he always acted on the first belief, and, whether from improved health or strengthened determination, with constantly increasing success; the interval between the attacks, at first rarely lasting more than a week or two, grew to months, at length extending over nine; and at the end of his life there was no relapse. This fact, even more than the physical and involuntary circumstances in which it began, seems to me to mark off Reuter's calamity from ordinary cases of drunkenness.

With these defects, the want of experience and the apparent want of steadiness, it is no wonder that Reuter's first attempts to earn a livelihood broke down. "He'll come to no good," was the universal verdict, which was approved even by his stern, old father, who had come to regard his son as a misfortune and disgrace. "I was far, far more wretched," he exclaims, quarter of a century later, "at this time than when I was in prison." And yet it is easy for us now to see that his very misfortunes were a preparation for his great and characteristic triumphs. He was cut off from any career adequate to his talents, and after the death of his father, who left him a very small legacy, he had to give up even farming from want of capital. For a moment he hoped to gain some post in the rising of 1848, but the success of the reactionary party left him out in the cold. Meanwhile he had asked the hand of Louise Kunze, the lady who afterwards became his wife ; and when she, moved by the sight of his agonies in one of his attacks, had overcome her natural objections to marriage with the deeply afflicted man, he was doubly anxious to establish a home for himself. In 1850, when he was forty years old, he found himself glad to accept the trade of universal school-master, with subjects ranging through mathematics, history, drawing, and swimming, taught at the rate of two groschen a week. A year later he married, and now another occupation became necessary as a source of income, even more than as an outlet for his powers. It was at this juncture that Claus Groth's Platt Deutsch poems appeared, and in their sudden popularity revealed the literary possibilities that lurked in the people's speech. And they were the occasion of Fritz Reuter's becoming not an author, but a Platt Deutsch author. Already he had planned, written, and even published—though certainly his printed productions were mere trifles; but he had invariably employed High German, save in a few almost extemporary verses intended for recitation at marriage festivals. This is the more noticeable, as the subjects of some of the works which then in High German lay ready in his desk were the same as those of his later Platt masterpieces; and the subjects of all of them were local and Platt. This bears out Reuter's own account of his poetical development. In prison the only substitute for actual entertainment was to be found in the play of fancy, and hence by continual exercise this power was trained to picture things with unusual clearness and precision. But with what could his fancy busy itself? Of all the twenty-three years of his previous existence, he had spent only six months out of Mecklenburg. Feeding on the past, and deriving from it his whole emotional nourishment, he had little choice but to digest and ruminate his Mecklenburg experiences till he had assimilated them as part of his consciousness. And as the shadows of his past took form and substance before him, it was almost a necessity that their lips should speak their native Platt, and that in it *his* lips should tell their story. The poetical style is only the finest, most perfect, most adequate form that an idea can assume; and here the Platt Deutsch was not alone most suited for the theme, it was also most suited for the author, who even in university and prison continued to talk it, and who could by means of it snare and hold the thought that in High German slipped from under his hands and left him with its vestment. That he should not at first have known where his strength lay is no more than happens with every author who has any strength at all ; and it was only natural that in his first Platt attempts he should follow Groth's example, and write short pieces, rather than at once set about recasting his more important works. Yet there is one characteristic difference between the two Platt poets from the very beginning. Both had, as it were, to originate a literary tradition ; but while Groth does so by imitating the foreign lyric of Burns, Reuter does so by adopting the little anecdotes that were in everybody's mouth, and giving them literary and poetical form. Gradually he put together a collection of such stories, of varied worth, in his worst touching Joe Miller, in his best, La Fontaine; of equally varied origin, some being the common property of Europe, some Mecklenburg household words, some incidents in his own experience. This collection, which he calls " Läuschen und Rimels " (" Gossip in Rhyme "), suggests sometimes Boccaccio without the immorality, sometimes a book of folklore, sometimes Ramsay's " Scottish Life and Character." But better and worse, native and foreign, all are Platt in colouring; and even in them Reuter is an original artist, precisely for this — that the Platt diction strikes the reader as the very best for this particular version of the story. It is this happy appropriation of the narrative that shows Reuter's genial instinct and that constituted his success. In this department he had not to work alone, his fellow Mecklenburgers past and present helped him, and despite the earlier High German drafts, it seems to me that his later and more ambitious works may be regarded as more and more artistic elaborations and combinations of simple Läuschen, and that they may best be criticised from this point of view.

The external success was proportionate to the internal. Reuter and his wife had embarked in the undertaking with many misgivings; he had to borrow money for it, and she had to fold and pack the copies herself : but their doubts were soon removed ; Mecklenburgers and Pommeranians rushed to buy the book that contained for the first time in print the old familiar stories, only narrated with more humour than ever before, and in six weeks the first edition was exhausted. A second collection some years later found the same reception. But meanwhile Reuter, now a famous man within a narrow area, had produced something far more considerable in his "Journey to Belgium." This may almost be regarded as a series of anecdotes strung together on the thread of a tour which two old peasants undertake with their two sons, for the education of the latter, one of whom has left a sweetheart at home. The maladventures of the travellers, who never get to their destination, are described with drastic humour. When the two youths are seeing the " Freischütz" in the theatre of a small town, the gallery on which they stand falls in during the thunder and lightning of the goblin scene. The whole party, in a Berlin theatre, are horrified by the discovery that the same piece is being performed, and they look forward excitedly to the accident, now three storeys more dangerous, which they understand as the crowning triumph of stage effect. They get into a train for the first time, to travel to Belgium, and by a series of accidents are dropped each at a different wayside station. They soon resolve to return to Berlin, where the sons meet by chance, but are presently arrested for a disturbance they innocently occasion. They are marched to the police office, and there find—their fathers, whose fate has been parallel. How comical is the imprisoned father's indignant salutation of the imprisoned son : " Sirrah, so you have been shaming me in these foreign parts !" And in contrast with these farcical scenes, to prevent the fun from becoming tiresome, we have the really idyllic picture of the native village, and little Dürten, the village bride.

Such passages were enough to show that Reuter, though his humour was sometimes broad and sometimes verbal, was nothing of a mountebank; but perhaps even his friends may have been surprised when his next work, "No House-room," appeared. "I wrote the book," he says, "with my life blood, for the sake of suffering mankind." It is a simple enough tale in verse, of what might any day happen in patriarchal Mecklenburg, where permission to settle had to be got by the labourers from the lords of the manor, and only those who had a "hüsung," were allowed to marry. A workman and his bride have been refused permission for long, and now it must be gained, and gained soon, or the girl will be put to shame. But their master hates them both, Mariken for refusing his own advances, Jehann for being preferred. His lady, whose help they ask, is painfully shocked at their trespass, and feels it would be wrong should they escape its consequences. Indeed, that is the feeling of all her circle in such matters. Pious pastor and profligate junker join in their wishes that the stool of penitence might be reintroduced— that is, of course, for the lower orders. Meanwhile there is no help, no escape for the unhappy pair, for Mariken's old father is bedridden, and even to save her fair fame she will not leave him. At last the old man dies, and Jehann returns from the burial, his grief hardly quenching his wrath and joy—wrath for the way the carcase has been stowed away like a dead dog,—exultation at the thought that now they can set out for America. Suddenly his master stands before him, casts at him evil words, and raises his whip to strike him. Jehann, in a transport of fury, lets fly a farming fork ; it hits, and his enemy lies dead at his feet. To his hiding, a fellow-servant, old Daniel—who typifies the submissive, as Jehann typifies the rebellious labourer—brings the hoard of the miller's wife whose child Jehann has saved from fire ; but he tells the murderer that now Mariken never can be his, and sees him rushing off to exile with curses on his lips. The miller's wife has meanwhile taken pity on Mariken, too, and tries to fend for her and the newly born babe. But the widow lady of the manor is guilty of no such moral laxity. She sends the deserted, one-day's mother word that she must turn out of her father's cottage, and unless she consents to part with the child, leave the service altogether. Poor Mariken staggers through the snow, to make one vain intercession, then rushes to the wood, where she is found cold in a swoon, but with her babe warm in her arms. Life, but not reason, returns, and eventually she finds the burial of a suicide. The poem closes with the momentary return of the wild-eyed father to fetch his son, now a boy of ten, to grow up in America, at least in liberty.

Even such a skeleton of the story will show to some, what tragic stuff it contains. But it is the detail that makes a poem live. The gathering fears, the flickering hopes, the final ruin of the young pair, must be followed from point to point before we gain full sympathy with them. We must be taught by Fritz's fine scorn who were their so-called betters, we must see how the most patient and most managing of their own class feel for them, we must accustom ourselves to the destitution and darkness of their lives, to the pettiness and unalterableness of their village existence before we recognize in Jehann the Titan struggling, like another Prometheus, against unworthy gods, and feel the spasm that Mariken must have felt at what was to her, not so much an act of blood, as an act of sacrilege. In this poem it is hard to find a flaw in the idea, or shortcoming in the solution. Each touch is true to actual nature, and each is instinct with higher symbolism. Even the peculiar double character of Jehann's deed, which, on the one hand, ruins his own life, and, on the other, we are led to understand, procures the happiness of his child, is *pace* German critics, clearly correct. His master, and all such, deserve their fate, but it was inflicted by Jehann, not as the righteous judgment of God for wrongs done to man, but in a moment of passion as revenge for an insult.

Still, despite these excellences, not to speak of the music of the numbers and loveliness of the descriptions, we hesitate to indorse Fritz's own opinion, "This is my best work." He himself finely says elsewhere, "Joy and grief are the warp and woof of life," and in works of the most human art, if the threads of the one were drawn out, the threads of the other would not hold. This is the case with Fritz's own later works, but hardly with the present. Humour of a somewhat sarcastic kind is allowed to season the pathos, as in the "Journey" pathos flavoured the humour; but they still lie together without being united at the same time in the same person. On the whole, then, these two longer poems should rank as companion but opposite monotones; and in treatment, though not in subject, and not with full success, Fritz essays a more complex, and therefore higher form of art, in his next and last verse tale, "Johnnie Snout." This poem celebrates the love of Johnnie, a blacksmith 'prentice, and the little Poodle, a maid-of-all-work, who have grown up together from childhood, and almost at the same time leave their little village for the hardships and temptations of the great world. In absence, they discover their fondness, remain true to each other despite threats and enticements, and come back to be man and wife in their old home.　It is a sort of rustic rendering into the circumstances of low life of Milton's idea in Comus :—

<blockquote>
" So dear to heaven is saintly chastity,
That when a soul is found sincerely so,
A thousand liveried angels lacky her."
</blockquote>

But in this story of birds and men, the heavenly ministers wear liveries that belong to a lower, not to a higher kingdom than that of man ; and starlings, nightingales, and storks watch over and hasten and modify the fates of the pair of sweethearts.　That a strong fantastic spice is here introduced is pretty clear, and sometimes it does not go very well with the other ingredients.　Reuter pictures his world of birds with such realism, that his world of men becomes occasionally rather unreal; but sometimes he quite transcends the difficulty, as in the tender and humorous passage where Johnnie is taught by the song of the birds what a sweet loving maid he has left behind him.　" That's a fine salad we've tossed up for ourselves," cries the male starling, Jochen, as the lad tramps off; " he has understood every word, we've spoken."　"Stuff and nonsense," says Lotte, his wife, " no man understands our bird-speech."　" My child," returns Jochen, "I am pained by your remarkable ignorance."　And then, in the style of Chaucer's

Chanticleer, he learnedly expounds the matter, how men, before they were so stupid as to write and print, used to know the language of star and bird, and how even later sages, in India, retained something of the art; but such linguists are scarce, for the conditions of the knowledge are manifold, and, indeed, range from being loved unwittingly by a pure maiden, to having eaten a stout sandwich, on the first of May, before going to sleep under a thorn.

When Reuter published this book in 1860, he was no longer the needy school-master, who eight years before could scarcely screw up courage enough to face the expense of his first modest venture. Each book had been a treasure-ship for him : he was already well-to-do, and was rapidly becoming wealthy. His holiday trips, at first confined to a run to his true and constant friends the Peters of Thalberg, gradually extended in compass, and were soon to bring him to the Golden Horn of Stamboul. His changes of residence, almost as frequent as in his "fortress time," always meant a more commodious house, a finer garden, and a livelier neighbourhood. They were soon to end with his settlement in the pretty villa near Eisenach, with its picturesqueness of scene and wealth of roses, where Reuter was to enjoy the fruits of his labours, and, surrounded by friends, expect his end. His circle of acquaintance had already grown in numbers and distinction, and the time was near when the ex-convict was to correspond with the grand duke in terms of equality, and receive from Bismarck, chief minister in the State which had so deeply injured him, a letter of hearty recognition. He had not yet reached the summit of his fame, but already in 1860 he had, not to speak of his dramatic, journalistic, and miscellaneous essays in prose, produced one work that had carried his name into the upper and High German circles. This was his "Story of the French Period," —the first of that series of semi-biographical prose tales to which he brought his maturest powers, and which, moreover, both in form and matter corresponded most perfectly with his genius. Reuter's writing is emphatically based on facts, experiences, a wealth of realistic detail. His verse is generally pleasing and sometimes truly poetical, but it is not the obvious channel for the flood of humorous particulars in which he delights; and in much of it we feel that he has rather overcome a difficulty, than chosen the natural way of prose, which at last he adopts. And again, his excellence lies not so much in inventing fictitious plots, incidents, and circumstances, as in working up, by judicious selection and expansion, what he has seen and heard and experienced for himself. For example, the "French period" owes its peculiar interest to the description of the plannings, doings, and sufferings of his own native Stavenhagen during the great French retreat of 1813. The *dramatis personæ*, the Amtmann Wewer, Town-councillor Herse, Fritz's own father and mother, are for the most part real. The Stavenhagen volunteer regiment, in which the great difficulty is to get any one to march in the second rank, is probably real too. The main plot is very simple and has also every air of reality. A few marauding French chasseurs arrive at the castle. The Amtmann, afraid to use force, frightens away the rest, and intoxicates their leader, who is carried off in a miller's cart, and, in somewhat undress condition, thrown out on the road. His disappearance leads to a military investigation, held by the captain of a more regular French force that passes by, and a few of the chief townspeople are arrested. It might have gone hard with them, had not the chasseur's booty been restored by the miller, whose servant Friedrich found it in the cart, and had not the same Friedrich managed to trace the plunderer and deliver him up to justice. Friedrich, of cast-iron countenance, infinite composure and infinite contrivance, is, perhaps, the hero of the book. He would have held it no crime to kill the chasseur, but is scrupulous to give up to his master all the booty, except eightpence, which sum another chasseur had once stolen from him; and his cunning in detecting, beats even the female cunning that would conceal, the missing culprit.   The other incidents—for example, where the honest housekeeper, Madam Westphalen, is prevailed upon to hide herself in the smoke hole, as a person specially objectionable to the French government, or when Fritz's own father profits by the bad roads to make his escape—have the vividness of witnessed scenes, which probably they were.   Fritz's own personal power, the rare power of the good narrator, lies in knowing what to leave unsaid, what to say and how to say it—which, after all, permits as much scope to the imagination as to the judgment, for the artist must improve and recast. In this book the balance, is pretty evenly held between historical reality and poetical fiction; the main plot is sacred to the one, the subplot of the loves of the miller's daughter and nephew to the other.   Just because of this balance, however, it seems to me that the plan of the book is not quite perfect.   When the French catastrophe is past, the story should cease; the extra episode of the miller's craze, that postpones the young people's union, stands in no organic connection with the rest.   In the " French Time " we have no thorough fusion, but only imaginative history, plus realistic fiction; while in the first of his next works, " My Fortress Time," we have the one, and in the second, " My Farmer Time," we have the other; and these rank higher, therefore, as works of art.

"My Fortress Time" is a biographical sketch, to which a few invented jests have been added. "My Farmer Time" is a novel into which a few real persons and incidents have been introduced. Of the former, I need speak no further here, as I have already used it as an authority. Of the latter, it is almost impossible to speak, its plot is so loose, its incidents and characters so many and so true. It is the work of Reuter's that has been oftenest translated, and yet continues to defy translation. One reason of this is, that it has never been rendered into dialect; and a second is, that the diction and manners are so truly Platt, that not even another dialect could reproduce them. It marks the flood-tide of Fritz's production. On the strong foundations of reality, which his genius required, he has freely shaped from personal observation, from the experience of others, from the villagers' stories, a sort of district biography in its humour and pathos, which only for lack of a better name we call a novel. Its characters are multitudinous, its area wide, its time extending through three generations, so that those whom we first meet as lisping infants we leave as middle-aged mothers with children of their own. It is "Platt Life and Character," woven into a connected whole, but a whole whose limits are prescribed by no recognized form of art. We may call it the memoirs of a whole country side; its unity is to be found in the gradual success of deserving men and families, and in the strong portraiture of certain typical characters, who are the chief doers and sufferers throughout. One of these is the honest capable farmer, Hawermann, who, twice ruined by the arts of a pettifogging parvenu, only in his old age gains his share of worldly good. Another is his sister, the energetic Frau Nüssler, whose management maintains the farm, while her well-meaning monosyllabic oaf of a husband can hardly see it through the fumes of the pipe that constantly dangles from his lips. But the chief person in the book is, undoubtedly, the overseer Zacharias Bräsig, old friend of Hawermann, old sweetheart of Frau Nüssler, whose red face, stout figure, and out-turned toes are as impossible to forget as the strange mixture of Platt and Hoch Deutsch called Messingsch, to which he has recourse in his efforts at polite speaking. He is Reuter's favourite and the most excellent of his creations. He appears in a number of the author's previous sketches, notably in a series of letters and an autobiography; in the latter, giving this account of his own origin: "I was born, and of a truth in the season for killing geese, sometime near Martinmas, year unknown, as the Frau Pastor used the register leaves to wrap the geese in. My aunts got a balance, and as they had just been slaughtering, tied me to the one end and a fat goose to the other, and—would you believe it ?—I was parallel with the brute, weighing therefore thirteen or fourteen pound roughly told."   In these early essays, however, Bräsig is merely a comic figure; in the " Stromtid " we learn to love the gentle heart, and to respect the shrewd sense concealed beneath his meddlesome laughable exterior.   To the very end he excites our mirth with his reminiscences of his three sweethearts, his hydropathic experiences, his amateur duennaship and the like.   Who can peruse with gravity the description of him in the pastor's coat, so exceedingly scanty that he has to hold the coffee-cup at arm's length, like an athlete poising an enormous weight, and goes about as though he were a philanthropist, eager to embrace the whole world ?   But his indignation with all that is mean and cowardly strikes a deeper chord, and his death scene may almost be compared with Falstaff's, as he murmurs his last words, of course in Messingsch, to his friend Hawermann : " But I always *was* ahead of you in composition."   Round these a host more are gathered, figures grave and gay, worthy and despicable, but all human.   The full-bodied pastor's wife with her duster ever ready for the cleanest places, and Hawermann's fair daughter blossoming into womanhood like a lily opening in the sun ; Fritz Triddelwitz, prince of all calf lovers, and Moses, most Christian of Jewish money-lenders ; Lining and Mining, the two maidens like as two bunches of grapes, with their suitors, the two theological candidates who respectively believe and do not believe in the devil,—these are characters, that once known are never confounded or forgotten.

Reuter's next longer work, " Dörchläuchten "—the familiar diminutive of " His Grace," or, as Carlyle would render it, " His Translucency,"—and his last, " The Journey to Constantinople," show increasingly his genius on the wane. It is almost as though the Mecklenburg of his own day were sacred to him, within that circle none daring walk but he, while change of time or change of scene broke his magic. The change of time is the less fatal. " His Grace," dated in the later half of the eighteenth century, humorously contrasts the absurd, almost idiotic, Gallicism of the petty German princeling, with the healthy, if often trivial life of his Teutonic subjects. That life not being very different from the present is well depicted, the characters of the subrector and his housekeeper are attractively drawn ; but we feel that the comical relations of Æpinus and the Duke of Mecklenburg-Strelitz are not so typical of the time as the tragic relations, say of Schubert and the Duke of Würtemberg. Even the last romance of all, founded on Reuter's own journey to Turkey, is not without

its ·merits. The characters at least, are, Mecklenburgers; and the scenes in Mecklenburg—notably the
panic produced in the school-master's house by the
reading of some of the horrors in Sue's " Mysteries of
Paris "—are in the author's best vein.

But that vein was for him exhausted. His life had
been hard beyond that of most men. To the stagna-
tion of his prison years had succeeded the excitement
of his author years, and the alternate strain was too
much, even for his iron frame. A new romance that
he began seemed to him made up of repetitions, and
he abandoned it. A couple of ballads on the fallen
soldiers of 1870–71 closed his literary career, and in
1874 his many friends and admirers were lamenting
his own death.

So simple that he could see facts, so kindly that he
could judge them, so brave that he could proclaim
them, Reuter as a man is easily known, and when
known must be loved. This intimacy with what is
real, is the basis of his literary power. Without a
profusion of actual experiences to work on, his fancy
becomes fanciful and his invention is weak. The
most original of his works, the " Primeval History
of Mecklenburg," is also the least interesting. The
similes of this people's-poet are often as far-fetched
as the conceits of Donne and Cowley. The crisis of
an important episode in the " Farmer Time " is brought

on by a misspelling, of the subplot in the "French Time" by a slip in grammar, of the main plot in "His Grace" by a mispronunciation. When his imagination seeks a harvest from the Elysian fields, it thrashes straw, but the broad acres of Mecklenburg yield it golden grain. The life of his countrymen, from his early exclusive acquaintance with it and his later exclusive rumination of it, he was able to reproduce almost perfectly, and he wisely availed himself of the language and form that experience offered to his hands. This form, as we saw, was the anecdote, and some of its features remain with Reuter to the last. In his mature works the characters are so true and vivid that they seem almost alive, but they are hardly exhibited in their growth or interaction. They are to make the story intelligible and interesting, not by the story to be analyzed and explained; they exist for it, not it for them. In short, Fritz Reuter is a great artist in truthful, pregnant story-telling, which never becomes frivolous. "In prison," he says, "one may not get to know men, but one does get to know man;" and this dearly bought knowledge of universal human nature gives a certain depth to his slightest sketches. In a word, his country, his history, his character have made him the chief narrative, as Burns is the chief lyrical, poet in dialect.

Perhaps a sentence may be added as to the language

of his works. Its uninflected character, its contact with English, its regular letter-change as compared with High German, make it simple reading to any Englishman who is fairly acquainted with the latter, and after a few pages he needs notes and vocabulary only for individual words and phrases. If he treats it more thoroughly, he will be constantly interested by its contrasts and resemblances with the history of his mother tongue.

ANGLO-SAXON JOCOSERIA.

[The riddles of Symposius are edited by Riese in his " Anthologia Latina." Those of Aldhelm, Boniface, and Alcuin may be found in La Migne's " Cursus Completus." A few examples from Tatwine are printed in Hook's " Lives of the Archbishops of Canterbury," and in Wright's " Biographia Literaria Britannica," but for the collection as a whole, as well as for all those of Eusebius, we must go to " M.S. Reg.," 12 c. 23. The Anglo-Saxon specimens are included in Grein's " Bibliothek der Angelsächsischen Poesie," but his readings are not always adopted. Ebert has some valuable remarks on the subject in his " Geschichte der Literatur im Mittelalter," under the above names.]

IN the literature of untamed and aspiring nations we are accustomed to expect, if something of art, little of artifice. Elaborate oddities like anagrams or acrostics, literary puzzles that rest on remote and fanciful analogies, seem by their very nature to belong to later times, when leisure is more plentiful, wit more practised, and the great demands of life less certain; they, far more than gorgeous or significant romance, are what one would anticipate from the " idle singers of an empty day." Experience, indeed, hardly confirms these expectations. In the spacious days of great Elizabeth we find a critical treatise laying down laws for the manufacture of poems in the shape of eggs, lozenges, and pillars; and Cowley, the contemporary of the serious Milton, surpasses all his brethren of the fantastic school in wire-drawn and far-fetched ingenuities. An eager and earnest age does not therefore exclude from all its range the productions of a merely formal wit. Still, we should have thought that in early Anglo-Saxon days the struggle for existence was too pressing to leave time or inclination for quips and quibbles; and it is therefore with surprise that we· learn that our countrymen were nationally notorious for their riddles, and that the earliest and greatest of their vernacular poets has left a collection of almost a hundred. Nor is this all; into his sublimest verses he weaves his name by means of a kind of spelling puzzle, and he is not above arithmetical catches. And the taste for such conceits was no vulgar one, to be satisfied merely by profane gleemen. Scholars like Aldhelm, archbishops like Tatwine, missionary saints like Boniface, educationists and philosophers like Alcuin have all made their contributions to the Old English miscellany of acrostics, riddles, and other whimsicalities. So this literature of trifles, as we are accustomed to consider them, was the work, not of triflers, but of the best and greatest men of their time. How did this come about ? Probably in two ways. First, the examples and models existed in the later Latin literature, and in most other departments of civilization as well as in religion, England was the humble pupil of Rome. It would have been presumption to criticize the utterances of the teacher : whatever was offered in the almost sacred tongue must be accepted as admirable, especially when, as in the case of acrostics, it had the sanction, not merely of the ignorant heathens, but of the Christian apologists.

Still, this of itself would not explain why Anglo-Saxon writers adopted and developed, often in quite original directions, the Latin contrivances. Another and deeper reason lay in their own mood and attitude. They were waking to the mysteries of the universe, the whole world to them was a collection of puzzles. The strangeness and wonder of common things had not been dulled in their eyes. They looked on earth and sea, on their beliefs and legends, on their arts, on their very tools, and recognized much in them that they could not explain and that defied full expression. By metaphors and analogy they strove to penetrate to the inner meaning; they delighted in experimenting with their new accomplishments; they were never weary of expatiating on the marvels, the enigmas that daily life contains, or of reiterating in strange figures their salient aspects. Thus conceit

and conundrum, play with letters and masquerade
of thought, things that before and since have been
but a pastime for the idle, were to them an intel-
lectual exercise in which head and heart had equal
share.

Perhaps this may be made somewhat clearer by
an instance from another class of literary oddities.
Macaronic verse, whether of the kind that mixes
different languages in the single words, or of the
kind that alternates expressions from one language
with those from another, has latterly been employed
merely for a comic purpose. Thus Dunbar in his
" Testament of Kennedy " writes—

> " I will na preistis for me sing,
>   Dies illa, dies iræ ;
> Nor yet na bellis for me ring,
>   Sicut semper solet fieri ;
> Bot a bag-pyp to play a spring,
>   Et unum ale whisp ante me ;
> Insteid of torches for to bring,
>   Quatuor lagenas Cervisiæ.

And such verse, so used, is common in English literature, from the days of Skelton. Probably the earliest
macaronic of this description occurs in Cynewulf's
" Phœnix," freely rendered from a Latin poem falsely
attributed to Lactantius. This was the poem in
which previous stories of the phœnix first received
their typical and final modern form, in which the
phœnix first typifies the immortal human soul by

rising from its ashes, and first typifies Christ, in so far as all the birds follow it as their lord. This is sufficient guarantee that nothing of levity intrudes in the bilingual verses with which, in the Anglo-Saxon version, the poem concludes :—

Us released has	Lucis Auctor,
That we may here	Merere,
By godly work,	Gaudia in Cælo;
And that we may	Maxima Regna
Seek and possess :	Sedibus altis
Live in delights	Lucis et pacis,
Own the abodes	Almæ Lætitiæ,
And bide in bliss ;	Blandem et mitem
The sender of victory see,	Sine fine,
And loud sing his love	Laude perenni,
Happy with angels.	Halleluja !

Or, entirely in English :—

Us released has	The Light-giver,
That we may	Merit on earth,
By works of justice,	The joys of heaven ;
And that we may	These mighty realms
Seek and possess :	Seated on high
Live in delights	Of light and peace,
Own the abodes	Abounding in joy
And bide in bliss ;	The bland and gracious
Victory sender see,	Ceasing never,
And loud sing his love	With lauds eternal,
Happy with angels.	Halleluja !

Here it is obvious that the Latin is employed to give a sublimity, a mystery of which the vulgar speech was thought incapable, much as we have borrowed the closing word, or the *amen* of our prayers. If we are to seek a later illustration of the same feeling we must look, not to Dunbar's macaronics, but to the solemn refrain of his lament for the makers; *Timor Mortis conturbat me.* Latin was thought to have, and on account of its religious associations did have, a majesty, a sacredness, which even more than its sonorous harmonies, exalted it above the daily speech. And just as Cynewulf's macaronic differs from our ordinary conception of the macaronic, so the Anglo-Saxon quirks and riddles differ from those that precede and succeed them.

This becomes very obvious when we consider the history of the acrostic. This tasteless trick of a wit not even verbal, but only orthographical, had been much in vogue with the less important Christian writers. Sometimes it was worked out to the last degree of pedantry—the initial, the middle, and the final letters, when read downward, forming some apposite phrase. Sometimes the initial letters repeated vertically the first line. Sometimes, when the poems were also riddles, the acrostic formed the answer,—an expedient specially associated with the name of St. Boniface. Very frequently the name of the author or of the recipient of the verses was thus indicated; and it is this variety which claims our special attention. It was employed by Aldhelm, and before him by St. Columba; and readers of Edgar Allan Poe will remember that it is not incompatible with a certain flavour of grace and fancy.

But though Anglo-Saxon writers in Latin make use of the acrostic, it is far less characteristic than the riddle, and, in the vulgar tongue, though not exactly obsolete, it is at least so changed that it cannot at first be recognized. The reason for this is probably to be sought in the strangeness and unfamiliarity of writing. In the first place, to analyse a word into its letters and entertain one's self with them, needs probably greater experience and skill in spelling them than the *scóps*, or poets, possessed. Even after an alphabet has come into use, in which sounds, not ideas, are indicated, some time must elapse ere the letter is so entirely divorced from the word in which it stands that it can be isolated and experimented on by itself. The writing with which the German tribes before their conversion were acquainted was the Runic, the mysterious, a knowledge of which was assuredly not very wide-spread, and which, by the very difficulty of reproducing it (by incisions on wood or bone), was protected against the playful impertinences of an acrostic. Perhaps no better instance can be given of the orthographical helplessness of the Anglo-Saxons, than the riddles in which we find parallels to St. Boniface's practice of giving the solution in acrostic form. That seems to make the puzzle simple enough, but what can the modern reader, who perhaps has been present at a spelling-bee, think of a conundrum like this ? "Hasting hence, I beheld on the track D. N. U. O. H." Another riddle commences, "W. O. B. is my name, only reversed." And there are several examples of the same kind, in which we have "R. E. E. P. S.," "E. S. R. O. H.," "N. A. M.," in the question, to help us in discovering the answer, *speer*, *horse*, and *man*.

Yet the chief reason for the collapse and reorganization of the acrostic lay in the marvel that was felt to be in all writing. Not only the native, but in a certain sense all letters were Runes or secrets. Their phonetic value was a wonder. That they should represent parts of a word, and therefore parts of an idea, was miraculous. They were matters far too serious to jest with. English writers in Latin might presume so far by the mere instinct of imitation, but English writers in English were too profoundly impressed, as well as too little experienced, to do so, although one would have thought that in their alliterative verse the temptation lay very near. The letters of their native alphabet were no mere orthographical signs, but mystic symbols named from the products of art and nature, and from man. Sometimes they were personified as wonder-working agents; sometimes the name of the letter was explained, as though it were the thing itself. In the drawing of lots, the Runes were used, and those which chanced to be seized were interpreted according to their designation. In one of the finest of the Anglo-Saxon lyrics, "The Husband's Message," the man, who has been driven by his enemies into exile, sends his wife a staff with certain Runes inscribed on it; and the poem concludes by mentioning them;—

> " United I set S and R together,
> EA, W, and M, to maintain with an oath
> That he the treaty and loving troth
> Which ye in yester time used to swear,
> In faith will fulfil for the time he lives."

It is now impossible to be quite sure of the connection and significance of these Runes. But they were probably to be interpreted by some allegorical exposition of their name-marks. And thanks to the dignity with which spelling was invested, the names of the Runic, or Futhark alphabet (so-called from its initial characters, as we talk of our A B C), are not as a rule doubtful. The Latin alphabet was regarded with far less awe, yet even it was chosen by St. Columba as the subject for a poem, which in many ways resembles our humble modern nursery series, " A was an Apple-pie," etc.; and a manuscript in the British Museum contains a similar fragment " by a certain Scot." Corresponding to them, and probably formed on their model, we have a remarkable Anglo-Saxon poem, called the " Rune Song," in which the letters are enumerated and described according to the value of their names. But the fact that they *had* names creates a great difference between the Teutonic Futhark and the Roman Abecedarium, and permits a certain depth and impressiveness in the former to which the latter must always be strange. For to the Anglo-Saxon, A was no mere sign, but the Ash, the tall tree that furnished the thegn with his lance ; and B was the graceful Birch, lovely among its twigs. Let us take a few of the characters and describe them by the explanatory verses of the old poem.

K was styled *Kén*, the resinous wood which we now call by its Latin name, *pine*, though in German the old word *kien* is preserved.

> " Kén shows its kind to men's ken in the fire.
> Blazing bright it burns most often
> Where children of chiefs their cheer are mending."

Y was denoted by *yr*, an obscure word which, however, most likely meant either money or a bow.

> " Yr is to earls and athelings all
> Winsome and worthy, well-loved on horse-back,
> In travels true among trappings of war."

Need stood for N :—

> " Need is narrow on the breast, oft none-the-less to children of men
> It is both help and healing, when they hearken to its words."

F

E was named *Eh*, a word for *horse* which has now entirely disappeared, but which we may remember from its connection with the Latin Equus :—

> " To an earl of athelings is Equus a joy,
>   The horse proud in hoof, when, the heroes together,
>   The choice ones on their chargers exchange their words ;
>   And ever is it easement to any that stay not."

Wén, the same as our *weening*, stood for W, but it had the sense of *hope :—*

> " He wants not weening whom few woes have touched
>   With sorrow and sadness, and himself who hath
>   Bloom and bliss and buildings in store."

Ur for U, is another word which has been nearly lost. It was the wild forest ox, or bison, now generally called by the Germanized form of its name, Aurochs, or by the Latinized Urus. The Rune is sometimes used with special reference to its mighty horns :—

> " Undaunted is Urus, and, armed with horns,
>   With his forehead fights this fearful beast,
>   High haunter of moors ;—hardy is the wight."

Lake stood for L :—

> " Lakes are long looked on by men
>   Ere they dare go down to their dancing skiffs,
>   And the foam of the sea frights them much ;
>   And the horse of the sea heeds not its bridle."

F was named *Fee*, which originally meant cattle,

and was at this time used, in a wider than the modern
sense, for wealth or fortune :—

> " Fortune seems fair to not few among men ;
>   Yet shall each surely share it with many,
>   If, when God shall give doom, he guiltless would stand."

My reason for selecting these special Runes is that
together they form the name Cynewulf. We have
seen how St. Boniface's practice of indicating with
acrostics the answers of riddles is represented in
Anglo-Saxon. We may now see how much remains
of Aldhelm's practice of indicating the authorship of
poems by the same means. Two specimens will serve.
In the first, the Runes are simply personified without
reference to their meaning, much as we might per-
sonify X, Y, and Z. In the second, there is a very
obvious attempt to introduce them appropriately with
reference to their meaning. But in both there is no
mistaking the deadly earnest, the absence of everything like idle and frivolous ingenuity.

The first occurs at the end of " Juliana," a poem
which describes the perils and sufferings of a Christian
martyr, for the sake of her faith and her chastity.
In vain worldly persecution, the rancour of demons,
and death itself have assailed her. She has endured
without fainting, till she has attained the heavenly
realms of peace and joy. And then the poet adds,
" I shall have need of her help when my soul leaves

this body on its journey, even I know not whither, to its unknown lodging."

> " Sadly go about
> Kén, Yr and Need ; the King is enraged
> The victory-spender ; and sin-stained await
> Equus, Weening, and Urus, with anguish o'erladen,
> What He will award as the wage of their life
> In doom of their deeds.   In dread, Lake and Fortune
> Are sighing and shivering."

The other example occurs at the end of "Elene," a poem on the legend of the discovery of the true cross. Cynewulf tells how, till he was blessed with a vision of the " wondrous tree," he lived in care and strife, and then proceeds—

> "Aye, till then was the man
> With care overcome—his Kén fire burned ill ;
> Though treasures were his, trinkets of gold,
> Many in the mead hall.   Mourning was Yr
> Neighbour of Need ; gnawing cares did he dree,
> Unknown ills where'er Equus might bear him,
> Measuring the mile paths, mightily rushing
> In wire-woven bravery.   Weening is weakened,
> Young joy with years and youth are fled far—
> Yon gladness of yore.   In yestertime Urus
> Was boast of the boy,—bygone now,
> When the due time is done, are the days of his years ;
> Lost in his life-joy, as Lake streams glide past
> Or floods flowing swiftly.   Fortune to mortals
> Is lent for a little, the land's adornment
> Wends 'neath the welkin like wind from us here,
> When high on the heaven it howleth aloft,
> Climbs with the clouds, clamorously passing,
> And soon of a sudden is silent again."

These are the typical representatives of the acrostic in Anglo-Saxon. What a change is here! The neatness and regularity of art are gone. Little remains but wonder at the strange magic in those cuttings that communicate thought, and the feeling that the introduction of them will not degrade any theme, but rather add to its solemn mystery. From this oracular enigmatical use of them we may fittingly pass to the consideration of the riddle.

This, like the acrostic, though by no means unknown in earlier times, as we may remember from the stories of Samson and of the Sphynx, seems to have been especially cultivated in the later ages of Rome. A certain Symposius—of place and period so doubtful that some commentators have arbitrarily transformed him into a symposium, and ascribed it or him to Lactantius—has left a collection of a hundred, which are in their kind, perhaps, the happiest and most entertaining that have survived. With a well-trained, acute understanding, he plays with his subjects, makes them describe their salient features in a few witty touches, so that the solution is always more or less of a surprise, and yet at once we feel its aptness. In many cases they are hardly to be distinguished from epigrams, except in so far as we are left to find out the reference for ourselves. The following is on the nail of a boot:—

> " With sole foot above me clutching, onward on my head I pace,
>   With my crown the pavement touching, while behind it leaves its
>   trace ;
>   Yet at least there lack not comrades who endure the same sad
>   case."

Another, on sleep, is rather subtler, and later writers
have praised by plagiarizing it :—

> " Coming only at my pleasure, shapes I fashion manifold ;
>   Terrors without truth or measure, vain imaginings I mould :
>   But unless he close his eyes, myself no mortal shall behold."

Symposius was the acknowledged starting-point,
and continued the model, often without acknowledgment, of the earlier mediæval riddle till the days of
Alcuin and Cynewulf; and despite the very different
style of these writers, we shall have occasion to
remark in them a transmission of the Symposian
influence. From him, however, at an earlier date,
Aldhelm, Bishop of Sherbourne, Abbot of Malmsbury,
and famous teacher in the Malmsbury Cloister School,
learned the art; and in the preface to his collection
of riddles, appeals to Symposius and Aristotle, as well
as to the Bible, in justification of his method and
work. In choice of subject and general style he is a
close imitator of his immediate predecessor. The
natural history, especially, of the animal world real or
fabulous, but also the workshop, the landscape, and
the house supply him with his topics. Some of his
best verses are on a shell-fish, on a bee, on the load-

stone, on a mill, on the unicorn. The one on "Salt" is perhaps the neatest and compactest :—

> "With slimy fish my wave was stored of late;
>   But while I bore the hot flame's fervent throes
> My nature changed by new decree of fate,
>   And now I gleam like ash or like the snows."

This is written almost in the spirit of Symposius; but even here there is a difference between the two which elsewhere becomes much more striking. Aldhelm's riddles sometimes reach the length of fifteen or six-teen lines, and never fall below the number of four, while those of his original never rise above the number of three. Now this means that the Latin is more expert with his tools than the Englishman; for when the riddle is a mere *jeu d'esprit*, it cannot dispense with the "soul of wit." But it also means that Aldhelm's riddle is not generally a mere *jeu d'esprit*: the personified object sets forth its traits with a certain poetic pomp, and often with a touch of pathos; and the converse of this is that the descrip-tions rather lose in brevity and pith. Wright calls attention to the immense number of glossarial expla-nations with which in the manuscript Aldhelm's riddles are accompanied, and adds, "There needs no greater proof how complicated and far-fetched they are." But this shows not so much a deterioration, as the change of attitude from the polite and dexterous jesting of Rome to the wondering but somewhat awkward reverence of the Northern barbarians. The riddle on that characteristic subject of contemplation, the alphabet, will illustrate the tendency in both its aspects :—

> " Sisters seven and ten are we, powerless born for speech.
> Other six we reckon not : they are bastards each.
> We from iron spring (yet soon must by iron die),
> Or from plumage of some bird flying to the sky;
> Us three brothers got,—who bore, still in doubt must lie.
> Whatso suitor eagerly to learn our lore hath will,
> Him we swiftly give swift words, and yet are silent still."

Many expressions here would certainly puzzle a modern were he not helped by the copious glosses. One of these explains that the six bastards are the letters x, y, z, k, q, h; the first three objectionable as being Greek or post-Augustan; k and q as being redundant, and h as being merely the rough breathing. Was Aldhelm the first English spelling reformer? The production and destruction by iron refers to the opposite uses to which the two ends of the style were put, in forming and erasing the letters. Another gloss declares the three brothers to be the three fingers used in writing; but the phrase about the doubtful motherhood has bred a swarm of exposi-tions, and is in turn referred to the wandering mind or the uncertain hand of the writer, or to his pen, which may be crow-quill, or goose-quill, or a reed.

Next in the series of riddle-writers come Archbishop Tatwine and a certain Eusebius,* neither of whom has hitherto found a printer, though certainly they are not inferior to most of their class. In them their Latin and their English predecessor are both imitated, but especially the latter; for while only particular subjects and ideas are borrowed from Symposius, Aldhelm has prescribed the treatment as well. But they divert the riddle still further from its original scope by introducing what, for lack of a better name, we may call the ecclesiastical element. This is seen, partly, in their treatment of ordinary topics, as when Tatwine in his riddle on the " Sower " directly suggests St. Paul's metaphor for resurrection ; partly, in their choosing as subjects details of Christian theory like the virtues and the graces, or items of Church furniture like the crucifix or the altar ; and of course the description is invariably deeply serious. Of the three following, the first and second will serve to illustrate their secular, and the third their ecclesiastical style :—

I. An Ox, by Eusebius.

" Now plough, now work I, am devoured each year ;
Loaves fail me ever—not for lack of grain ;
The crops I tend, no drunkard's draughts I drain ;
My voice is sign to fill the town with fear."

---

* Who this Eusebius is I know not, but, from the style of the riddle, conjecture that he was an Englishman of the eighth century, who assumed the classical name, as Winfrith became Bonifacius.

The last references are to the use of the ox's horn in drinking, or in sounding the alarm.

II. A TABLE, BY TATWINE.

" I to all men various rations for their food am wont to share,
  Hence the happy generations have ordained that I shall be
  Fourfold in my feet, and garments of abundant beauty wear ;
  Yet do robbers oft lay hand on me in greed to plunder me—
  Snatch my spoils, and then abandon me with all my limbs laid
      bare." *

III. LECTERN IN EAGLE SHAPE, BY TATWINE.

" Many a time to the surrounding folk I serve celestial cheer,
  While the hollow throat with sounding words of wisdom fills their
      ear ;
  Yet no voice to me is given, nor any tongue for speaking clear.
  And on poise of double pinion am I staid in all men's sight ;
  Yet therein is no dominion that they should be used in flight,
  Nor for walking has the single foot I stand on any might."

The first letters of Tatwine's forty riddles make up a descriptive phrase; and in this, as in his moral and

---

* As most of Tatwine's riddles, with all those by Eusebius, exist only in manuscript, 1 may take the opportunity of quoting the text of Nos. I. and II.

" DE BOVE.

" Nunc aro, nunc operor, consumor in omnibus annis,
  Multæ sunt cereres semperque desunt mihi panes ;
  Et segetes colui nec potus ebrius hausi ;
  Tota urbs pallebat signum quo verba sonabam."

" DE MENSA.

" Multiferis omnes dapibus saturare solesco,
  Quadrupidem hinc felix me sanxerat ætas
  Esse tamen pulchris fatim dum vestibus orner ;
  Certatim me predones spoliare solescunt,
  Raptis nudata exuviis mox membra relinquunt."

theological leanings, he may have given an example to
St. Boniface, whose twenty *ænigmata* form a double
series—ten on the chief virtues, ten on the chief vices
of the Christian code, with the answer to each riddle
concealed in the initial letters of the lines. This is
the least interesting of all the collections, the characterization is both artificial and slipshod, and indeed
could hardly be otherwise, when the author elected to
tie his hands for so difficult a feat of metrical leger-
demain. Precisely on that account, however, his
riddles are of some importance ; for in the discrepancy
between their substance and their form they illustrate
the conflict between the traditional artificialism of
such devices, and the new wine of seriousness which
was being poured into them.

We next stop to report progress at the court of
Charles the Great, and find there that the tendency
towards earnestness has gone even further. To begin
with, we may notice the wonderful prevalence of the
riddle in this centre of power and studiousness.
Historians like Paulus Diaconus, litterateurs like Peter
of Pisa, exchange enigmas in their correspondence ;
and Alcuin, the Englishman, from whom probably
they caught this Anglo-mania, has left specimens of
more kinds than one.* The most interesting collection

* E.g. *Virtus* is treated as a combination of charade and spelling
puzzle : *vir*, the man, is contrasted with the *tus*, or incense for the

is contained in his educational handbook or catechism called, " Disputation of Pippin with Alcuin the Scholar." Pippin is Charles's son, with whose instruction Alcuin was entrusted, and the little manual was compiled by the tutor, with a view to training his pupil's thought and exercising his acumen. It is divided into two parts. In the first, Alcuin asks direct questions and receives descriptive answers, which are to all intents and purposes the theses of riddles. A few of them will serve for illustration :—

" *A*. What is the day ? *P*. The stimulus to work.

" *A*. What is mist ? *P*. Night in day-time, the vexation of the eyes.

" *A*. What is sleep ? *P*. The image of death.

" *A*. What are the hands ? *P*. The artisans of the body.

" *A*. What is the moon ? *P*. The eye of the night, abounding in dew, prophetic of storms.

" *A*. What is autumn ? *P*. The storehouse of the year.

" *A*. What is the year ? *P*. The chariot of the world."

worship of God; and the disastrous effects are noticed of dropping the fourth letter from the word.

The following clever play on *mălum*, *mālum*, and *mulam* can hardly be preserved in translation :—

"Causa necis fueram, tamen et nil nuncupor esse,
Ordine quisque legat recto me, comedet et me,
Me super ille equitet, transverso qui legat ore."

In this way many common subjects of knowledge, the body and its limbs, life and death, the stars, the seasons, the elements are characterized in picture or metaphor. In the second part, an acquaintance with this method of enigmatical explanation is presupposed in the pupil, and the character of question and answer is reversed, the teacher now propounding riddles for Pippin to answer. Sometimes he does this, not by directly naming the object, but by reciting another parallel description of it, *i.e.* he answers one puzzle by another. For example, to Alcuin's problem, "I saw the dead generate the living, and the dead were consumed by the breath of the living," he answers, "From the friction of wood is born the fire that consumes wood." Elsewhere Alcuin adopts a riddle of Symposius, quoted by Wright, to which one would hope the answer is not quite so obvious in this cleanly age as it used to be, but at any rate it is an odd question for a clerical tutor to ask an imperial pupil.

"*A.* I was with others on a hunt in which we took nothing back, if we caught anything; but what we could not catch, that we took home with us. *P.* This is the hunt on which peasants go."

Or again, borrowing from Symposius, he asks in regard to sleep, or Somnus: "Who is it that we can only see when we close our eyes?" And Pippin replies, "Whoever snores shows him to you."

This pædagogic use of the riddle will seem less surprising when we remember that modern school exercises are hardly different in character, save in their sacrifice of the literary element, and that a collection of mathematical problems has been irreverently styled a book of conundrums. Besides their application to the practical business of life, there are two other points in these riddles—one formal, the other very essential—which illustrate the continued inroads of the Anglo-Saxon spirit. This we see in passing from the Latin of Alcuin to the English of his somewhat younger contemporary and countryman, the famous poet Cynewulf. The first is that fashion of replying to the question, not categorically, but by a new statement of the case. Of course, in some sense, this practice is as ancient as it is natural; and we all remember how Samson's thesis, " Out of the eater came forth meat, and out of the strong came forth sweetness," was answered by the query, " What is sweeter than honey ? and what is stronger than a lion ? " But there are several indications that the Anglo-Saxons specially insisted on this, and we find Cynewulf constantly laying stress, not only on the acuteness, but on the eloquence and literary skill required to answer him. He often concludes with such turns as these: " Guess, if thou canst, Sage practised in words, what this creature may be ; " " Answer, prudent in heart, with sure speech, master of words ; " " If thou canst rede a riddle swiftly with certain words, then speak ; " " Whosoever will, let him proclaim with noble words what it is that I speak of." That these answers have not survived, is easily explicable. In the first place, they must have been of a much more extempore character than the riddle itself; and in the second, the authors probably stood far below Cynewulf in poetical talent; so that generally they would not be worth preserving. But the custom would be peculiarly congenial to the Anglo-Saxons, as they sent round the harp after meat in the hall. And it is just what we might expect from their use of the riddle, to stimulate a poetical appreciation of things, not to amuse by a momentary jerk of surprise.

The other point is more important. In many of Alcuin's delineations, *e.g.* of the mist as night in day-time, we feel that we are among the metaphors of Anglo-Saxon poetry, which constantly describes the sea as a swan-bath, a battle as the ash-play, an arrow as a war-adder, a ship as a sea-horse, and so on. This fondness for figurative paraphrase is a racial trait, shared by the Scandinavians, whose skalds talk in riddles as M. Jourdain in prose, without knowing it, and puzzle their readers with phrases like " wolf-rill " for *blood*, or " sea's bright sunbeams " for *gold*. Now, it is clear that this habit of mind could not but exert enormous influence on the production of intentional riddles; and this is one cause of, in both senses of the word, their *tropical* luxuriance in England. It shifts them still further from the sphere of wit into that of fancy and imagination, and Cynewulf runs riot in discovering analogies, not only with his subjects as a whole, but with their parts, their functions, and their origin. Sometimes this becomes the midsummer madness of metaphor, but more frequently he is protected from such a lapse by the depth and strength of his emotion. If he often bewilders by his profusion of imagery, it is not because he wishes to show off his own abundance, but because he is determined to bring home to himself and his audience all the aspects of that strange existence which he is trying to describe; and his sketches are always steeped in feeling. It may help us to realize the interval between him and Symposius in spirit, when we notice the difference in the size of their riddles. Cynewulf's longest contains more than a hundred lines, and only a couple are confined within the original number of three. One of these I have already given: it is the spelling puzzle on a hound: the other is on frost.

> " I watched a wight wend on his path ;
> Many the marvels his might performed.
> A wonder happed on his way—the water became bone."

But precisely these short ones seem to be the worst in

the whole quarry; the poet needs room to move before
he can show his power. He sometimes borrows from
Symposius, and when he keeps near the limits of his
original, is at a great distance in all other respects, for
he fails completely in point and brevity of wit; but
when he expands and recasts, he makes ample amends
by his emotional power and his feeling for the picturesque. To illustrate this we may place together
two pairs of riddles by the two poets. The subject
of the first is a book worm, which in Symposius
thus concisely describes itself:—

> " What a letter is I know not, yet of letters is my food,
> And in studïous zeal I grow not, yet are books my livelihood.
> And though I devour the muses, it has done myself no good."

Very long-winded and obvious in comparison is
Cynewulf's statement :—

> " A moth ate words. To me it seemed
> Matter of marvel when I marked this wonder,
> That a warrior's words a worm should devour,
> Like a thief in the night, with the noble speech,
> The stay of the strong. Yet the stealthy guest
> Was none the wiser for the words that he swallowed."

Here we feel and like the Anglo-Saxon's honest sense
of wonder, and notice his added simile, " like a thief in
the night;" but this is all we can say for him. But
take another pair of contrasts, this time on an anchor.
Symposius writes cleverly and happily as usual :—

> " On my crooked iron tressle bear I prongs to left and right.
> With the hurricane I wrestle, with the whirlpool's depths I fight;
> I explore the midmost waters, and the earth itself I bite."

G

Cynewulf is less neat but more poetical, for the mysterious uses of the anchor rouse his full enthusiasm. He belonged to a seafaring stock, and his soul was stirred when he sang of the safeguard of the dragon-bowed ship in the storm, as it hugged a dangerous coast, to be laid by again when the sky was clear, and the ship was scudding before the breeze, or beached on some hostile coast.

> " Where no one would ween I wander oft
> Through bellowing billows to the bottom earth,
> To the soil of the sea. In surge is the ocean,
> In fury the flood, the foam whirls round;
> The whale-realm is roaring, wrathfully raging ;
> Billows break shoreward, and batter the cliffs,'
> The steep rocks with stones, strew them with sand,
> With weeds and with waves,—while the wide sea-floor,
> The bosom of earth, I bite in strife,
> Weighed down with the waters. The waves that enshroud me
> I fling not from me till freed by the guide
> That wills all my ways. Oh, wise one! say,
> From the depths of the deep who draweth me forth,
> When ocean again has its anger stilled,
> And the currents are calm that covered me once."

But this race had latterly settled down to subdue the soil; and the same instinct of wonder, the same feeling of mystery that led heathen husbandmen to imagine a god of agriculture, led Cynewulf to celebrate its implements. This is how he describes a rake:—

> " Something saw I in resorts of men
> That feeds the farm-stock ; its face is its help,

> With treasure of teeth it travels face down.
> It harries but hurts not, and homeward speeding,
> Gripping the wall.grass, gropes after herbs,
> Finds without fail the unfastened ones,
> Leaves the lovely ones alone if well-rooted,
> To flicker and flash, to flower and green."

Or, to take another instance: in those days of war, of the battles of the kites and the crows, as Milton puts it, would not men be impressed with the secret craft that lurks in a bow; when it is strung and its arrow placed, an instrument of death, but without its twine as worthless as a willow wand?

> " I, creature of cunning, to conflict am framed!
> When bowing my back, from my bosom there flies
> A venomous viper, I verily drive
> The murderous mischief with might from me hence.
> When the warrior who wields me, and worked me this woe,
> Loosens my limbs, I am longer than erewhile,
> Till he gives me again the grievous drug
> And the venom vile I vomit anew.
> From this harm that I hint of, hard matter is it
> For man of the march to mend hereafter,
> If what flies from me forth he feel in such wise
> That the fighter forfeits force or life,
> For that drink of death, that draught I pour full.
> If I bide unbound, obey I none,
> So tie me tightly : and tell my name."

Or, again, how manifold were the uses of the horn ! With it the oxen fought; from it the wassailers drank ; in it the gleeman received his wage ; through it sounded the summons to the fight or to the hunt.

> " Once fought I weaponed ; a youthful wight
> Now gives me garb of gold and silver—

> A wire-drawn woof. Now warriors kiss me ;
> Summoning to slaughter now sounds my voice
> And calls the keen thegns. The courser now bears me
> Far to the forest, or fair with adornment
> I bound o'er the billows on back of the sea-horse.*
> My lap, some lady laden with rings
> Fills now for me ; or fallen I lie,
> Hard and headless, my hangings stolen.
> Once more on the wall where warriors drink
> Gilded and garnished with gawds I hang.
> Striding their steeds, as stately war-badge
> The warriors wear me ;—the wind then drink I,
> Burnished bright, from bosoms of men.
> Sometimes my voice sounds, the soldiers bidding
> To wine and wassail ; it wakeneth sometimes
> To reave from robbers their wrong-got spoil
> And fright the foe.—Speak forth my name."

Or, once more, what ineffable mystery wrapped round a manuscript of the Bible ! The mere writing would, for the half-savage, be invested with its customary awe, while all the processes through which the parchment had to pass would doubly impress the new convert in view of their wonderful result, the rescue of souls from the "ungentle ones," and their restoration to the fellowship of saints and angels.

> " From me my foeman filched my life,
>   Stole my world-strength, wet me then,
>   Dipped in water, drew me thence,
>   Set in the sunlight ; and there soon lost I
>   The hairs I had. The hard-edged knife,

---

* *Merehengest*, ocean-stallion, here for ship, as *fugles wynn*, the pride of the bird, in the next riddle, line 8, for feather.

Cinder-sharpened, shore me then,
And fingers folded. Freely bedewed me
The Quills of birds with drops of blessing,
Flecked my brown face with frequent traces,
Deeply drank the draughts of tree-dye,
Anon stepped on me, strod across me,
Travelling dark-tracked. Me next a trusty one
Sheathed within shields, sheltered in hides,
Girt me with gold, and gladdened me
With wondrous smith-work wire encompassed.
Now far be famed by fairness of mine—
My dazzling dwelling and dye of red—
The Prince of Peoples, not pines of Hell.
If mortal man has mind to use me,
In soul he is sounder, certain of victory,
Higher in heart, happier in mood,
Mightier in mind, with more of friends,
Lief ones and loving, loyal and good,
Trusty and true ones, who tenderly nourish
His fame and fortune and fold him round
With beauty and benisons, in love's embraces
Who compass him closely. How do men call me ?
Search for man's sake ! Sacred my name,
High-famed 'mongst heroes, holy itself."

Such riddles are so edifying, that one is almost
tempted to speculate on their purpose and audience,
and to conjecture that they were, like Alcuin's, used
for educational aims. But this is not the case: the
allusions to the wassailers and the mead-hall, and the
board where warriors drink, are too frequent to be
ambiguous. Yet we are left with a feeling of amazement. The old Anglo-Saxons can hardly have been
the barbarians of common imagination if at their
revels they were so entertained.

About a tithe of Cynewulf's riddles are on subjects now generally tabooed, but they express merely *naïf* wonder, not, I think, wanton indelicacy, or even marked jocularity. The rest take up natural phenomena, or the inventions of man; old myths, as of the dragon flying to its cavern of treasure; or new beliefs, as of the infinitude of the human soul. And in form the old conundrum character is so far transcended, that the riddle ranks among the best songs of the time, and we can only here and there prefer the professed lyric before it. Perhaps a civilian may be permitted to doubt whether the entertainment in the " hall where" our modern "warriors drink " is always much more exalted in character.

To sum up our history and characterization of these Anglo-Saxon curiosities: The old English scóp accepted the elaborate contrivances of Roman wit which he inherited, because he felt, perhaps too keenly and tremulously, the wonders of the world; but in accepting he transformed them, till, by adding weight and fire, he gradually converted the epigrams of Symposius into perfervid little lyric allegories.

SOLOMON IN EUROPE.

[Most of the materials for the history of these legends of Solomon are contained in Kemble's " Salomon and Saturnus " (Ælfric Society); in Hoffmann's paper in the *Sitzungsberichte* of the Munich Academy, 1871 ; in Jagię's paper in the " Archiv für Slavische Philologie," bd. i.; and, for the story of the elopement, above all in Vogt's " Deutsche Dichtungen von Salomon und Markolf," bd. i.]

HAMLET, moralizing on the skull of Yorick, exclaims " May not the imagination trace the noble dust of Alexander till he finds it stopping a bung-hole ? " Yet if the bodily change proclaims the hollowness of all earthly fame, perhaps the lesson is more clearly taught by the popular corruptions of that fame itself. Alexander the Great might overlook the desecration of his ashes. It would be harder for him to bear with the mediæval stories that accuse him of an expedition against Paradise to levy tribute from the angels, and of an inglorious retreat from before the walls. And he is no solitary victim. Virgil was for generations better known as a necromancer than as a poet. The politic Emperor Charlemagne appears in story as a fighting saint, angels and prophecies directing his wars, his followers forming as it were a noble army of martyrs.   And the subject of the present sketch is the checkered literary career of Solomon, in his wanderings from age to age and from place to place, with the wonderful adventures that have befallen him on the way.   We, as a nation, have borne a hand in transforming and distorting his original likeness, so it is only fair that we should grant him a little tardy sympathy.

But before proceeding to the Solomon of legend, we must recall the Solomon of history.   For no matter what mad pranks tradition may play with men and events, one thing must never be forgotten—it is always founded on fact.   It does not originate quite by chance.   There is some feature in the authenticated stories, some action or quality of the men, which gives rise to the later inventions, and round which they gather.   This may be seen from our previous examples.   Alexander, who is said to have wept because there were no more worlds to conquer, finds in the later romance a new field for his ambition. Charlemagne, the champion of Catholic against Aryan Christianity, who, moreover, repelled the heathens in the North and the Mohammedans in the South, becomes quite naturally the invincible hero of the Church, fighting for the faith, and miraculously inspired.   Virgil is credited with knowledge of the black art, perhaps from vague reminiscences of his story of the Descent to the Infernal Regions, just as this is one of Dante's reasons for making him his guide through hell. What, then, are the salient features of Solomon's true life and character?

He became king when the Hebrews were entering on a new phase of their history. The days were past when their religious exclusiveness could be rigidly maintained. That might suit a loose federation of tribes held together chiefly by their religious consciousness, which, when maintained, led them to harass the nations around, and, when lost, made it easy for the nations to harass them. But with the closer union under the kings, especially under David, came increased strength and wealth. When Israel became a great State it could not always war with the heathen; and with the growth of its riches the need arose to cultivate the graces of life. Solomon, succeeding in his youth to the supreme power, had the insight and sagacity to become exponent of these tendencies. He raised the royal authority, but took care also to raise the respect for it by justice and munificence. Himself a man of literary tastes, his knowledge or feeling uttered itself in shrewd sayings, songs, and parables; and in his court there was a patronage of art which had hitherto been strange among the Jews. The political side of this was that he lived in amity and commercial alliance with his heathen neighbours. He "made affinity" with Pharaoh; he cemented David's connection with Tyre; he had dealings with the surrounding kings, and intermarried with their daughters. The effect of all this on a nation hitherto either harrying or being harried was immediate. The country enjoyed unexampled tranquillity; stately buildings arose in Jerusalem; planting was encouraged; the precious metals flowed in. Nevertheless this prosperity had its dark side. The concessions to the heathen were in the spirit of compromise with far inferior views. The system of concurrent endowment, by which Milcom and Ashtoreth were subsidized along with Jehovah, was not calculated to satisfy the most earnest minds; and the expenses of the court, especially of the seraglio, would be apt to raise a party of malcontents. Solomon himself, like a kindred mediæval figure, Frederick II., the Wonder of the World, broke down in his plans, not only because they were above, but because they were below the sentiment of the age. Their over-catholicity alienated common religious feeling, which the harems of both, for different reasons, naturally failed to conciliate; and we are not surprised to find the popular revulsion expressing itself in Ahijah's announcement of the fall of Solomon's house, and in the subsequent disruption of the kingdom.

There are here three grand traits that rivcted the attention of contemporaries, soon became in a manner proverbial, and formed the nucleus of later myths: Solomon's wisdom, his glory, and his fall. To these we must give some attention as they appear in the original scriptural narratives, selecting such details as are important for the development of our special series of legends.

The references to his wisdom crowd upon us, from the first account of his choosing it before other blessings. In the Second Book of Chronicles it is stated that he "passed all the kings of the earth in wisdom," which perhaps is no great compliment; but in the First Book of Kings it runs less ambiguously: "He was wiser than all men; than Ethan the Ezrahite, and Heman, and Chalcol, and Darda, the sons of MAHOL" (the last an important name for us). "He spake three thousand proverbs: and his songs were a thousand and five." He spake of trees, of beasts, of fowls, of creeping things and of fishes. "And there came of all people to hear the wisdom of Solomon, from all kings of the earth, which heard of his wisdom." Such visits for instruction almost imply that the teacher would have to satisfy his guests of his pre-eminence—imply, that is, visits for debate. Accordingly, we hear that "when the Queen of Shebah heard of the fame of Solomon ["concerning the name of the Lord," adds the Book of Kings] she came to prove him with hard questions." "And Solomon told her all her questions," so that she exclaims: "Behold, the one half of the greatness of thy wisdom was not told me!" The story of this visit was not forgotten. Not only did it give rise to a separate group of Eastern legends, but, in the first and third Gospels, it furnishes Christ, whose images are never unfamiliar, with a comparison and contrast. Nor should we overlook the vanquished Queen's offering of gold, jewels, and spice, to swell the victor's wealth, nor his responsive liberality.

This leads us to a consideration of the King's magnificence, but we need not cite the innumerable instances of this trait; a few of the most noticeable will suffice. And not many are more noticeable among all the references to his servants and officers and their equipment, than his retinue of horsemen with their horses. Their number of twelve thousand, their four thousand stalls, the cities he appointed them, their rations, their maintenance, the traffic in them, are all items which are enumerated and referred to as of the first moment. But more important were his building operations. His own royal house that occupied thirteen, and the far more glorious temple that occupied only seven years in building, gave the Hebrews the splendour of a court and a capital. And Solomon's great way of doing things was seen as much in his methods as in his results. No unseemly bustle, says the story, disturbed the erection of the great national and religious fane. "The house, when it was in building, was built of stone made ready before it was brought thither, so that there was neither hammer, nor axe, nor any tool of iron heard in the house while it was in building." And the decorations were in the same grand style. Solomon, distrusting untrained Hebrew taste and skill, borrowed from his ally, the King of Tyre, a namesake and half-countryman of the Tyrian king, Hiram, or Hiram Abi, as the Hebrew chronicles style him, a worker in brass who "was filled with wisdom and understanding, and cunning to work all works in brass." He moulded all the metal utensils and ornaments; and here are especially noteworthy the lions about the throne, the oxen under the sea in the temple, the lions, bulls, and cherubim on the borders; above all, the two cherubim that stretched their wings over the ark. These cherubim we must bear in mind, and though Josephus says that in his time their shape was "unknown and not even to be conjectured," we must try to form some idea of what they were like. Without discussing the philology of the word, we may be sure that they had wings, and may suspect that they were quadrupeds, since in the eighteenth Psalm it is said of the Deity, "He rode upon a cherub." Perhaps we shall not be far wrong, then, when we remember their half-Punic designer, in imagining them like some of those winged centaurs of Oriental sculpture that are still to be seen in the British Museum.

But perhaps the chief instance of Solomon's Eastern state was his huge harem with its thousand inmates, from which we may at once pass to the story of the fall with which it was so intimately connected. Here, however, we must guard against a misapprehension to which our modern Western feeling exposes us. Solomon is blamed nowhere for the number, but always for the creed and kin, of his wives. In Kings (for in the more courtly Chronicles the whole episode is omitted) the writer laments Solomon's love, not for many women, but "for many strange women;" and Nehemiah, in the only other Old Testament reference to it, uses the story to point a moral, not against polygamy, but against marriages with the heathen: "Even Solomon did outlandish women cause to sin." And with the ensuing worship of his wives' gods, Moloch and the rest, is connected the opposition he encountered from Edom and Damascus, and especially from Jeroboam, who received his first impulse to revolt from the announcement of the offended prophet Ahijah. And this prophecy foretold more terrible things, the loss of the kingdom mitigated only by delay, limited only by the loyalty of the southern tribes.

We may now see how these hints have been worked out and added to by Josephus, who comes next in date among the more serious historians.

Fewest alterations have been made under the third head, but even here there are one or two worth noticing. For example, in the narrative of Kings we are given to understand rather that Jeroboam fled from the king as a precautionary measure, than that he had been guilty of an overt offence; but Josephus states that the youth already in Solomon's lifetime tried to make use of his position to stir up the people and seize the throne. Moreover, he takes up Solomon's polygamy in its moral as well as in its religious side, and while still most severe on the recognition of heathen charms, also accuses the king of sensuality and of uxoriousness—the last an inevitable but suggestive gloss: "he was governed by his wives." Perhaps more striking is his ingenuity in discovering an earlier backsliding of the king's. This was the transgression of the command to make no graven image, through the sculptures in palace and temple.

But for the temple itself he has only praise. The

difference of time in the erection of it and the palace is made the subject of another interesting comment. The former, though grander, was ready sooner, because in it "God co-operated;" that is, in it Solomon had supernatural help. And in describing its splendours he varies from the account of its erection without the noise of tools. "The whole structure of the temple was made with great skill of polished stones, and those laid together so very harmoniously and smoothly, that there appeared to the spectators no sign of any hammer or other instrument of architecture, but as if without use of them the entire materials had naturally united themselves together, so that the agreement of one part with another seemed rather to have been natural, than to have arisen from the force of tools upon them." Thus, to combine the two accounts, the temple, both in process and completion, would seem to be erected without tools.

Nor in treating of Solomon's other glories is Josephus at all lacking in enthusiasm or minuteness. Thus, in regard to the horsemen, he tells us that they were the king's attendants on steeds the swiftest and finest in the world, that they were in the flower of their years, larger than most men, with long flowing locks, which were daily sprinkled with dust of gold to make them brighter.

But the weightiest additions are certainly those that refer to the king's wisdom, and of these the bulkiest and most emphatic deal with those contests of question and answer of which we have seen the germ in the episode of the Queen of Shebah. Now, however, Solomon's antagonist is Hiram, king of Tyre. Josephus seems to have been much occupied with the story, for he narrates it as well in his "Antiquities" as in his treatise "Against Apion," and in both cases quotes two versions. The passage in the "Antiquities" runs: "The King of Tyre sent sophisms and enigmatical sayings to Solomon, and desired that he would solve them, and free them from the ambiguity that was in them. Now, so sagacious was Solomon that none of these problems were too hard for him, but that he conquered them all by his reasonings, and discovered their hidden meaning and brought it to light. Menander also, who translated the 'Tyrian Archives' out of the dialect of the Phenicians into the language of the Greeks, thus makes mention of these two kings when he says thus: 'When Abibalus was dead, his son Hiram received the kingdom from him. Under this king was Abdemon, a very youth in age, who always conquered the difficult problems which Solomon, king of Jerusalem, commanded him to explain.' Dius, also makes mention of him: 'When Abibalus was dead, his son Hiram reigned. Solomon, who was then king of Jerusalem, sent riddles to Hiram, and desired to receive the like from him; but that he who could not solve them should pay money to him that did solve them. And Hiram accepted the conditions, and when he could not solve the riddles he paid a great deal of money for his fine; but afterwards, he did solve the proposed riddles by means of Abdemon, a man of Tyre; and Hiram proposed other riddles, which, when Solomon could not solve, he paid back a great deal of money to Hiram.'" The statements in the treatise "Against Apion" are to the same effect, with the following introduction, which implies that the tournament was between friends. "There was another passion, a philosophical inclination of theirs, which cemented the friendship that was between them, for they sent mutual problems to one another, with a desire to have them unriddled by each other."

In these accounts we have to notice the agency of Abdemon. For the rest there may be a basis of truth in the story, yet it is exactly the sort of development that we might expect in legend. For the Biblical records quote a correspondence between the two kings, and mention their singularly intimate relations, which seem only once to have been disturbed. Then Hiram was in some sort famous for his temple-building among the heathen, as Solomon for his temple-building among the Jews; and this, which made each a representative of his racial religion, would invite tradition to confront them with each other. For we must remember that while such a pictorial opposition of rival sages has many parallels both before and since, from the story of Moses and Pharaoh's magicians, to that of Friar Bacon and Jacques Vandermast, the contrast, whenever Solomon was involved, would be far deeper than between this man and that. When Bacon closes the contest by having Vandermast carried off bodily by a demon, we have simply the victory of one magician over another, coloured a little perhaps by national feeling. But Solomon's victories (and Josephus, when speaking in his own person, mentions only victories) would always mean the triumph of the Jewish wisdom over the Gentile, of the sacred wisdom over the profane. Hence he could not have a more fitting antagonist than one who laboured for the cult of Tyrian deities, whose names Josephus renders by Jupiter, Hercules, and Astarte. And that the contest should be in enigmas need not surprise us, when we remember the narrow line that separates the parable from the riddle. In Proverbs, the king insists on the wisdom of being able to "understand a proverb and the interpretation, the words of the wise and their dark sayings." And Jesus, son of Sirach, apostrophizes him in Ecclesiasticus : "Thou filledst the earth with parables and with enigmas. Thou wast in the admiration of all lands by thy songs, thy proverbs, parables, and interpretations." Even the wager that accompanied Hiram and Solomon's match would have its precedent in the Queen of Shebah's tribute; and from the stake that Samson laid on *his* riddle, we may see how this feature, too, could be a natural popular expansion.

Hitherto we have seen Solomon, according to Hebrew narrators, chief among mortals in wisdom; but now, by another addition, he is made master of unseen intelligences. "God gave him skill to expel demons," says Josephus, and goes on to relate that he himself witnessed such exorcisms effected before Vespasian and his troops, by a Jew, who made use of Solomon's incantations and of a ring containing one of the roots Solomon had described.

Now, supposing these two traditions of Solomon's disputes and of his relations with the spirit world were brought into connection, the central idea of the former might obviously be strengthened and relieved. For the contest would be even more glaringly between religious wisdom and questionable demonic power. In point of fact, the dealings of the great king with those intermediate spirits, the Hebrew Shedim, the Mohammedan Djins, are recounted in a multitude of Eastern legends. Perhaps the best known in England are those tales of the " Arabian Nights," one of which, *e.g.*, describes a Genie imprisoned in a jar by the impress of Solomon's seal on the lid. In regard to the building of the temple, indeed, it was hardly possible that such stories could fail to arise among a people who held these beliefs. In Josephus we have the supernatural acceleration and the toolless appearance of the work ; and a Rabbinical legend, to which we now pass, accounts for these features by the assumption of demonic help. Nor is this all; the same story assists us in the history of the two other Solomon characteristics, his wisdom as shown in his contests, and his fall.

Solomon, we are told in the Talmud, after subduing the other Shedim, or demons, to his will, is still thwarted by their prince, Ashmedai, or Asmodeus. But his help is specially required by Solomon for procuring the serpent Shamir to cut the stones for the temple. Now the demon every day soared to the firmament to examine the laws of heaven, then dived down to examine the laws of the earth, and then refreshed himself by drinking from a cistern of water. This Solomon drains, and fills with wine. Ashmedai, compelled by his thirst to partake, is overcome by slumber, and fettered with a chain which bears on it the name of God. He now has to do Solomon's bidding, and answer *in colloquy all his questions*.

But the king, anxious to see the demon's power, unwarily sets him free, and lends him his own ring, when Ashmedai hurls him away, a distance of four hundred parasangs, and, assuming his shape, occupies the throne. Ashmedai now reigns at Jerusalem, master of the kingdom and of the harem, while Solomon wanders about as a beggar, crying, "I, the preacher, *was* king at Jerusalem." The Sanhedrim, surprised at his persistence, investigate and discover the facts of the case, and restore him his ring. Then the demon flies in fright, and the king enjoys his own again.

There are many legends of this kind, Hebrew, Mohammedan, and Hebræo-Greek. In one of these the fatal ring is described as giving Solomon power, not only over the creatures of air and earth and sea,—perhaps a reminiscence of the natural-history parables ascribed to him,—but over the demon-world as well. Some of the demons, however, were not very submissive: and Solomon had constantly to struggle with the worse ones, who are pictured as of monstrous shape, half bestial, half human; some of them with bodies of horses and heads of men. One story tells how, with an army of these demons and birds and men, he goes against the most truculent of their number. Generally speaking, these apocryphal traditions describe Solomon's relations with the intermediate powers, whether in the way of supremacy, colloquy, or strife. For the Western cycle of tales the first of these points concerns us no farther; in other words, we need not follow at greater length Solomon's legendary magnificence. The two other points we must notice more closely, at least in so far as the legend of Ashmedai illustrates them.

First, then, in regard to the dialogue, we should observe that, according to the early Christian practice of identifying evil spirits with pagan deities, the way was paved for representing Solomon in dispute with a heathen god, a fitter antagonist even than Hiram, because the very head and impersonification of heathenism. Second, however, the legend represents Solomon as the questioner, and the demon as compelled to reply. This differs from the early types, in which Solomon's victory rather lies in his readiness and his antagonist's inability to answer, and the same change has taken place in all the apocryphal dialogues between him and the spirits, especially in the cosmological discussions between him and Ashmedai. But the alteration is due to Solomon's new *rôle* of master forcing secrets from sometimes reluctant servants. If the story changed back to a trial of skill, the form would change back with it.

Turning to the other form of the legend, we find that the story of Solomon's fall has undergone a very important modification. In the Bible the mitigation of his doom lay in its being postponed and partial, here, however, in its being temporary. And the occasion for the change was furnished by the expression in Ecclesiastes: " I, the preacher, *was* King of Jerusalem," whence it was inferred that at one time he had lost sovereignty ; and Jeroboam's unsuccessful attempt at revolt, which Josephus mentions, may have given a *point d'appui* to the invention.

On the other hand, the legendary fall in this version is not attributed to the king's wives, though it is expressly stated that his enemy gains possession of them. But elsewhere this gap is supplied. Indeed, in a Mohammedan story, it is one of the wives that procures the ring for the demon, whose ensuing triumph punishes Solomon for worshipping, to please his Indian queen, the statue of her father.

To sum up, we find that the account of Solomon's wisdom has given rise to stories of wit-combats in which he joins with heathen sages, and of conversations that he holds with a demon-prince who, perhaps, may be transformed to a heathen god. The account of his fall has given rise to stories which represent him as vanquished through his uxoriousness by the same demon-prince, who seizes his wives ; while Solomon goes about in beggary, till, recovering his magic ring, he also recovers his State.

Now, tradition continued to run on independently along each of these lines, the story of the debate chiefly from east to west, the story of the fall chiefly from south to north, till, strangely enough, they are found in some sort of combination or, at least, contact in Germany.

We shall proceed on one line till we reach the junction, and then return to our starting-point by the other.

In the history of the dialogue, not the earliest (for it belongs to the twelfth century), but the most convenient transition link is a notice by William, Bishop of Tyre. He mentions tales of a certain Abdimus who, in chains, solved Hiram's riddles for Solomon, and then proceeds: "This, perhaps, is he that the fabulous stories of the vulgar name Marcolf; of whom it is told that he solved Solomon's riddles, and replied, propounding in like manner riddles to be solved in their turn." Abdimus is thus identified with Marcolf, but how are these names related? and why were they selected?

For the first, we can hardly fail to seek an origin in the Abdemon of Josephus. But how did Abdemon, who interpreted for Hiram, come in legend to interpret for Solomon? It has been suggested that he was confounded with Hiram's other cunning servant, the Hiram Abi of Chronicles, who was sent to help the Hebrew King in his brazen works.   But the description of him obeying the king's behests in chains, suggests, besides, an additional confusion, viz. with Ashmedai himself, who was forced in chains to assist and answer Solomon.   Both were engaged in the structure of the temple, and if we remember that Hiram Abi shaped those figures by which Solomon transgressed, he may well correspond with the mythical assistant and assailant of Solomon's glory.

This, however, becomes more probable when we consider the second designation, Marcolf.   This (in its various forms Marcholfus, Marcoul, Marcon, Marolf, Morolf) was the usual name for Solomon's disputant in the West, and, since traceable as far back as Notker in the tenth century, must have been in use at a still earlier date.   But though Western in sound it is really Eastern in origin, and possibly, like Abdimus, contains a reference to more Eastern personages than one.   It may have been confounded with *Mahol*, that sage Hebrew whose sons Solomon surpassed in wisdom. But at any rate it implies an earlier form, Marcolis, corrupted from Malchol, Moloch, or Milcom.   To this god, Solomon sacrificed to his ruin, and to such a god, as we saw, Ashmedai might easily be converted.

But the proof becomes stronger if we turn to a third name by which, in Europe, Solomon's antagonist is known; and this the one which, though quite singular and isolated, is also the earliest on record. In the fifth century we have mention of a *Contradictio Salomonis*, but the contradictor is not named; in the tenth, the more widely spread Markolf comes to the surface; but we still have two fragmentary Anglo-Saxon dialogues written in the ninth, which represent Solomon in dispute with *Saturn*. Here, at any rate, there can be no question about the personality of the heathen god, and it need not surprise us that the appearance of the Syrian deity in the West should be ambiguous, now with his name translated into a classical form, now with his person rendered by a classical proxy. And that Saturn is after all no other than Ashmedai is also apparent. In the poem he calls himself Earl of the Chaldeans, but the country he describes, to which no flesh may come, is not Chaldea, but a magic realm. He is sprung of dreadful race that has fought against God. And in the one poem, the cosmological argument is a modification of Solomon's cosmological instruction by Ashmedai; while the other, as frequently happens in the Eastern apocrypha of Solomon, treats of the subjugation of demons.

In the older fragment Saturnus, who enumerates all the countries through which he has wandered, engages Solomon in a conversation on such subjects as death, fate, the fall of the angels, and the conflict of the good and evil genii of men. In the later dialogue, Saturn, after studying the books of all Islands, the history of India, the science of Lybia and Greece, comes to Solomon for an explanation of the Paternoster. Solomon solves his difficulties in a mystical and cabalistic exposition, which fills Saturn with admiration and delight, but which, to a modern reader, is a good deal more puzzling than the original subject of discussion. Thus, for example, he separates and personifies the letters that make up the Paternoster, with them, as with a charm of Runes, to subdue the powers of darkness.

The eccentric description of Saturn, as Earl of the Chaldeans, need not detain us. His subjects have been selected for him on account of the fame and antiquity of their speculations; and his brevet of rank is no more extraordinary than that of Duke Eneas, or Dame Venus, or Jupiter the Great Enchanter, as they appear three hundred years later, in the romances of chivalry. It is a more abrupt transformation that makes of Solomon a Christian expositor, whose inspired insight renders him wise beyond the stores of unregenerate culture, and who vanquishes the demons by the might of Christian prayer. Yet there still remains the essential idea of the legend, the contrast between the sacred and the unhallowed, the higher and the lower wisdom; only change of time and clime has brought consecration to the tenets of a new creed.

Another change, far less obvious, contained in it germs of more important consequences. In occasional details, *e.g.* in the description of the demons, who here and there approximate to our English elves, the Oriental ideas of the poem take a certain local colouring from the Teutonic West. When this process once began, it was bound to go on. Indeed, the mere form of the story made it peculiarly susceptible to such influences. The dialogue, with its sharp interchange of question and answer, of thesis and antithesis, of problem and counter-problem, was a favourite form for poems of moral and religious content among the Teutonic tribes, and goes back to heathen times. Perhaps its classical example is the "Vafthrudnismal" of the verse "Edda," in which Odin seeks out the giant Vafthrudnir, and agreeing that the vanquished shall pay forfeit with his life, they try to pose each other with hard questions on the fates of heaven and earth. Despite a partial similarity of tone, it would be wrong to think that this poem had any connection with the story of Solomon and Saturn, which, as we have seen, is of undoubtedly Jewish origin. But the latter may have gravitated towards a native myth, a process which the dialogue form and the attitude of the speakers would render easy, and which would account for the Teutonic leaven in some parts of the discussion. At any rate, in the next version we have to consider, the Teutonic element has displaced the rabbinical. The Anglo-Saxon " Salomon and Saturnus" is still Oriental, with a flavour of English ideas. There may be Eastern traits in the German " Salomon and Markolf," but in the main it is a product of Germany.

For we must now skip over more than three hundred years, and cross to the Continent. The changes the poem has undergone in the interval are so great that it can scarcely be recognized. Of course the continuity is not broken. Through all the accumulations and *débris*, the main lines of the legend may still be traced. But the action of the Teutonic element is now undisguised, and the mysticism of the poem has been rejected for broad popular humour.

This change seems to have begun in Flanders towards the close of the twelfth century, and one reason for it may have been that the name Marcolis, in its corrupted form Markolf, was dangerously German in sound, and no longer suggested any very mysterious or superhuman personality, but rather the slow, sly peasant, who was everywhere around. But if Solomon were confronted with an antagonist of rustic name, the contrast between the higher and lower wisdom would cease to be between the sacred and the profane, and could only come to mean a contrast between theory and practice, between learning and shrewd mother wit. We have a saying that star-gazers are apt to break their shins. Solomon's mind is here of the star-gazing order, so he may still be taken to represent the nobler wisdom in opposition to the baser-souled Markolf, who is fully alive to the advantages of keeping his shins whole. This character he everywhere preserves. The French versions of the dialogue, *e.g.* " Les Dictz de Salomon avecque les Responses de Marcon " (1530), soon take an original direction by transgressing all limits of decency, but do not essentially change the cynical cunning of Markolf's character. And in the English collection that belongs to the end of the thirteenth century, known as the " Proverbs of Hendyng," the speaker, who is worldly wisdom incarnate, calls himself " Marcolves Sone." But the classical example of the opposition between Solomon and Markolf is the German dialogue of the fifteenth century, with the Latin dialogues on which it was based, and which in their turn probably render a lost Low German original.

The German version contains three divisions. In the first, which introduces Markolf as a slovenly and deformed boor before the magnificent king, the antagonism is worked out with considerable humour, and in great detail. Solomon, with frequent use of scriptural phrase, makes some highflown declaration about himself, or virtue, or woman, which Markolf contradicts or parodies or caps with some shrewd homely proverb. Thus the king begins by announcing, " God has given me wisdom more than all men." " Praise yourself if you have ill neighbours," answers Markolf. When Solomon goes on to boast that he is the chosen monarch of Israel, Markolf, nothing daunted, rejoins, " In the land of the blind of course the one-eyed is king." Solomon quotes, " To him that hath shall be given;" Markolf infers, "Therefore let us pluck and rob the poor to enrich the man of means." And so on, through a series of statements and contradictions, Markolf lavishing special contempt on Solomon's gallant praise of women. In the end he is dismissed with gifts.

In the second part, the opposition between Solomon's theorems and Markolf's knavery is even more drastically exhibited, but now rather in narrative than in dialogue. Solomon, when hunting, finds Markolf in his hut, is greeted with riddling answers to the questions he puts, and summons the peasant to court. But Markolf misconducts himself so impudently that the king condemns him to death, unless he can watch with him the whole night through without giving way to sleep. Markolf, however, continually falls over, and always excuses himself with the plea that he has been meditating. The king tells him that if he will escape execution he must prove the results of his meditations, among others that a woman cannot keep a secret, and that nature is stronger than habit, the next day.

Now, to his sister Markolf confides, under the solemnest pledges of silence, that he is plotting to kill the king. He then goes off to Solomon and brings a charge against this sister's good fame. Of course she is indignant, and retaliates by disclosing his treason; and the sham conspirator has proved his first point. Again, Solomon has a favourite cat, which he has trained to his will, and which every night at supper sits on the table supporting his silver candlestick. But Markolf brings in three mice in his sleeve. He lets the first escape: the cat sits steady. The second runs across the table: the candlestick sways to and fro, but the cat, admonished by Solomon, manages to control herself. Then Markolf despatches his last mouse. This is too much for the virtue of the cat; nature triumphs over habit; off she goes, dragging in her wake a chaos of goblets, candles, and plates.

Solomon, cheated of his revenge, but still indignant, now forbids Markolf the court, and threatens that if he ventures to return he will set the dogs on him. Markolf is not disconcerted, and when the dogs are about to tear him in pieces, lets a hare slip from his pocket, which immediately diverts the attention of the kennel from himself. In the presence-chamber he makes himself offensive by spitting, and is told (a curious hint as to the manners of the age) to spit on a bare place, whereupon he selects the bald pate of an old courtier. He is present at the judgment of Solomon, which he makes light of; and when Solomon follows it with a panegyric on women, Markolf dissents, not respectfully, and foretells a day when the king will change his mind. This, too, he is set to prove, and does it by spreading a report that Solomon has ordained that every man is to have seven wives. The next time his majesty shows himself abroad he is greeted with a storm of abuse from every female he meets. At first he tries with a soft answer to turn away the wrath, but at length loses patience, and renders railing for railing in a way that rejoices Markolf's heart. But this trick is not to be forgiven, and Markolf is forbidden to show his face to the king again on pain of certain death; and when he breaks the spirit of this command while observing the letter, Solomon is inexorable—Markolf must die; only, when the guards lead him off to be hanged, as a last favour he may choose his own tree. After a while the culprit returns and complains that he *can't find a tree to his mind*. Solomon is duped, and in the end has to grant him a free pardon.

There are some points here that call for notice ere we proceed to a consideration of the third part, or appendix. The Teutonic conquest of the Eastern legend is now complete. The answers are forced on Markolf at hazard of his life, like those of the mythical contests. Some of the incidents are common German heritage, and are found elsewhere in no connection with the Solomon legend. The final incident, for example, is told of James I.'s fool, Archie Armstrong, though the threat of summary justice shows, as Kemble says, that it arose in a more primitive stage of society.

Again, the dialogue form is at last abandoned, and we have instead a narrative of helpless inefficiency contrasted with thorough experience of affairs; the man of wiles fulfilling the behests of the royal woman-worshipper, who in wisdom can now at most claim to be, like his British namesake, the wisest fool in Christendom. Now, in the third part this is carried further and worked out in a sort of romance, in which Markolf, instead of obeying Solomon in malice and guile, helps him as his brother and general factotum. There is, however, a fuller and independent version of this story in a German poem, " Salman and Morolf," to which we must first turn.

It exists in texts of the fifteenth century, but evidence internal and external assigns it a much earlier date. It belongs to the large class of gleemen's poems which were most in vogue at the end of the twelfth century, and originated, perhaps, in the crusaders' camps for the delectation of rank and file. All these poems have a striking family likeness in form and matter. They show equal fondness for jest and earnest, equal respect for cunning and valour, and they love to introduce some chief actor under the person of a gleeman. They all deal with an expedition to the East for an Eastern bride. Above all, they delight in the repetition and multiplication, with only slight variations, of the main story as well as of subordinate episodes.

It used to be thought that the present poem was a further development of the dialogue, occasioned by the transference of its personages to the legend of an old Frankish king, whose name, Salman, might give opportunity for the confusion. This is not so. It is, rather, the most corrupt and far-fetched version of the other branch of the Solomon tradition, the story of his fall, or his overthrow by Ashmedai; and its final corruptions are due partly to the gleemen's habit of variation, partly to the absorption of independent tales, partly to that view of the chief characters which the comic debate had introduced. But the essential origin of the poem in the Oriental myths will appear if we examine its contents and, with the

help of earlier versions, gradually reject the inter-
polated elements.

Its substance is as follows. Salman, head of
Christendom, and king of Jerusalem, carries away
by force Salme, the heathen princess of India, bap-
tizes, and weds her. Meanwhile, the great heathen
King Fore (Pharaoh) consults with his lords where
he can find a fitting match, and is advised to seize
Salme for himself. He agrees, and comes against
Jerusalem with a huge host. But Salman and his
brother, the wily Morolf, beat the heathen with a
smaller force, and take Fore captive. Morolf now
counsels the death of the prisoner, but Salman determines not only to spare him, but to hand him over to
the custody of Salme; despite Morolf's remonstrance,
" Whoso puts fire near straw, kindles himself a big
flame." Morolf, nevertheless, is right. Fore presents
his gaoleress with a magic ring, which immediately
rouses in her a passion for the giver. They agree that
in six months a gleeman is to fetch her; and, meanwhile, she helps her prisoner to escape. Morolf taxes her
with this, but the gallant Salman refuses to believe.
After half a year the gleeman comes, and gives her a
magic herb, on tasting which she falls to the ground
as though dead. Morolf suspects a trick, and pours
molten gold through her hand; but when this does
not wake her, he is driven from court, and she is

magnificently buried.   When, however, the coffin is found broken and empty, the distressed king turns to his brother, and begs him to seek the fugitive. Morolf consents, and sets out, personating a Jewish beggar, in which disguise he obtains alms from Salman himself.   After seven years, he comes as a pilgrim to Fore's capital, and recognizes Salme without himself at first being recognized.   Strangely enough, however, after having found the queen's whereabouts, he does not leave at once, but waits and interviews her.   On one such occasion, while playing chess with her, he observes the burn on her hand, and is now, for the first time, quite sure that this is she. A song that he sings betrays him, and his death is at once determined.   Twice he escapes by drugging the guards, the first time to be caught again, but the second with more success. Returning to Jerusalem, he again, as a pilgrim, escapes recognition by the king (an incident which, with slight variation, is repeated a third time), and at length disclosing himself, they plan the recovery of Salme.   They cross the sea with an array of ten thousand chosen heroes; and while these are concealed in a firwood, Salman (such is Morolf's scheme to prevent the escape of Fore or Salme) sets out with some reluctance for Fore's castle, clad in palmer's weeds, which conceal his weapons and a horn. Salme, informed of his arrival by Fore's sister, suspects who it is. Finding her surmises correct, she rejects his prayers to return, and declares her preference for Fore, who shall himself condemn Salman to the gallows. Salman, now confined to an ante-room, sees through the curtain how Salme welcomes her heathen husband home, and hears how she exhorts him to treat his rival without ruth. It is, therefore, rather needless for Fore's sister, who is always friendly to him, specially to come to Salman with these tidings. He is now asked by Fore, how *he* would act, were their positions reversed. This is what the wily Morolf has foreseen, and Salman replies, he would keep him captive for the night and publicly hang him the next morning. Fore, to Salme's delight, exclaims that this shall be Salman's own sentence, and rather inconsistently commands that his captive be fettered, in the very breath with which he bids the sister tend him courteously. The maiden throws away the fetters, and Salman tells her that his angels in the forest will save him. Next morning, the Christian king is again condemned to death, this time in open court, and the procession sets out for the wood, Fore's sister wiping the sweat from Salman's brow. Arrived at the gallows, the condemned is allowed, as a last favour, to blow three blasts on his horn, that St. Michael may come to rescue his soul. At the first blast, his army, in three divisions, hastens forward, and already at the second, is on the spot, and the fight begins. The Christians are victorious; Fore is hanged on his own gallows; Salme, against Morolf's advice, forgiven and restored; Fore's sister conveyed to Jerusalem, and baptized.

But soon the queen breaks faith again; this time with the heathen King Princian, who gains her love with a magic ring, and carries her off. Again Morolf sets out to find her, and meets with many comic adventures, when disguised in succession as cripple, pilgrim, gleeman, butcher, and pedlar. He finds the queen, and, returning at the head of an army, slays Princian and regains Salme, whom he bleeds to death in Jerusalem, while Salman weds Fore's sister.

Perhaps one's first thought, on reading the poem, is given to the sad deterioration of Solomon. It is hard to recognize in this handsome nullity, the great king "who was wiser than all men." Still, there is no change without its good side, and in some respects he has benefited by his tour in Europe. At least he has lost his taste for polygamy, and shows wonderful fidelity to his wife in somewhat trying circumstances. Indeed, almost the only original trait he has preserved is precisely this, that he is woman-ruled. On the other hand, Morolf is a decided improvement on the Markolf of the dialogue. He is no longer a boor, but an accomplished man of the world, still a little sly and tricky, but valiant, practical, and quite a mechanical genius. No doubt even anointed kings are the victims of his horseplay. No doubt he steals and assassinates without turning a hair. He is even a common sharper when he plays chess with Salme, and by ostentatiously displaying his ring diverts her attention, and purloins two pawns and a knight. But his boat would excite the envy of modern engineers, for it goes equally well above water and below; his accomplishments are beyond count, and his readiness of resource inexhaustible. He, indeed, is an embodiment of the gleeman type. The writer feels this, and spares no pains in describing the qualities he and his class possessed: wit and impudence, courage and coarseness, varied skill, and unscrupulous cunning. But all the personages in the poem, not Salman and Morolf alone, are well constructed and consistent; the scenes are vivid, some passages even rise to beauty, and the melody of the verse is always pleasing. In these respects, and in general tone, this is perhaps the best extant of the gleemen's poems.

But such merits cannot appear in an analysis, which indeed displays only the great and obvious defect of the whole. This is its "damnable iteration." That repetition in which the gleemen delighted pervades the entire poem, equally as regards the main plot and the most trivial parenthesis. At the end of the first part, when the business is happily wound up and Salme restored, the whole embroglio begins once more : again there is a magic ring to win her love, again an elopement with a heathen king, again the detective expedition of Morolf incognito, again his return at the head of an army. And so, too, with the details : Salman's disguise, Morolf's disguises, his druggings and escapings, his warnings and the neglect of them, give us the feeling that with all the progress of the story, we never stir from the spot. But even the exasperated reader does not, at first, guess how deeply this repetition is imbedded in the stuff of the story. It contains some contradictions, two of which I have noticed—Morolf's need of seven years to find out Salme's residence, despite his foreknowledge that she would make off with Fore, and the useless interposition of Fore's sister ; and these are due to this same minstrel crotchet. For there were two other popular stories somewhat like that of Salme's elopement, and parts of these our author incorporated in his own work without pausing to see if they were exactly suitable. One of them tells how a lady absconds with a heathen prisoner entrusted to her care ; the husband follows for revenge, is recognized, and would be executed but that his son and followers come to the rescue. From this quarter the story of Fore's expedition and captivity has crept in. Were it omitted, the wily Morolf would have some excuse for his delay in finding the queen, who would then have made off with an unknown admirer. The other story describes a similar elopement, but in it the avenging husband when captured is tied to a pillar in the hall, and forced to witness his wife's fondness for his rival. But that rival's sister cuts his bonds, and returns him his sword with which to right himself. Here we have the episode of Fore's sister, and her throwing away the fetters, which becomes unmeaning when combined with the original *dénoûment* of the rescue at the execution.

Now, it is obvious that if we eliminate such reduplication and superfœtation of motives, we shall restore the story to a less corrupted form. And such a form it wears in the third part of " Salomon and Markolf." This appendix seems to be a *resumé* or synopsis of an earlier version of the romance, but either that version was faulty, or the analysis has omitted some of the most important traits. In it the story runs as follows :—

Solomon's wife secretly loves a heathen. To procure her he sends two gleemen, who place in her mouth a magic root, that immediately stupefies her. All believe her to be dead except Marolf, and his attempt to expose her by pouring molten lead upon her hand fails through the potency of the magic; so the queen is carried off. Marolf, disguised as a pedlar with a number of nick-nacks, sets out to discover her, and at length, before the gate of her new lord's palace, identifies the runaway by her burned hand as she buys of him a pair of gloves. He hastens home to report, and by his advice Solomon, in palmer's weeds, enters the castle of the heathen, while Marolf waits with the troops to rescue the king at the sound of the horn. Meanwhile the faithless wife sees through her husband's disguise and delivers him to her paramour. Asked what he would do were their positions reversed, Solomon replies that he would hang his rival on any tree he liked to choose. When this sentence is about to be executed, he begs leave to blow three blasts with his horn. At the third, Marolf appears on the scene, the heathen is hanged, and the queen bled to death.

There can be no doubt that this compact, concise, prose narrative is earlier than the complicated lumbering poem, though the latter, as we shall see, has preserved some original traits that are here omitted.

But meanwhile there is another simplification to be made ere we can trace back its growth any further. Morolf, Marolf, Marcolf, or Marcolis probably represents, it will be remembered, Solomon's antagonist

Ashmedai.   Now, in these tales he appears in the *rôle* of Solomon's friend and brother, but at first we may be sure this would not be so; if mentioned at all it would be as foe and seducer, while Solomon would have to do all the discovering and recovering of his wife for himself.   We cannot follow up the story to this earlier stage in Germany, but now the Russian legends come to our assistance.   A high authority remarks that a striking feature in the folk-lore of "Holy Russia" is the great abundance and comparative purity of the "Christian mythology" which it contains; and under this designation he includes stories from the Old and New Testaments, and legends apocryphal or non-apocryphal.   It is therefore what we might expect, that the Solomon tradition should retain in the Russian versions a maximum of its Oriental character; and the relationship of the ballad, analyzed as follows, will not be dubious.

The Emperor Vasilj Okuljivič drinks with his lords, and bids them suggest a bride worthy of his hand. A certain Ivaska offers to procure Solomon's wife Salamanija, and sails to Jerusalem in a magic ship. Solomon is not at home, and his wife coming on board to inspect the treasure, is drugged and carried away to Vasilj, with whom she lives three years.   Meanwhile Solomon collects an army of winged horse-bodied men, and instructs them at the first blast of his horn to saddle, at the second to mount, at the third to hasten to his aid.   He himself, disguised as a pilgrim, reaches his wife's new home, is recognized by her, and confined in a chest.   On Vasilj's entrance she advises the execution of the captive.   Solomon begs, as a last boon, that he may blow three blasts of his horn, as he used to do in his youth when he fed cows.   At the first blast, while he is on the first step of the ladder, all beasts and birds approach and his men saddle their steeds.   On the second step he blows again, the trees tremble, the sea is stirred, the horsemen mount so that the earth quakes.   At the third blast they arrive ; Salamanija, Vasilj, and Ivaska are hanged.

Here, besides the simplification before noticed, we remark that some traits which in the prose appendix were lost are as distinct as in the German poem. Such are the project of the abduction ; the queen's relation to that event—at first, under the compulsion of drugs or magic, quite involuntary, but afterwards enthusiastically favourable ; the separate purport of three horn-blasts.   We have also to notice that there are supernatural traits which, in both German versions, have been rationalized away.   Such is the sympathy of earth, air, and sea with Solomon in his need ; such, too, those winged centaurs whose significance has, even in Russia, been so nearly lost that they are bid saddle and mount.   On the other hand, one trait which the German poem preserves, the heathenism of Solomon's wife and her lover, is not found here; and while in the German the latter is suggestively called Fore, or Pharaoh, the father of the woman who led Solomon astray, in the Russian his name has no particular importance. But in another older Russian version, in Latin prose, we find this want supplied. Here it is Solomon's brother Cetovrasus, or Kitovras, king of men by day and of beasts by night, who steals Salamanija. Now Kitovras is a regular corruption of the Greek Κένταυρος, and that Solomon's weird rival should be named Centaur clears up many things. In the first place, we remember Solomon's sculptures, so offensive to Josephus, and the mixed shapes of the Shedim, some of them too with bodies of horses. Again, not only is the prominence given to his horsemen true to the first notices of Solomon, but the description of them as winged centaurs—that is, of the same race from which his enemy is named—suggests the Eastern legend of his going to battle against one demon with an army of others. This of itself would justify the conjecture that Kitovras was a fourth alias for Ashmedai, and in a Russian version of the old Talmudic story of the temple building, we actually find Kitovras in that demon's place.

If the robber is really Ashmedai, many difficulties

are made smooth. In the first place, we see how the story can have risen from the distorted tradition of Solomon's fall. Then the attitude of the wife is explained, for Solomon's heathen consorts did not knowingly ruin him, and yet were in the interests of the false gods, or demons. Again, the German version, which humanizes throughout, has substituted for the superhuman rival a heathen king, but it calls him Pharaoh, with a vague memory that Pharaoh, through his daughter, was concerned in the disaster. Solomon's pilgrim disguise recalls his mendicancy, when he went about crying, "I, the preacher, was king at Jerusalem." And the horn that roused the inhabitants of earth, air, and sea, besides summoning the demon hosts, may be a Western version of that ring, of the same fourfold power, with which, in like manner, he regained his sovereignty.

The common story, perhaps of Byzantine authorship, which must have lain at the root of both German and Russian versions, probably contained the following as its chief episodes. The demon prince steals away the heathen wife of Solomon. Solomon, disguised as a beggar, sets out to search for her. At length, after being nearly murdered by the demon and his bride, he summons with his talisman his natural and supernatural allies, and obtains victory and revenge. This does not seem very unlike those tales from which we set out. Indeed it merely digests and combines their various elements; the disastrous heathen marriage, the usurpation of the evil power, Solomon's vagrancy, his expedition against the djin, and final triumph.

We have seen how Solomon, great in his wisdom, great in his fall, gradually sinks to an effeminate carpet knight. We have seen how Ashmedai, subtlest of his traditional foes, splits in two, and, in so far as he is subtle, does yeoman's service against himself in so far as he is hostile. All this is very strange; and in conclusion, since we have been discussing the fates of Ecclesiastes, the preacher, it may be permissible, if not to preach, at least to draw a moral. After tracking the Solomon story through the centuries and across the Continent, and seeing what shapes it has assumed, we should be prepared for other discoveries of the same kind. There are traces of ancient belief and stories and customs in many corners of our modern life. Tradition carries them down, as birds in their flight bear with them undigested seeds, from country to country, from clime to clime. This is no isolated case. We need not wonder if we find traces of old heathen observances in the festivals of the Church, bits of primeval myths in the legends of the saints, fragments of old religion in lingering superstitions and nursery rhymes. Our present life is joined with the past by hundreds of such little unseen threads, which become visible through the lenses of philology, literary history, and comparative mythology. The present development is one of the most amusing and convenient as an illustration. But it is not important in itself, and it leads to no important results. There are other stories of wider scope and with wider issues that bring us face to face with great problems.

THE THREE
CYCLES OF MEDIÆVAL ROMANCE.

[The authorities in this subject are too numerous to be mentioned, yet many romances remain unedited, and few critical questions are as yet finally decided. We are still waiting for some one to do for the Arthurian and Carlovingian legends what Weissmann did for those of Alexander, even with imperfect materials, in his "Alexanderlied."]

IN mediæval times we have an international language descended from classical Latin, with an international religion supplied by the Western Church; and, from the middle of the eleventh century, we have some approach to an international literature radiating out from France.

This, its point of departure, is interesting and significant. The raw materials are contributed by German and by Celtic tribes, by the new and by the antique world; but they obtain completion and currency only when transfused in the crucible of Romance thought. Their recognition is quite local till they receive the stamp of the French spirit; thereafter they pass at once into European circulation. Something of the same kind has happened more than once since then. Again and again, and in every sphere, has France been the instructor and lawgiver of the West : but not last century, when its "illuminated" led the fashions in philosophy,—not a hundred years earlier, when its dramatists invaded every stage,—had its literature so universal a sway as at the zenith of the Middle Ages. For then it penetrated into every neighbouring land, and was adopted by every neighbouring people ; and though modified by the genius and language of each individual nation, kept the distinctive marks of its origin to the last, and remained emphatically a Romance literature.

And this designation is important on another account. It is not unparalleled to have an international scientific literature, and, in so far as this genus existed at all in the Middle Ages, it belonged to all Western Europe. But these times possessed as well, and this is what seems strange, a common stock of imaginative work, of poetry and fiction, which, in its great narrative type, always elaborated on the lines laid down in France, was rightly called the Romance. This, of course, was only possible when the literary classes of all Europe were impelled by a common spirit towards a common ideal, when this ideal was more clearly realized in France than elsewhere, and when certain stories were found to express it in special perfection.

Now, the ideals of those days were almost all summed up in what we style chivalry. It would be wrong to call all the romances chivalrous, for, as we shall see, only the latest group fully answers this description. But at least they are all of chivalrous tendency, and aim at embodying its conceptions. And those conceptions were essentially ideals. It has once and again been shown that there never was an actual age of chivalry, and that when in the fourteenth century people tried, as they thought, to restore it, they were attempting to import into practical life what was in truth a minstrel's dream. Nevertheless, since it was a dream that flitted before the eyes of many generations, it was in its way a very substantial reality. There never was a time when the feudal knights were exactly knights errant, but there was a time when the best of them wished they might be such; and that time was nearly dead when the third Edward became patron of its semblances and outward trappings in his Orders of the Garter and Feasts of the Round Table.

The real meaning of chivalry was something deeper. It had arisen as a compromise between the ascetic theology of the mediæval Church and the unsanctified life of the world, which that Church condemned as wholly bad. It is sometimes described as the projected shadow of feudalism, and so it is, but only because in the upper feudal ranks there was most need felt of a *modus vivendi* between practice and belief. The masses of the people are never much swayed by airy doctrines. The exigencies of their position keep them near a course of life that may be rude but is not unnatural. In the present case, with a certain varnish of Christian theology, and some real education by the spirit of the Christian faith, on the main they acted on traditions of conduct, the heritage of the race from heathen times. But this stubborn placidity was not within the reach of the upper classes. They had the same heritage, but could not have the same rest in it. They were taught to consider the religious life the highest, yet what could be more opposed to their ancestral habits and lawless passions than the three monastic vows of poverty, chastity, and obedience? To poverty they preferred plunder, like their fathers who ravaged Britain and the Empire. Their traffic in female slaves shows their rude disregard for the second vow. As for obedience, that must have existed within the narrowest limits, when each little mark was jealous of its independence, or when a great exodus from Norway followed its union under one king, or when every petty lord strove to be a petty sovereign. The literature of the unsubdued Teutons illustrates these traits. Our own Beowulf and the German Hildebrandslied' show their greed for gain and fierce self-assertion, and the older story of Brunhilde's wooing lets us take the measure of their delicacy.

No doubt this society, even in its wildest phase, contained the germs of a higher life. Roman observers remarked among those barbarians profound feeling for the sanctity of wedded and family life, and unshrinking loyalty among the pledged companions of a prince; nor was wealth coveted at the expense of feelings like these. And when the popular mind was enlightened and elevated, however gradually, by the new faith, its nobler principles received new stimulus, and shone forth in poems, which grew up scarce brushed by a dogma of the school, but not therefore quite destitute of Christian sentiment. Thus, in the popular story of "Havelok," the loyalty of Grim, the honest fisherman, is contrasted with the treason of the usurping Godard; in the "Kutrun," the heroine's chaste constancy in love receives a foil from the fickleness of the duchess; in the "Niebelungen," Siegfried wins by valour and virtue the treasure which Hagen filches with force and fraud. All these poems are more modern, though more rude in feeling, than the international romances, but for that very reason are less representatively mediæval. Characteristically they achieved only a local success, and not till our own day have they begun to enjoy an European reputation. The truth is, the healthy ethics of lay life which they expressed, lacked all basis in and reference to the received theological standards. They could obtain the sanction of religion only if they were baptized into it, and modified in the direction of its code : since they lack such sanction, they fail to express the spirit of the age; but had they obtained it, they would have ceased to be what they are, and would have lost much of their vigorous truth. But the adaptation of lay ethics to clerical ethics is the problem of the higher ranks, and its solution is chivalry.

The transition is marked above all by this picturesque trait, that the hero becomes a knight. This short statement implies a very important change, which is symbolized in the complicated ceremonies of knightly investiture, very different from the few simple rites that used to accompany the Teutonic youth's assumption of arms. The young candidate spends the time with priests, and receives the sacrament; he is led to the bath and endued with a white robe, to signify his change of life; his sword is blessed and his vows are taken. Thus the knight, if belonging to lay life, partakes in the character of a monk, as mediæval writers clearly saw and frequently explained. His admission to the order is a religious service, and brings with it duties which, though differing from those inculcated by the three monastic vows, are analogous, and almost as fanciful. Thus, if he be not pledged to poverty, and is allowed his share in the world's goods, it is on the understanding that he may be called at any moment to surrender them. He is required to swear that he will always be ready to fight for the Church against the infidel; at mass, when the gospel is read, he must point his sword to the book to show that he is its sworn soldier; and especially he must give up all for the defence or recovery of the Holy City. Lands and goods must be left when the Church has a crusade on foot, kingdoms abandoned in quest of dreams. Again, it would have been impossible to exact complete obedience from men of such strong self-consciousness as the feudal knights, but neither are they left to their isolated and uncontrolled self-will. The principle of honour is introduced, which appeals to the individual's desire for preeminence and mastery, but which gratifies it only if he submit to a certain code of conditions. His valour must be carried to an extravagant pitch—he must seek out adventures, and face the greatest odds; he must refuse advantages, and show mercy to the suppliant and courtesy to all; his quarrel must be just, and he must succour the poor and distressed. Far removed is the knight from the old heathen, who fought and fled, waylaid and slew, precisely as it pleased himself. And in the third place, while only some of the knightly orders were pledged to celibacy, all knights were bound to uphold the honour of women; and gradually without oath they submitted themselves to that strange kind of gallantry known as the Service of Love, which at this distance of time strikes one as the most obvious feature of the chivalrous character. This fantastic fashion, in which the love *par amour* usurped the place of marriage, at once gave scope for the devotion of the knight, and suited a society in which marriage was regarded as at best a necessary evil.

If the attempt to harmonize the demands of lay Teutonic life and Latin ecclesiastical theory originated these ideas, it is easy to see why they were specially developed in a nation to which Teutonic and Latinized races have given its mingled blood. In France we find the prerogative phases of mediævalism —the feudal, the scholastic, and, among others, the chivalrous; and there the first, the most persevering, and the most successful attempts were made to express the last in successive cycles of romance. Three such groups, French in fabrication, but European in circulation and development, progressively advance in expressing the life of chivalry—the romances of Charlemagne, of Alexander, and of Arthur. If we remember that chivalry sprang from the union of mediæval religion and secular morality, we may thus describe their relations. In the lays of Charlemagne the ecclesiastical predominates, in the lays of Alexander the secular; only in the Arthurian stories do both sides, as it were, come to their rights.

The earliest poems of the earliest cycle, the epics of the great German emperor, give the knightly ideal on its monastic side. From the first, Charlemagne is emphatically the hero of the Church. His historical career, indeed, made this almost necessary. He owed a great part of his success to his championship of the Catholic faith, against Arian heretics on the one hand, against heathens and Mohammedans on the other. In the old poems he is notably a religious personage, a soldier of the cross, a crusader in the best sense of the words. Nowadays we are apt to look for the Charlemagne of poetry in such love romances as "Amis and Amiles," or even "Huon of Bordeaux." But these are of a later growth. In them he is no longer the chief person; when introduced at all, he figures as a wilful tyrant. Such tales arose when chivalry was finding other channels of expression; they took his great name as a sort of centre, but he himself no longer suited their wants; and he was thrown into the background or criticised. But in the early romances he is the proper hero, and, whenever hero at all, he is an ecclesiastical one.

Of all his wars none was so famous in song as his expedition into Spain. By request of the citizens of Saragossa, he marched thither against the Arabs, and was winning his usual victories, when a new eruption of Saxons compelled his return to the North. On his passage through the Pyrenees, the marauding Gascons surprised and destroyed his rear-guard, only one of whom escaped. This massacre took place on the 15th of August, 778—it is not often we can give so precise a date for an event so mythical,—and in one version Einhard, Charlemagne's biographer, commemorates among the slain, " Ruodlandus limitis Brittanici prefectus." This is the first mention of the famous Roland, and as yet there is nothing very remarkable about him ; he has no magic horn, he is not nephew to the emperor, he is not so much as commander of the force. But the bald narrative soon becomes legend, the theme of poems, the delight of warriors. Already, on the battle-field of Hastings, Taillefer sang a song of Roland ; and probably before then the story had undergone a change, in conformity with the ecclesiastical character of the cycle, which made it more specifically Christian, and increased its artistic unity. This was the substitution of un- believing Saracens for the Gascon robbers who surprised the Franks. Thus Charlemagne was shown at war with the infidel, Roland and his comrades became martyrs of the faith.

This is the case in the "Chanson de Roland," which is the oldest extant epic in the series, and cannot be dated later than the end of the eleventh century. It comes to us from the obscure dawn of the Middle Ages, its sources are unknown, its authorship uncertain; but despite all inequalities and repetitions, in its existing form it bears the impress of one man's mind. It is written in *tirades*, or stanzas of varying length, composed of twelve-syllable or ten-syllable lines, bound together by assonance, or a common vowel rhyme in the last syllable; and this metre, though not very polished, is perhaps, by its freedom and continuity, better suited to a narrative poem than rhymed couplets of any description. To the verse the matter of the lay corresponds in its unfiltered unity and strength.

For seven years Charlemagne has been busied with the subjugation and conversion of Spain, and all the kingdom has yielded to his will, save Saragossa, where King Marsile still holds out. And even Marsile is sorely pressed, and in his extremity sends an embassy to Charles with offers of submission—to be thrown off when the time comes. Roland and others mistrust the proposals but are overruled, and now it is debated which of them shall bear the conditions to the Saracen king. First Roland offers himself, but the emperor thinks him too fiery and incautious: then he suggests Ganelon, who, to his great wrath, is accepted, and who henceforth suspects Roland's motives and determines his death. At first doughty and faithful, after a while he falls in with Marsile's designs, and hastening the return of the Christians to France, contrives that Roland shall be left at Roncevaux, in command of a small rear-guard. Soon the little detachment espies the approach of a huge Saracen army. In vain Oliver prays Roland to summon help with a blast of his wondrous horn,—they must fight the fight alone, in their own strength and the strength of God. Archbishop Turpin blesses and exhorts them, and they quit themselves like men in the battle, yet all their valour is of no avail. Host after host of the heathen is annihilated, but ever new supplies pour in, and the peers begin to fall. At last, Roland consents to blow his horn, but long ere succour can arrive he lies dead beside his fellows, concealing his sword, since he cannot break it, beneath his own corpse. There needed not the precaution, all his enemies were slain or fled.

Meanwhile Charlemagne, thirty leagues away, has heard the note, and is filled with forebodings. Ganelon tries to reassure him. "Roland is hunting," he suggests; but the emperor only commands to bind him hand and foot, and begins his countermarch into Spain. Yet all his haste is vain; he can do nothing but take double vengeance, short and swift, on the authors of the wrong. The heathen are wasted with fire and sword, and Ganelon, worsted in the appeal to Heaven, is tied to the tails of wild horses and dragged, back and breast, through thorns and stones and briars.

The chanson, with all its bareness, has some of the best qualities of a good epic. It possesses wonderful unity of purpose, for its action is united, its feeling even too uniform, and in presence of its great, strong definite characters, there is no fear that our attention will lose itself among the details. First and greatest is the figure of the emperor in its inviolable repose,— "a little stiff," says W. Grimm, when discussing the German version of the story, "like the earliest statues, which sit but do not walk;" yet always majestic with the consciousness of a Divine mission. He is always still and deliberate; when others offer their counsels he sits silent; his words, when they do come, have the weight of Divine commands. For he is in constant communion with God; his prayers can change the course of nature; like another Joshua, he commands the sun to stay. If this character be translated from the gravity of age into the impetuous ardour of youth, it is that of Roland. Otherwise, uncle and nephew are much alike. Roland, too, is the favourite of Heaven; he, too, has miraculous gifts and enjoys the intercourse of angels; signs and wonders accompany his death, such as happened at the crucifixion. He, like the emperor, is soldier of the faith, but his championship is all fire and motion. These and the remaining characters have their foil in Ganelon. God is not in all his thoughts: he is not imbued with the Divine enthusiasm of his comrades, he gives room to personal interests, he has leisure to be suspicious. And though interests and suspicions are not un-natural, this does not save him from ruin. There is no middle place for these men between the highest and the lowest. Ganelon suspects, betrays, and dies a traitor's death.

We have here, then, bold impressive types, but do they conform to the ideas of chivalry? This question must be answered chiefly in the negative. They are not knights, but mere soldiers of the Church, mere fighting monks. They are strong, absolutely fearless, they slay their thousands. But they do not joust for the pleasure of it, they do not crave adventures for the honour to be gained, they want the splendid courtesy of the chevalier; and, above all, they have no sense for the service of ladies. Only two women catch our eye in the whole poem; the heathen queen who welcomes the Christian faith, and Aude, the betrothed of Roland, who falls dead without a word when she hears that he is slain. But he never spares her one thought. At Roncevaux Oliver urges him for her sake to blow the horn, but the appeal has no effect. And at his death he thinks of God and country, he blesses the emperor, and bids his sword a tender farewell, but the name of Aude does not cross his lips. We have here to do with men like Cromwell's Ironsides. When not in the fight they are on their knees; they have no time for ordinary human emotions. They are constant in their prayers and exhortations, and have a tendency to preach. In conscious antagonism with the infidel, they are prophets in his presence and impress him with awe. Ganelon may blench before the peers, but even he compels the respect of the Saracens. These men do not know the meaning of earthly love. Only in a later age does Roland the Christian warrior become Orlando Innamorato, under the hands of an Italian who no longer believes in his story, but mocks at it.

Here the chivalrous ideal is very far from being realized, but still we are on the way to it. With soldiers it is impossible entirely to exclude the principle of honour. Here it appears in Roland's affection for his sword, in his refusal to summon aid, in the rather carnal desire he and his friends disclose to pay their death-stroke with interest, in his words when Oliver rails at the treason of Ganelon: "Hush! he is father of my wife." Again, though love is absent from the men, it is sketched with depth and pathos in Roland's bride, whom no ambitious lures can restrain from death. And, lastly, despite all opposition, the heathen are regarded with no polemical hatred. They receive full credit for their valour; their chief faults are rashness and presumption—points which it would not in those days be hard to forgive. Ganelon's doom is recorded without pity; but one of the Saracens provokes the exclamation, "What a man would he be were he only a Christian!" Thus the orthodox profession does not shield a man from contempt, nor does heathenism make admiration impossible. We are here on the threshold of an ideal very different from the military monasticism of the chanson, and need not wonder that to the epic of Charlemagne succeeds the epic of Alexander.

The hero of the antique world, the pupil of Aristotle, the imitator of Achilles, the enthusiast for Homer, in his own age remained to all intents and purposes unsung. Though the completer of Hellenic life, no great epic of Hellas celebrated his prowess. Nevertheless there, and wherever else he penetrated, tales of him remained and grew. Egypt especially strove to claim a share in his glory, and in Alexandria, perhaps under the Ptolemies, Egyptian legends of his origin ran together with others from Judea, and possibly from further Asia. Nor did the Greeks forget him. They seem to have invented for him, as for Phalaris, epistles and rhetorical disquisitions; and even in the Western world one of these apocryphal letters, on the wonders of the East, survives in an Anglo-Saxon version. These and other materials were collected and digested at Byzantium, not later than the end of the fourth century, in a work that falsely bears the name of the historian Callisthenes. They soon spread to Western Europe in the Latin translations of Valerius and Leo; and in the second half of the eleventh century passed into a Romance vernacular in the version of Auberi of Besançon. This has, unfortunately, been almost entirely lost; but about the year 1125 it was rendered into German, probably by a priest named Lamprecht, and to him we must go for the story in its earliest as well as its best romantic form. The other versions in Germany, France, England, and Scotland are too numerous, and, for our purpose, too unimportant to mention.

Thus Alexander was seized on to embody the conceptions of mediæval chivalry, but in many ways he was an unsuitable subject. His character was essentially Greek, yet here it is interpreted, not even by a knight, but by a priest; and the discrepancy of the title-page is the discrepancy of the book. The verse, still very unpolished, is the octosyllabic couplet usually employed in the later romances of chivalry, which, despite its "fatal fluency," is rather apt to break up the flow of a narrative. And in accordance with this, the poem is merely a chronological life of Alexander— a disjointed series of episodes held together by the strong personality of the hero. It contains three parts, each with its distinct class of adventures. The first of them is historical, or at least is based on history. It rejects the story, which appears in other versions, of Alexander's generation through the magic wiles of Nectanabus, but mentions the prophetic portents of greatness that accompanied his birth. Then it describes his early exploits and, in greater detail, his refusal of tribute to Persia and his ensuing invasion of Asia. He routs the generals of Darius; Tyre falls before him; he avenges his adversary's gift of a play-ball, as, in later tales, Henry V. requites a similar insult from the Dauphin. Soon Darius is overthrown, his kingdom shattered, his wife and daughter made captive. Yet still he defies Alexander in his despair, till, defeated anew, his spirit is broken, and he dies by treason ere his ally, Porus of India, can arrive. With the defeat of this new comer in single combat, and the expedition to Scythia, this section concludes.

The second part is quite legendary. Alexander marches to the end of the world, where nought remains but the abyss, and where the heaven revolves like a wheel round its axle. There he is seized with a longing for his home, and writes to his mother, Olympias, and his teacher, Aristotle, an account of his adventures on the road. His letter tells of giant men and fabulous beasts, of magic waters and wonderful woods, of his visits to the voluptuous Candace and to the warlike Amazons.

The third part is allegorical. Victorious to the ends of the earth, he is still unsatisfied, and marches against Paradise to take tribute of the angels. He perseveres through many mishaps till he reaches his goal, but fails to gain admission. At length an old man opens the door, teaches him that only meekness finds entry there, and dismisses him with a magic stone. He vainly seeks to learn its secret from his wise men, till an ancient Jew shows him how its little bulk outweighs any load of gold, but a handful of dust and a tuft of down turn the scale. "Such," declares the sage, "is the human eye: the wealth cf the world cannot appease it, but add a sprinkling of ashes, and it is not worth a feather." Alexander lays the warning to heart. He becomes humble and devout; and when he dies, and of all his conquests retains nothing more than the meanest hind, then his sins are forgiven him.

A poem of this kind with so rambling a plot depends for interest on the vividness of its episodes and the truth of its central character. In both respects the Alexanderlied stands high. All the scenes are graphic and strong. In battle the two armies face each other and roar like the sea; they leap together like wild swine; no helmet holds out, the green fields grow red, the furrows are manured with corpses. So at news of the defeat the sister bewails her brother, the mother her son; the infants weep in their cradles; the boys leave their playing in the streets. But the best-known and by far the finest passage in the poem is the unique adventure of the fairy forest. Alexander writes home :—

"After a while we saw standing there a noble wood of manifold marvels. As we went by, we heard from within many clear voices, and the noise of the lyre and harp, and the sweetest song that ever was found of men. Right gladsome was the shadow of the trees: there sprang flowers and grass and divers herbs; I ween never wood was so adorned. It was long and broad, as I tell you, and lay in a fair meadow. From out of it ran many streams, clear and very cool. I and my swift heroes had there wondrous pleasance; I will conceal no whit but diligently tell you all.

"The trees were high, the branches thick and broad, never might the sun shine through. We left our steeds and went to the wood, the time seemed long till we reached it. And there we saw wonders. Troops of fair maidens were playing on the green clover, a hundred thousand and more. They sprang and played and sang so sweetly that we all, small and great, for the sweet clamour of the wood, forgot our pain of heart and our great labours, and all trouble and all the anguish we ever had known. Methought I had never been sick, and was whole from all sorrow, and would fear death no more.

" Would you understand the nature of these women you will greatly marvel. Soon as winter passed and the summer came and the leaves grew green, many fair and stately flowers sprang up in the wood. They glistened as the light, and shone far off in their white and red. They were round like a ball, fast shut and wondrous large. When they opened from above, mark this well, perfect maidens lay therein,—I tell you what I saw. They lived and walked and had the senses of men; they spoke and asked questions as were their age about twelve years. They were shapely in their bodies, never saw I women of fairer aspect nor eyes so well placed. Hand and arm was white as ermine, with leg and foot. They were well nurtured and merry, and laughed and sung with voices sweeter than human.

" And, would you trust me ; these women had their health in the shade; if the sun shone on them they died. The wood echoed with sweet noise, for birds and maidens sang therein; how might it be blyther early or late ? Their raiment grew on their body, and was red like the flowers and white as snow. We pitched our tents in the wood, I and my men, and lay amid the music, and were glad for our strange brides. We loved them and abode there, and had never such joy since we were born. Alas, that we so soon must lose our great joyance! Three months and twelve days I and my heroes dwelt in the green wood and its pleasant glades by the fair women, and lived in ease and delights. Then came ill worse than I can mourn. When the time was full, our joy fled; the flowers rotted and the fair women died ; the trees left their greening, and the brooks their running, and the birds their singing. Then my heart was stricken with grief for the plight of the fair women. Oh, but it was woeful each day to see them die, and the flowers wither ! Then I parted thence in sorrow, I and all my men."

Alexander's personality is brought before us with no less vividness. His hair is red and shaggy, his one eye blue, his other black. In his earliest weeks, if roused, he is like a wolf standing over its prey. When a man, he mows down an army like grass, and fights like an angry bear baited by dogs : " what thing it can reach with its claws, on that it wreaks its rage." But brute valour is not his only or his chief excellence. He is truthful and high-souled, and studies the law of the land that he may deal justly. Darius is thankless for his courtesy to the captive queen, and this is Alexander's reply : " What kindness I have shown thy wife, that she owes to my mother, for whose sake I gladly serve all women,—not for thine : thy talk of rewards is idle." This is just the man who at the world's end turns home-sick, and writes to mother and teacher. His self-respect and genial wisdom appear in another incident. Pleased with the frugal simplicity of the Scythian shepherds, he bids them ask a boon. The only thing they want is immortality. " How can I give you that," he asks, " when I myself am mortal ? " The petitioner retorts, " Then why turn the world upside down, when soon you must die and leave it all ? " " God has shaped men variously," answers Alexander : " while I live, I must still be doing something. What were the good of life, if all thought like you ? "

The question remains whether this vigorous character corresponds to the chivalrous conceptions, and the answer cannot be wholly in the affirmative. On the one hand, it is too healthy and human,—on the other, too little religious, for a knight of the Middle Ages. During the whole poem the ecclesiastical side is neglected; then, at the last, it is recognized and all that precedes is condemned. The old Jew admonishes Alexander that his mind is greedy as the gulf of hell, and Alexander owns it and repents.

Nevertheless, we are in the Gentiles' court of the romance of chivalry. Alexander is rather ambitious than adventurous, yet he has a store of adventures in love and war. He respects women for the sake of his mother, not of the Virgin; and there is, perhaps, a want of etiquette in his treatment of the forest maidens *en masse*, without specializing their names, their lovers, and their several fates; yet courtesy to women is one of his chief traits. The march on paradise he undertakes in no spirit of devotion, but none the less it procures him heavenly lore, and is not altogether unlike the great mystical quest of chivalry. These points only needed further elaboration to give mediæval knighthood what it required. And they are more fully worked out in some other of the antique romances, but in general merit these remain far behind the lay of Alexander.

Chivalry, therefore, whether seeking its ideal in German or in classic story, had failed to express itself in its purity.   In each case the hero had a character too obstinately historical to be merely chivalrous, neither more nor less.   But a warrior at length became known whose name and deeds belonged by invention or tradition to obscure and sequestered tribes, and whose figure was vague and formless as the mists on their own hills.   This hero was the British Arthur.

Two things strike us about the new competitor as in curious contrast with those who preceded him.   No one doubts or thinks it necessary to maintain the historical existence of Alexander and Charlemagne, and we know the exact day of the battle which gave rise to the great romance about the latter; but who is bold enough to assert or deny that the Briton was once a man among men?   Again, there is little question as to the general growth of the Karlovingian and Alexandrine legends, but it is by no means undisputed whether there were even popular Celtic traditions of Arthur long before the twelfth century.   Probably in this the mania of Teutonic scepticism has been carried too far, as in its denial of Celtic mixture in modern English blood.   Many characteristic traits in the Arthurian romances—the agency of fays, the enchanted forests and lakes, perhaps the Round Table itself—are authenticated as genuine by classical writers : some touches, like the increase of Gawain's strength till noon * and its decrease thereafter, are not of the kind that mediæval writers add : and the prevalence of Arthurian place-names on Brythonic territory is hard to explain, were the legends of Arthur merely a late invention.   And if they contain a mythical element, it is easy to see how it should be transferred to some leader in the Saxon wars; just as we see, in the case of Beowulf, the historical hero absorb the myth of Beowa.   If something of this kind be true, the Celtic stories must have been very pliant and undecided, or else strongly predisposed to the chivalrous ideal, for in any case they express it perfectly. And this makes our task easier.   Whatever their remote origin may have been, it justifies us in treating the Arthurian romances as the inventions of chivalrous writers, and in neglecting the north-west passage of Welsh antiquities for the safer overland route of Latin and French authorities.

Among these, the first mention of Arthur's name occurs in Nennius, whose account must not be dated earlier than the ninth century.   Although many are more noble than he, the magnanimous Arthur is twelve times chosen leader of the Britons against the Saxons, and is as often conqueror.   At the battle of

* This trait recurs in the description of other knights, especially of him of the Red Lawns, whose connection with the sun has been preserved as a "fool's allegory" even in Tennyson's idyll.

Gurnion, he bears the image of the Virgin on his shoulder; in one interval of quiet, he has time for a pilgrimage to the Holy Land; at Mount Badon, nine hundred and forty fall by his hand, none but the Lord assisting him.   "In all these engagements the Britons were victorious, for no strength can avail against the will of the Almighty."   This is the whole story; for the prophecy of Merlin, or, as Nennius calls him, Ambrose, the youth reputed fatherless, refers rather to the future total expulsion of the Saxon white dragon, than to actual achievements of the red dragon of Britain in the days of Arthur.

There is here little to distinguish the new hero in character from the great Frank emperor.   Both are quite ecclesiastical, fighting for faith and fatherland, bearing sacred armour in the sacred cause, performing prodigies of valour through miraculous help.   Indeed one touch, the pilgrimage to Jerusalem, seems directly borrowed from the legends that gathered round Charlemagne, as Nennius' derivation of the Britons from ancient Troy repeats the fictitious pedigree of the Franks.

This tendency is carried still further by the next writer in the series, Geoffrey of Monmouth, the patron and sponsor, if not the father, of Arthurian romance. In his "History of the Britons," completed in the year 1135, Arthur wages not only a defensive but an offensive religious war.   He is not alone, but is surrounded by worthies, like Kai and Bedver, Gawain and Peredur, to whom Owen was soon to be added,—names not less famous in later story than those of the peers themselves.   His exploits extend from the island to the mainland, he breaks the power of Rome and grasps at the crown of the world.

Yet, on the whole, Geoffrey's additions are more suggestive of Alexander than of Charlemagne.   The mighty continental empire is common to both.   But Nennius's hint of Arthur's disadvantage in birth Geoffrey explains away with a tale of magic like that of Nectanabus;[*] Merlin's craft endues Uther with the shape of Gorlois.   Further, Merlin's prophecies are pressed into service, and Arthur's greatness is not less clearly foreshadowed than that of Alexander.   Again, Nennius has told of Arthur's superhuman prowess; but Geoffrey makes him win kingdoms, like Alexander, in single fight.   And as Alexander refuses Darius's claim to tribute, and retorts it on its author, so Arthur treats the Roman demand, not without reference to the capture of Rome by Brennus and Constantine.

But Geoffrey also contributes material that we do not find in either of the earlier romances; and all of

* It is perhaps no accident that we find this tale adopted in the best English Alexandrine romance.

it has the genuine chivalrous stamp.   Arthur engages
not only a champion but a giant in duel; and looking
at the carcase, exclaims, "I have found none of so
great strength" (as though this sport were matter of
his daily experience) "since that Retho who challenged
me to fight on Mount Aravius," and who made himself
furs with the beards of the kings he had killed.   Arthur
was bound to punish this unknightly foible; and so,
too, in the present case he has sought out the monster
at his feet to avenge an injured damsel.   To encounter
giants, to put down ill customs, to maintain the cause
of women were all chivalrous traits, and in the court
at Caerleon, there is even some approach to the
usages of mediæval gallantry.   The ladies give their
love only to those who have approved themselves in
three combats.

And Arthur's final doom fits in with the story
of his life.   Perhaps no man ever lived in less fear of
historians than Geoffrey, but even he may have
shrunk from making his British parvenu conquer
and keep the empire of Rome.   Yet he must be
pictured too great for overthrow by any foreign
power.   And since he is the champion of the Christian faith, the dignity of knights, and the honour of
women, what instruments so fitting for his destruction
as those who betray his religion, his love, and his vows.
His enemies are those of his own house, his wife and

nephew, who unite in guilty love and call back the heathen foe from over sea.

About the year 1155 Geoffrey's Latin passed into the Norman-French of Wace, who adds a few details, of which the most important refers to the Round Table and its origin, and generally vivifies the narrative, but in all essentials closely follows his authority. The successive titles by which his work has been known are rather significant. First, it is the "Geste des Bretons," which cannot fail to suggest the "Chansons de Gestes," as the Karlovingian poems were called. Then, with an acknowledgment of its Celtic connection, it becomes the "Brut [Brittanice, Chronicle] d'Angleterre." Lastly, "Brut" was misunderstood as Brutus, the mythical Trojan who colonized Britain, and the name arose "Roman de Brut," which recognizes both its classical *point d'appui* and its really romantic character. Romance it is, in language, substance, and metre, and has a right to be regarded as the first in the Arthurian cycle.

To Uther, the great king of Britain, Merlin prophesies the future greatness of his house. Now Uther loves Igraine, the wife of Gorlois, and Merlin, to fulfil his word, lends him the semblance of her lord. Later, on the death of her first husband, Igraine becomes Uther's queen, and thus Arthur, despite his doubtful birth, succeeds to the throne as rightful heir. He at

once makes war on the heathen Germans and Scots,
and with the aid of Hoel of Brittany smites them from
shore to shore. He distributes the conquered lands,
and makes his brother-in-law Lot, father of Gawain
and Modred, King of Lothian, and marries Guinevere. But he does not rest on his laurels. He speedily
carries his arms into Europe, and subdues it from
Norway to Aquitaine. Gaul is the spoil of his own
hand, for he wins it in single combat with Frolle,
the hostile armies looking on from opposite banks, as
they fight it out alone on the island of the Seine.
The conquered lands are distributed anew, and Arthur
holds high feast at Caerleon in celebration of his
victories, summons round him his most famous
knights, and, to avoid the danger of dispute, insti-
tutes the Round Table, at which all the places are
equal. The feasting is broken by the arrival of
ambassadors from Rome, who demand the intermitted
tribute. In full assembly it is refused; and Arthur,
leaving Modred in care of queen and kingdom, sets
out with his knights and vassal kings to enforce his
counter-claim. On the way a dream prefigures his
victory over a lustful giant, which he achieves alone.
Resuming his march he carries all before him, for
the emperor's Grecian and Eastern allies avail little
when confronted with the chivalry of the West. In
its ranks Gawain takes the first place, and next to

M

Arthur becomes henceforth the hero of the tale. But the Britons are checked in mid-career. News comes that Modred has married Guinevere, usurped the kingdom, and strengthened himself with heathen troops. When Arthur arrives a great battle ensues; Gawain is killed, but the rebels are routed. Guinevere flies to a convent, Modred retreats to the West, whither Arthur follows him in grief and wrath. In another battle the chivalry on both sides is annihilated; Modred is slain, Arthur mortally wounded, but not, as in later versions, by each other's hands. Arthur bequeaths the crown to Constantine, and is carried to Avallon to be healed; but there is as yet no word of his return, which first appears in Layamon.

This account, eked out with more or less picturesque additions, sometimes with, sometimes without the prophecy of the second coming, became source and model for all the more primitive romances that look on Arthur as the blameless king, the type of all that is good in knighthood. This view still prevails in the English alliterative "Morte Arthure," of the beginning of the fifteenth century, and has been revived with a difference by Mr. Tennyson in our own day.

His wonderful fulfilment of the requirements of chivalry and of the wants of the day, is shown by one fact. British romance was practically unknown on the Continent before 1145, and can scarcely have been widely known for ten years later, for Gaimar's lost work was probably not equal to that of Wace. Yet at once it was seized on by the best writers, and it became as customary in those days to tell and retell Arthurian stories, as it was a few years ago for young Englishmen to translate " Faust," or as it now is to write constitutional histories.

But these other romances contain a great deal of new material, and illustrate the knightly life with far more fulness and richness than the original biography of Arthur. No one person could completely exhaust the possibilities of chivalry, and the idea must have lain near to supplement the career and character of Arthur with those of his favourite followers. We have seen, indeed, how prominently Gawain has already come to the front, and in some respects he and his fellows were even more suitable for this treatment than their chief; for they were knights, while he was king; his exploits were necessarily on the large public scale, while they had more leisure for the private individual adventures of errantry. They lent themselves to the representation of the chivalrous life in its various aspects, and are thus treated in the first great group of additions to the Arthurian story.

In describing them as the first there is no intention of dogmatizing as to date; the connection indicated is rather one of thought than of chronology. Yet it must be borne in mind that the two chief of the class, " Eric " and the " Chevalier au Lyon," have not been traced further back than Chrestien de Troyes; and though Chrestien's works come later than the prose Arthurian romances, yet he seems never to write without authorities; and as the sources for this pair of legends have not yet been discovered, they may turn out to be of very early date.

As Chrestien treats them they are two companion pictures, portraying respectively the knightly duties of love and honour, setting them in mutual opposition, and showing that neither can be neglected without danger to the other.

The story of Eric Mr. Tennyson has adopted for his Geraint. While riding to avenge an insult of the queen, the knight chances on Enid, clad in mean attire, and winning her love with his own, weds her and sets her amid the glories of the court. But in its round of distractions and duties he has no leisure to indulge his fondness. He takes leave for his own land, and there forgets all knightly prowess at the side of his bride, till the people cry out against him, and Enid herself is bitterly ashamed. Her remonstrance is misunderstood by her husband, and he drives her forth before him when he rides out once more in quest of strange adventures. On the way she is his guardian angel, still warning him of attack and ambuscade, though he threatens her with the whole weight of his wrath if she open her lips. At length he is wounded, and they are both borne to a castle, where Eric awakes from his swoon at the right moment to save Enid from the insults of their unknightly host. In new adventures he is more courteous, and on their return to the court is greeted with the plaudits of all.

As we are apt to fill in this sketch from Mr. Tennyson's poem, it may be worth while to point out that the modern idyll is subtler and truer than the mediæval romance. Chrestien does not clothe Enid for her rough journey in the faded silks of their first interview. Eric leaves the court merely in quest of a tranquil retreat, not in suspicion of an atmosphere grown foul; he takes the road in resentment of his wife's criticism, rather than in mistrust of her faith; and with less motive for estrangement than Geraint, he has also fewer moments of remorse. But the main idea of the poems is the same; the knight leaves the world for his lady's love, and ends by treating her like a stable-boy.

The story of Owen is just the reverse. He has undertaken the adventure of the enchanted fountain, splashed the water about it, till, as foretold, a storm beat on him and a warrior spurred against him. He has slain the champion and won his lady. But her love cannot keep him from his knightly work, and at most he plights himself to return to her side with the year. But in the excitement of action he lets the time slip by, and finds, to his agony, that he has missed his day. His lady, too, denounces him as traitor; his misery is not to be borne and he loses his reason. On his recovery he goes about, in company with a lion that he has saved, redressing human wrongs and slaying monsters, till his broken faith is expiated, and it is ordered in the train of events that he regains his lady's favour.

Thus Owen by zeal for honour soils his honour, as Eric in following love betrays it. But the second romance is far deeper than its neighbour. Eric jauntily overlooks his offence, but Owen realizes the sacred duties of a knight, and cannot easily forgive himself for failing in their observance. And their difference in character leads us to the two next great branches of Arthurian romance.

We saw that chivalry was a compound of the code of the Church and the code of the world; but this did not exactly settle the question. It was still possible to fulfil its obligations in a carnal or a spiritual way, to a profane or a religious end. And so there was room within it for knights of the Holy Virgin and knights of a lady's garter. And this divergence is expressed by two stories which had originally nothing to do with Arthur or his Table Round, the legend of the "Holy Grale," and the romance of "Tristram and Iseult."

The grale was properly the cup from which Christ partook of the Last Supper, and symbolized the sacrament of the Eucharist. Hence the further expansions of the story. In it some drops of Christ's blood were caught as he hung on the cross—a clear reference to the doctrine of transubstantiation. And since by this process man was united with God and fitted for a celestial throne, the chalice was said to be made from a stone that dropped from the crown of the falling Lucifer, to supply whose place man was created.

The earliest extant legend on this subject is the "Petit Saint Graal," of Robert de Borron, written some time between 1160 and 1170. It recounts how the Arimathean Joseph, in his captivity, was miraculously fed from the mystic vessel, and how it was brought to the West by Bron and his children. Neither in this nor in the "Grand St. Graal" is there an actual connection established with the chivalrous romances, but in the latter progress is made in this direction. The cup is brought to Britain by Joseph and his son, who turn the land to the faith, and in a manner bequeath it the holy treasure. Here there wants but a step to introduce the grale into the career of Arthur, and it is taken in the prose story of "Percivale," whose name corresponds with Geoffrey's Peredur. In this form Chrestien got hold of it, and set himself to his usual work of versification and reconstruction. But he left his poem unfinished, and we shall get the best idea of its spirit, not from his French continuators, but from his genial German translator, Wolfram von Eschenbach. Something of definiteness, indeed, it loses by crossing the Rhine. Chrestien, from artistic motives, had reserved his explanation of the grale for the climax of his story, and meanwhile merely described it as a miracle and mystery. But he never got the length of the *dénoûment,* and Wolfram has the vaguest ideas as to the precise nature of what he always calls the "wondrous thing." He knows its strange qualities, how the sight of it can keep men in life, how its presence brings each man his wish, but he does not know exactly what it is or what it is like; and perhaps his ignorance increases his reverent awe. It is strange to find that just as the German mystics arose in opposition to the dogmatism of the Church, so the great mystical poet of chivalry does not recognize the dogmatic basis of his theme. With him the grale stands for something like the Divine presence, but not in any narrower ecclesiastical sense; and while this circumstance somewhat changes the direction of the story, it does not make it less fit to illustrate the religious side of knighthood.

The grale is tended on the Savage Mountain by an order of spiritual knights who are vowed to the monastic life. Only their king is allowed to wed, and even he must give love the lower place in his heart. The last of them cried "Amour" in battle, and for this was wounded well-nigh to death. He lingers on from year to year, kept in life by the might of the grale, and often wishing he were dead. But when a wandering knight shall be his guest, and ask the meaning of what he sees, Anfortas shall be healed, and the stranger made king in his stead. It is Percivale who is predestined to the quest.

In his boyish years there is little promise of his future achievement, for his mother, widowed of her lord, has fled to a lonely wood, and there brings up her son in solitude, determined that he at least shall be kept far from the perils of knighthood. He knows nothing of arms and war ; he can only make himself rough weapons for killing birds, but their woodland melody makes him leave even this. His mother tells him their song is the gift of God. "What is God?" asks the child. "Son," she replies, "I tell you true, He is brighter than the day, who took on Him the shape of man : son, pray to Him at need ; His truth is still the succour of the world. .And one is called the Lord of Hell, who is black and full of guile; from him turn thy thoughts, and from the fickleness of doubt." In later years, in his time of trial, Percivale forgets this counsel, but now his heart is full of the brightness of God. One day he sees a company of knights in shining armour ride through the forest glades; he falls on his knees, and cries to their leader, " Help, God, for Thou art rich in help;" but they mock him, and pass on. Another, in shirt of flashing mail, surprised at the greeting, disclaims the honour, and explains that he is a knight. Percivale thinks he has not been respectful enough, and hastens to correct his familiarity. " Sir God," he begins again, " why is your body covered with these small rings?" The boy's fancy is now fired with what he hears of armour and chivalry, and the life at Arthur's court. He runs to his mother, and demands leave to go. She gives a distracted denial, and at last will send him forth only in the livery of a fool, thinking that by ridicule he will be driven back to her side. She understands his sensitive pride, but has not measured his unblenching resolve. His fool's dress suits well with his awkwardness and inexperience, and he makes many blunders rich in comedy and pathos. The *jeunesse dorée* of the court can only scoff at him, but Arthur and Gawain see the greatness of his soul. He puts us in mind of those other knights

of the grale, our great geniuses, our Schillers and
Shelleys, who come to transfigure the world, and are
for long the jest of worldlings. But Percivale does
not rest till he has the outward polish as well as the
inward worth of the court and the lists. An ancient
knight instructs him in all courtly usages and noble
manners. Such gains often imply a corresponding
loss, and Percivale, in acquiring the accomplishments
of the world, forfeits something of his open sense for
all that is great and wonderful. Among other things
he is told that he asks too many questions; a knight
should be able to see strange sights without always
inquiring their meaning, — an instruction of fatal
result. Meanwhile he goes out on adventures, rescues
the Queen Conduiramurs and weds her, but immediately passes again to new enterprises. He comes to
the Savage Mountain, and sees all the pageantry of
the grale, the bloody lance at which all lament, the
grale itself borne behind a procession of maidens, the
wounded king reclined on his couch ; but, mindful of
his lesson, goes to rest without question asked. His
dreams are hideous ; he wakes to find the castle empty ;
only one old servant lets him out, who curses him for
his clownish silence. Thus Percivale, by his schooling
in the great world, has lost his triumphant innocence
and wonder, his power to feel the grand mysteries
of life. At first no ill overtakes him, and he returns

in safety and honour to Arthur's court. But there he is appealed of treason by an ill-favoured damsel, who says he has played the churl on the Savage Mount. Gawain, too, is attainted on another charge, and the two knights must avoid the fellowship till their fame is cleared. Gawain is careless and confident, he knows that his cause is just, and bids his friend the cheerful farewell greeting, "God give thee luck." But Percivale is in despair. "Alas!" he returns, "what is God? Were He great, lived He in power, would He have fastened this reproach on us twain? Since I understood His grace I have followed His service. Now such service I renounce. If He bears hate, so can I."

Gawain is now chief person for a large portion of the story. His prowess is stainless, but it is the prowess of the world. He suffers no religious eclipse, and the world's honours fall thick upon him. But through his bright career of jousts and rescues we have glimpses of Percivale, gloomy and reckless, forgetting God or defying Him. At last, one Good Friday, his heart is softened. He thinks, "What, indeed, if there be help with God? Now for the last time will I prove it. Truly this is His day of grace." He leaves himself to the guidance of his horse, which brings him to a lonely hermitage. Here the worldly lessons of the old knight are counteracted by the religious lore of an old anchorite. Percivale is re-proved for his ambition, and dismissed into the great world with his sins forgiven. Restored to simplicity and meekness, he is also restored to all he has lost. Once more he is welcomed to his seat at the Round Table. Once more he is called to the Grale Mountain and made its king. Best of all, once more he is re-united with Conduiramurs his wife.

This crowning bliss of love is the starting-point of the other supplement to the Arthurian cycle, the great romance of "Tristram and Iseult," perhaps the best known and most cherished of all the series; which in the Middle Ages penetrated to the Greeks, and even to the Slavs, and in our own days has attracted the genius of the greatest poets and musicians. As to its early growth we are left in doubt, but at least the Provençals knew it in the middle of the twelfth century; and in North France, besides the versions of Berox and Thomas, Chrestien made it the subject of a poem which has unfortunately been lost. It has survived in many different languages and in many different forms, which apparently may be grouped in two main branches; but its main features are common to all. In English literature, the metrical romance of the thirteenth century conforms to a higher type than Malory's prose narrative, and this type has, on the whole, been favoured by the greatest mediæval and modern poets. Perhaps the best of the elder versions is the poem begun by Godfrey of Strassburg, and completed by Henry of Freiberg.

Who does not know the story of Tristram, the child, the knight, and the slave of love ? Born on the battle-field, and left orphan of both his parents, he is bred by his foster-father in ignorance of his descent. His beauty makes him the prey of pirates, but they fear their own crime, and leave him free but an outcast on the Cornish coast. His skill in venery and min-strelsy makes him the favourite of his uncle, King Mark; and when his birth is declared, he becomes the acknowledged heir of Cornwall. Then follows his rejection of the Irish claim to tribute; his slaughter of the Irish champion in single fight; and his voyage to Ireland, in minstrel disguise, to be healed of the wound he has thus received. He returns full of the praises of Iseult, the fair princess who has wrought his cure, and readily undertakes to procure her as wife to King Mark. He sets out on his second voyage, gains his point by the slaughter of a dragon, is recognized and all but murdered by Iseult, as the slayer of her kinsman. Nevertheless he fulfils his task, and, despite her reluctance, bears her back to Cornwall. Now comes the fatal mishap with the love-philtre. It is intended for Iseult and Mark, but accidentally drunk by Iseult and Tristram, and henceforth the fate is laid on them to love each other. To this passion they surrender themselves, and breaking all other ties, respecting no other claims, become the mediæval type for all true lovers. And if dangers faced, hardships endured, sacrifices joyfully offered for their love were claim enough, they should be entitled to all praise. Their deception of King Mark was only the inventiveness of love, their flight to the forest only its enterprise, which was also its exceeding great reward. Tristram's marriage with another lady, the fair one of the white hands, is palliated by her suggestion of his absent mistress; and this partial lapse, besides bringing him to his death, is expiated in passionate remorse and implicit revulsion to his early love.

We must be careful not to read in the mediæval romance the misgivings of modern thought. One great modern poet treats it as a story of free and careless desire. No doubt Tristram is brave, courteous, generous, and sacrifices all for love. But this love is an unlawful passion that leads him to violate every obligation of life, and is so essentially ignoble, that he cannot remain true even to it; he betrays all for Iseult, and is not faithful to her. Another modern view is, while admitting this, to lay the accent on the love-philtre, the compelling cause that lay outside Tristram's free choice, "the sinless source of all their sin," and to interpret the magic potion as the passion, the irrational basis of man's life, the dark power of nature which he must follow to his doom. In Wagner's opera the overture opens with the voices of the ocean, on which we seem to float, weeds without a root; and Swinburne leaves the lovers, their dust, their tomb, the land of their sojourning, engulfed in the waves on which they had sported and tossed :—

> "Peace they have that none may gain who live,
> And rest about them that no love can give;
> And over them, while death and life shall be,
> The light and sound and darkness of the sea."

But these are the glosses of a moralizing age, which has lost the power of seeing the chivalrous tales eye to eye. In a certain sense, Ascham was right when he complained of Tristram and his fellows, " Those be counted the noblest knights that do kill most men without any quarrell, and commit fowlest aduoulteres by sutlest shiftes;" and unless we consent to forget for a time some of our ten commandments, we shall never find in the mediæval stories just what they offer.

For his own age, Tristram was the ideal of worldly chivalry. Even in his outward appearance he is the image of a knight, tall, strong, and beautiful. In all courtly accomplishments, from hunting to minstrelsy, he excels the experts in the craft. He gives away kingdoms as other men give alms, he is grateful and true to his friends, his bravery is without a flaw. And lastly, all his powers, all his prospects, all his merits he sacrifices to the service of love, to the lady of his heart. No wonder that his was the favourite story of chivalry, and that he was the darling figure of romance. To compare a man to Tristram, was the highest honour that could be paid him, and grave seniors recommended Tristram as the best model for the youth of the day. It has been said, with happy infelicity, that his relation to Mark is a coarse doublet of Modred's relation to Arthur. It is, perhaps, unnecessary to discuss its coarseness, but it may be noticed, that, if a doublet, it is one in which our sympathies are inverted. It takes the side, not of the uncle, but of the nephew, and thus represents the point of view more native to an age that licensed the service of love. If Tristram commits a fault, it is not by loving another man's wife, but by following in a weak moment a criminal impulse towards marriage. Yet this is but a brief eclipse of his gallantry, as Percivale passes through an eclipse of his faith. Despite their temporary lapse, they remain respectively the great types of love and devotion.

It must be noted that both knights, though tending away from the centre of chivalry to the two modes of life which it had joined, do not actually transgress its limits. The drift of Percivale's life is to holiness, but he is not insensible to human affection, and the summit of his bliss is reunion with his wife. Tristram is the Paladin of love, but he is pattern of the other knightly virtues as well, and he, too, feels the stirrings of religion. Yet we feel that here there is some inconsistency. Percivale alone, of the grale knights, is allowed to wed, but precisely the exception is unintelligible, for he is their chief: surely in those days, if the highest life were the goal, the monastic vows must be observed. Similarly, though Tristram is the flower of worldly knighthood, he does no doubt show that faithlessness to sacred ties, that prostration before headlong passion, which modern feeling so eagerly remarks. If the perfection of chivalry, he is also its disgrace; his story, if its pæan, is also its dirge. Yet this aspect of the question is, in his romance, quite overlooked.

If the quest of the grale, the search for absolute union with God, were described in real earnest, it would have for its hero one who did not yield to the compromise of chivalry, one who knew no earthly love, and who could not rest in the half-hearted compliances of the Round Table. And thus in later romance Galahad supplants Percivale in the achievement of the grale. On the other hand, if the unconditional surrender to love which the age demanded were pictured in its naked truth, it would be shown

over-riding, but not with impunity, all other knightly
duties of honour and religion, and leading to the disruption of chivalry, the dismemberment of the Round
Table.   In this respect Lancelot, who for the sake of
his queen betrays his king, who is not worthy of the
grale for which he yearns, whose life is a losing
struggle, and who ruins the knighthood that he
adorns, takes the place of the cheery and unhesitating
Sir Tristram.   The search for the grale weakens
Arthur's fellowship: on Lancelot and his kinsfolk that
fellowship makes war.

And meanwhile Arthur himself, who at first had
gathered up in little all that was good in chivalry,
was changed and desecrated, and became the author
of his ruin, the father of the nephew who was to
accomplish his fall.   Thus in his own person, as in
the order of the Table and the idea that they both
express, we see the union of warring principles, the
mingling of unsanctified passion and overstrained
religiousness, which could not blend, and which in
their disruption meant the overturn of the old ideal.

These, the last significant accretions of the Arthurian romance, are represented in the prose stories
of " Merlin," attributed to Borron, of " Artus," and of
" Lancelot du Lac " and the " Queste del Saint Graal,"
both attributed, perhaps rashly, to Walter Map.
These were developed in almost entire independence

of each other, and only some of them in isolated parts passed into poetical romance : thus Chrestien's " Chevalier à la Charrette," and the fine fourteenth century alliterative poem, " Syr Gawayn and the Grene Kniȝt " are episodes from Sir Lancelot. It is characteristic that the first experiment in gathering the loose threads together again, and assigning to the adventures each its proper place in the one great tragic scheme, is made under Edward IV., that king who destroyed the "last of the barons," and in whose reign the new principles of society begin obviously to work. Sir Thomas Malory made this attempt, and made it pretty easy for himself. He aimed at no great solidarity in his work, was rather capricious in his insertions and omissions, and often leaves an adventure half told. Yet he must be allowed to have given the story of the British king, so that none of its pathos and terror is lost. The son of the Christian champion Uther, he is the fruit of a lawless amour; and though hallowed and chosen by heaven, in his first love he violates the common instincts of mankind, and ruthlessly but vainly seeks to shun the consequences of his guilt. Yet for long all seems to go well with him. He weds the fair Guinevere, and with her receives the Round Table, founded to bring back the holy grale among the people. He fills its seats with knights of unmatched prowess, some of whom excel himself in games of chivalry, and he does his *devoir* in purging the world of ill. Yet, amidst all his pomp and magnificence, his weird is slowly fulfilling itself. Lancelot, his best knight, his best friend, is but his " dearest foe." As Arthur's truant passion has its fruit in Modred, born to be the scourge of the order by his villainy, so Lancelot, in his one breach of faith to the queen, becomes father of Galahad, born to be its scourge by his holiness. For this attracts once more the holy grale to the haunts of men, and while the fellowship breaks itself on a quest which is only for the virgin knight, Galahad disappears to be grale king elsewhere. Never again does the Round Table feast so goodly a company, and soon the discovery of Lancelot's love divides it against itself. When Arthur is warring against him over sea, the traitor Modred seizes kingdom and queen, avenging his origin with equal wrong; and though Arthur returns to take swift vengeance for this baser treason, vengeance does not mean redress. In that weird last battle the great king and his nephew son fall by each other's hands.

Thus the Arthurian stories, after expressing the beauty and fulness of chivalry, end by expressing its dissolution. That this ultimate phase was necessary both in the ideal and in its literary reflection, we may see, if we recall what chivalry was, and how it found utterance in song. It sought to establish a compromise, an equipoise between the opposing forces of religious monastic theory and irreligious lay life. The scales dip to the clerical side in the " Song of Roland," to the mundane in the " Lay of Alexander; " only in the career of Arthur, and its elaboration in the adventures of his knights do we find anything like an exact balance. But since there was mere adjustment and no real fusion in chivalry, at best it was in unstable equilibrium, liable at every moment to be destroyed. In the added romances of Percivale and Tristram we find the fine poise disturbed. In the reconstruction of the story, which makes Arthur in his own person represent the conflicting forces, and Lancelot and Galahad follow them out to the uttermost, the whole contrivance breaks up.

And this was the fate of chivalry as a guiding principle, because it was unequal to the problem which it undertook to solve, and men soon saw that it merely professed to give the answer. Yet it remains a great attempt to reconcile man's impulse to self-indulgence with his impulse to self-denial; and the fictions to which it gave rise retain, in like manner, and for the same reason, a certain depth and breadth which gives them a charm even now.

THE MINNESONG.

[Hagen's " Minnesänger," 1838, contains the complete series of songs with lives of the authors. Since then the works of individual minnesingers have been more accurately edited, *e.g.* in Lachmann's " Minnesanges Frühling," in Pfeiffer and Bartsch's " Walther v. d. Vogelweide," in Haupt's " Nithart," and Ettmüller's " Frauenlob."]

THE contrast between the position of women in ancient and in modern times, among the Germanic and the " classical " races, has often been explained ; and if it has lost nothing in literary descriptions, is yet very real and important. The Greeks, who were always children, regarded women as boys regard girls : even when deepest in love, perhaps then most of all, they were blind to the higher claims and qualities of those they admired; and their characteristic lyric celebrates stray amours rather than permanent attachments. They had clearer eyes for female beauty than for female character and worth, and their feelings at their healthiest had more of instinct than of spiritual sympathy.

For the more refined and typical minds of recent

Europe the reverse of all this is true. Before the Middle Ages have begun, the Anglo-Saxons sing of the man's longing for his absent wife or the wife's for her banished lord, and deal with none but wedded love; and thus early strike the ground note of the later lyric. Not as though modern poetry of this kind were all or most of it put in the mouths of married personages. The pursuit has inspired more verse than the fruition. But in it generally, and by preference, "the bent of love is honourable, and the purpose" might be "marriage." It often touches its highest levels in uttering the hope of life-long union or the feeling of reverential respect; and few, by comparison, are the pieces that we find in absolute conflict with these ideas. Moore does not take the most ideal view of love, but see how differently Moore and Horace contemplate the fading charms of their mistresses. Lyce is insulted with sarcasms:—

> " Quo fugit Venus ? heu! quove color ? decens
> Quo motus ?   Quid habes illius, illius,
>   Quæ spirabat amores,
>   Quæ me surpuerat mihi."

But Moore only sees a new demand and a new opportunity for his affection :—

> "It is not while beauty and youth are thine own,
>   And thy cheeks unprofaned by a tear,
>   That the fervour and faith of a soul will be known,
>   To which time will but make thee more dear."

If we select a greater modern poet for the comparison, the contrast becomes more drastic. Horace tells us how Glycera aroused his sleeping love :—

> " Urit me Glyceræ nitor
>   Splendentis Pario marmore purius,
>   Urit grata protervitas
>   Et vultus nimium lubricus aspici."

Coleridge's lines to Genevieve could not be more diametrically opposed were they written in conscious protest :—

> " Maid of my love, sweet Genevieve,
>   In beauty's light you glide along,
>   Your eye is like the star of eve,
>   And sweet your voice as seraph's song.
>   Yet not your heavenly beauty gives
>   This heart with passion soft to glow,
>   Within your soul a voice there lives——
>   It bids you hear the tale of woe.
>   When sinking low the sufferer wan
>   Beholds no hand outstretched to save,
>   Fair as the bosom of the swan,
>   That rises graceful o'er the wave,
>   I've seen your breast with pity heave,
>   And therefore love I you, sweet Genevieve."

Erotics ancient and modern have thus their several and well-defined spheres. But a third variety, hardly inferior in beauty of form and content, the mediæval lyric of Provence and Germany, is more ambiguous in character, often more remote from our sympathies, and therefore less amenable to our judgment. If the classical view of love was boyish, and the modern be manly, the mediæval may perhaps be described as youthful. But as Keats says, " The imagination of the boy is healthy, and the mature imagination of the man is healthy; but there is a space of life between, in which the soul is in a ferment, the character undecided, the way of life uncertain, the ambition thick-sighted; thence proceeds mawkishness." These words are severe in their criticism of youth, and doubly severe if transferred to the criticism of the Middle Ages; yet they are not without a deep measure of truth. And just as many men retain more feeling for their boyish open-air life than for their youthful dreams, so the world has more at heart the direct appeals of the classical than the harebrained fancies of the romantic age.

So far as these fancies prevail in the domain of love, they are marked by two salient features, their frivolity and their extravagance.

If men's homage fell to professional beauties in ancient, and to possible wives in modern times, it was paid in the Middle Ages to other men's wives. These, at least, had the preference, and in more rigid circles only the pursuit of them was strictly entitled to the high name of love. To judge from their poems, the chivalrous singers served for very tangible reward, and thus, far more than the *naïf* worshipper of Aphrodite, broke through what are now regarded as the most primary demands of social morality. They themselves do not feel that their conduct is at all out of the way. They pay a certain price of devotion for which they expect remuneration, and complain when remuneration is withheld. Attempts have been made to show that all this literary gallantry had nothing corresponding to it in real life. But such attempts have a great body of evidence against them, and were this otherwise, they would hardly succeed in rebutting the charge of levity. It is a question whether the man who spends his life breaking the marriage vow cuts a sorrier figure than one who is always constructing fictions how he has broken and is going to break it.

But this theory of love had at least one advantage for the knight errant. It opened the floodgates for a lavish waste of devotion. To this, indeed, they were already inclined. Unlike the boy, who is some-times conceited and tyrannical by reason of his strength, the troubadour almost seemed to find his strength standing in his way. He was not satisfied unless he could spend it to the uttermost, not for his lady's real good, but simply in token of his own self-surrender. Her weakness was her imperial title, her merest whim was his law. His love-making was rightly styled the service of women. And how could the servant display his devotion so well as to a mistress, removed by rank or distance, or above all by marriage? Thus there were more difficulties to overcome, more dangers to surmount, a great many more chances of posturing and keeping his passion on the *qui vive.* If the whole thing after all were much ado about nothing, that did not greatly matter. The main point was gained, he had plenty of scope to throw himself away in the very asceticism of love.

This extravagance was, however, very excusable, and in a way very laudable. When the world or when a man begins to feel the might of a new idea, the result is apt to be a one-sided enthusiasm, often carried to ridiculous lengths. Every principle develops through opposite excesses to the golden mean. And the new-born reverence for women was no exception to this rule. Western Europe, through the combined influences of race and religion, was beginning to perceive what dawns on a youth as the result of his physical and mental growth. The surrender of love to be complete, must be as much in feeling as in fact; and the feeling cannot be evoked save by sympathy, self-sacrifice, and service. The vagaries of chivalry are eternal, because they are renewed in successive generations of youthful lives.

Neither is the frivolous nature of the end proposed very mysterious. The Church of those days set celibacy above wedlock, and the upper classes, among whom the service of love found its chief votaries and minstrels, could not but be affected by the teaching of the Church. The lower orders might do their own will, marry and be given in marriage without question asked, and sing simple love songs on their rustic courtings and quarrels. But the nobles could not help being a little *doctrinaire*, and attempted a compromise between their natural bent and their authoritative ideals. This compromise was the service of woman, which is a sort of middle term between free love and marriage, or between both and continence. That it should enjoy such universal favour need not surprise us when we remember that a Templar who violated the statute, *de osculis fugiendis*, was yet by common estimate a more sacred person than a wedded layman.

But, indeed, the best interpretation of this theory, too, is found in the feelings of youth. Love's young dream is concerned rather with episodes than with the whole future life,—*that* it leaves to other young dreams of ambition, knowledge, work, perhaps religion. The dreamer pictures himself oftener as lover than as husband; indeed, of all his castles in the air, perhaps the least frequent is the Englishman's castle of his own house. Thus, with all his reverence, he divests love of what alone can entitle it to reverence, for he seeks its ideals outside the family. He lives in the atmosphere of the Middle Ages.

Not that the spirit we have described was the only one to express itself in the literature of that day. We have also much that is antique, much that is modern in feeling, the former originating chiefly with the travelling scholars, the latter chiefly with the people at large. Students still sing in the spirit of the one " Vivant omnes virgines, *faciles*, formosæ," and read the refrain of the other :—

> " An hendy hap ichabbe yhent,
> Ichot from heuene it is me sent.
> From all wymmen mi loue is lent
> And lyht on Alisoun."

In England, indeed, which has never accepted Continental impulses till they have lost something of point as well as of violence, it is impossible to say that the service of love distinctively existed. And in Germany, the land of Volkslieder, we find traces of an earlier and yet more modern style of love-song, which was displaced but not destroyed by the encroaching spirit of the age. How simple and heartfelt, for instance, is such a stanza as this :—

> " Thine am I, mine art thou,
> That is firm and sure, I trow.
> Locked thou art
> In my heart,
> And within must ever be ;
> For I've lost the little key."

Some of these anonymous verses betray a certain contempt for the theatrical devotion that was to carry the day against them. Thus, in one of them, a knight tells a lady how he found her sleeping, and, struck dumb with awe, feared to awake her. " Mischief take you ! " replies the fair one. " Did you think I was a wild bear ? " But such lays are few and unimportant. In Germany, which is so apt to ponder, as in the romance lands which are so apt to act, on the impulse of the day, the dominant lyric, when once imported from Provence, is the lyric of chivalry.

If we remember that the fundamental feeling in the service of love is exalted devotion to an insignificant end, we may thus describe the relations of the Northern minnesinger and the Southern troubadour. The Provençal clearly realizes the aim towards which he works, and fears not to insist on it; but the German is taken up with the means, and dwells on the emotion, the self-sacrifice of his service. They are contrasted as the professional fisherman and the amateur angler, as the commercial traveller and the holiday rambler. If the one is more steady and direct in his purpose, the other has more sense for the marvels and beauties of the way.

And from this many consequences follow. First,

the German is by far the more reverential of the two.
It is not uncommon to find the troubadour, after a
while, writing satires on his lady; but the minnesinger is respectful to the last. The minnesinger has
delicacy enough to mention no names, while the
troubadour gossips to all the world who is mistress of
his heart. In Germany, the service of women was
connected very closely with the service of the Virgin.
She was made very human, they were made very
divine. It has been said of the hymns and love-
songs, that, with title covered, one could hardly know
whether they were addressed to "the Queen of
Heaven or a Queen of Hearts." The younger Reinmar says, "Pure women are the world's treasure,
God's own body was born of a maid," and elsewhere
he compares the service of love to the quest of the
grale. Such reverent mystical touches come naturally
from the German, who, absorbed in his feeling, broods
over and tends it with a kind of religious care.

This brings us to another point of difference between the two love-songs. The Provençal impresses
us with his active personality. He is aggressive and
pushing. He will fight for his lady and maintain
her beauty against the world. But the German retires
within himself, he communes with his own feelings,
they fill him with wonder, he meditates on them and
tries to exhaust their meaning. *Minnen* and *minne*,

the mediæval words for love, are from the same root as the English *mind*, and at first meant, the verb, to bear in mind, to think upon ; the noun, remembrance or reverie. And so the *minne*singers, in their poetical meditations, ask, " Is Minne man or wife, is Minne body or soul ? " and rifle a passage in Veldeke's " Æneid," where the fancy-free Lavinia first hears of love, its contradictions, its potency of joy and pain, and proclaims its mystery by confessing that she can make nothing of it. In the same way, Friedrich von Hausen, far off in the crusades, is perplexed in mind because he cannot forget his cruel lady : often in his reverie he wishes people " good-night," instead of " good-morning ; " often he thinks of her instead of his sacred mission ; " God forgive me ! " he cries, fairly puzzled, " but why has He made her so fair." " Woe is me," says another, who gives it up with a touch of irritation ; " God has done me great wrong in shaping so goodly a lady ! "

And from this constant occupation with their feelings arises a third great difference between the Germans and the Provençals. The latter sing about everything : they take up theology and politics, social and literary criticism ; they abound in satire and invective. But with the exception of one, Walter von der Vogelweide, though strangely enough he is their chief, the minnesingers sing only of minne : they cannot leave the circle of their ruling feeling; if they look at the world at all, it is through the medium of their love; their whole universe is their adoration. The literature of the South has thus greater variety, that of the North greater depth, but also a vein of wearisome iteration. With the monotony of matter it is hard to avoid this, but a remedy is at least attempted by constantly varying the form. And this leads us to speak of their Metric.

The measures of the purely native minnesong were very simple, and hardly ever went beyond rhymed couplets, common four-lined stanzas and their easiest modifications. But under the French *régime* all this was exchanged for a new store of elaborate and complex harmonies. There was a more intricate arrangement of rhymes, more variety in the length of the lines, the whole structure was made more artistic and complete within itself, and as such, suited better the wants of lyric poetry. But just as we saw the Germans while accepting the French matter, modify it in the process, so now they modified the form. This they did by their observance of two canons, which have been called the Laws of Variety and Triplicity. Of these, the first was quite unknown among the Provençals, and the second was, at least, by no means universal.

The first is an extraordinary phenomenon, probably

quite unique in literature. Every verse-form was regarded as belonging to the man who invented it, and its use by another was infringement of the rights of property. This law forbade such infringement, and enacted that every one should fabricate his own stanza. The reason for this strange regulation must be sought for in the fact that, so long as the single feeling of love was the subject of every song, there were few chances of originality save in the form. And no doubt it did produce infinite variety. Men were even afraid to plagiarize themselves, and continually strove to diversify their own metres. The result was by no means satisfactory. Very many of their stanzas are mere metrical experiments, eccentric and surprising, but not in the best sense of the words original. In no department does the effort after novelty, the craving to be different from one's predecessors and neighbours, result in anything of real worth. The greatest works of the greatest geniuses are original in the sense, not that they are brand new, but that they disclose a richer significance in old and well-worn themes. Even Shakespeare has his sources, and more of them than a smaller man. And, for the case on hand, this is illustrated by the Provençal way of working. The troubadours were hampered by no such oppressive and harassing legislation. They could freely appropriate the results of other men's labours, and by constant development of the best forms bring them to perfection. To these, men return even now; but of the countless German stanzas, though some of the less adventurous are very fine, hardly one is remembered. The choice selection of the Provençals is better than all the motley stores of the minnesingers, where the real gold lies half hid in tinsel and pinch-beck.

This variety, however, was not allowed to be utterly lawless. A certain element of resemblance, a certain type, was preserved and enforced by the Law of Triplicity. According to it each stanza must contain three parts, the first two of which, as in the sonnet, should exactly correspond, while the third should be on a different model. This triple framework is, no doubt, necessary to the most perfect verse-form: the repetition of the first part impresses it on the memory and leads up to the variation in the last, which brings cadence and completeness. But it was a mistake to insist on such a model, however good, for a whole generation of poets. The second law of the minnesong brought back, as it were, the monotony of which the first tried to get rid. The stanzas may contain three lines or thirty; the lines may contain one foot or ten; but the arrangement is always in the obvious and glaring threefold scheme. We have, indeed, endless variety, but it is within a narrow range, and one sometimes gets to long for any common couplet or quatraine. Despite, therefore, of the first promise to the contrary, the fault of the matter returns in the form. There the minnesingers rang the changes on the single emotion of love; here they force the strangest metres into the single triple mould; but in both cases the result is apt to weary. These poets are fond of calling themselves nightingales. "Certainly," says Jakob Grimm, "we could not find a better simile than the song of birds for their exuberant melody, which we can never anticipate, in which every moment the old notes return in a new modulation;" but they remain the old notes.

Since this is so, an historical account of the minnesingers is apt to be tedious and indistinct, and may be compared with a sail down the Rhine in rainy weather. The impression it leaves behind is like that of a long series of hazy headlands, each repeating the same fine slope, each surmounted by its knightly castle, and all obliterated and ghostly in the mist. The authors were almost all men of rank, the sons of stirring times, in which they must have led adventurous lives. But seldom are these reflected in their verse, which mirrors only the clouds and brightness of their one vast overhanging thought. It is well to look less at the crowd of individual singers and more at a few of the typical kinds* of song, which arise in some sort chronologically ; and then to trace the growth and decay of the feeling which these songs evince. Perhaps only one great aspect of our subject will thus escape us, viz. its tediousness; but *that* it is impossible, were it desirable, to reproduce in any selection or brief notice. Hence it comes that outsiders often have a higher opinion of this poetry than those who have actually waded through its interminable stream of languishings and longings.

The minnesong, in its most general undeveloped phase, simply ran through the whole gamut of love; its despairs and raptures, its lamentations when favour is withheld, its wonderment when favour is accorded. This love-song of moods remains with the minnesingers to the last, but in the earlier period it has a more exclusive sway, and is marked by a certain shrinking reverence, a certain tender submission, which gradually becomes more rare. What lover was ever more religious in accepting his lady's frowns than the Burggrave of Nietenburg in this little snatch? But for the disturbing reference to sex it might be a hymn of Christian resignation :—

> " Since she wills to chasten me
> I shall count it for a grace,

---

* In selecting these types, I have not in all cases adopted the technical species of mediæval art.

> And like gold I thus shall be
> That within the fire we place
> To approve it well;
> Whence it doth excel,
> Fair and clear and pure.
> This my song is sure."

Freidrich von Hausen's lines on his absent mistress, if not so meek, are even more delicate :—

> "Full many a time I ponder,
> If I again should meet her,
> The words that I could say.
> It helps me, as I wander,
> In fancy to entreat her
> To lift my load away.
> Thus falls it day by day
> Men think my life the sweeter,
> And ween my heart is gay,
> While but with dreams I play."

But even the patience of the minnesingers would have been tired out by songs of this simple kind; and we early find a variety in which the words are placed in the mouth, not of the knightly author, but of his lady. Generally the motive is grief at the absence or joy in the worthiness of the lover. "The Falcon," attributed, perhaps rashly, to "Him of Kürnberg," as the earliest known minnesinger is rather vaguely styled, is a lay of this kind, and belongs to the very oldest period of the art, while yet it was hardly touched by foreign influence. Its versification, rough but not unmusical, with the peculiar halt in the last line, is popular in character, and is also employed in the great German epic, the "Niebelungen Lied :"—

> "I once reared a falcon a year and more with me,
>   And after I had trained him as I would have him be,
>   When gay was his plumage with gold from my hand,
>   He soared aloft right freely, and flew to seek another land.
>
> "In fair flight my falcon saw I once more,
>   And silken were the leashes that round his foot he bore,
>   And all of his feathers were ruddy with gold.
>   God send those together that love each other from of old!"

When the poets' imagination had grown so dramatic that their songs claim to be the utterances of ladies, the idea must have lain near to increase their vividness, by giving them the form of a dialogue between the knight and his lady. And this step was soon taken. The example I quote is, indeed, rather a couple of monologues than a single dialogue; but elsewhere there is a closer approximation to actual conversation. The two quatraines, modelled like the preceding, seem certainly to be by the Kürnberger; and few other pieces illustrate so well how, at first, in Germany the self-sacrifice of love was placed before its gratification :—

> "Full late in the night-time I stood by the wall,
>   And far underneath me I heard a knight call.
>   Like him of Kürnberg sang he, in the self-same measure,
>   The land he must void me, or else I yield me to his pleasure."
>
> "Now bring me and stay not my steed and weeds of war,
>   Since I for my lady must hie me hence afar.
>   Forth she drives me from her because I love her well ;
>   For this she, too, surely without my love must ever dwell."

When once the form of dialogue became established

it received further modifications. For instance, the lady appears in discourse, not with her lover, but with her lover's messenger. Perhaps this device, by its indirectness, gave the author greater opportunity for the praise of his constancy and devotion than he could becomingly find so long as he spoke in his own person. The "Messenger's Lay," given below, was written by the elder Reinmar, the teacher of his greater pupil, Walter von der Vogelweide, who, however, hardly overtopped him in the praise of contemporaries. Despite the utter self-abasement of the knight, it is plain that the idea of the wage is nearer the minds of all the parties than in the songs hitherto quoted.

" ' Say, for guerdon of my giving,
Hast thou seen the man I love so well ?
    Is it true he still is living,
As they say and I have heard thee tell ? '
    ' Lady fair, he dwells at rest ;
His heart beats ever high, nor shrinks from your behest.'

" ' I forbid him joyance never ;
Yet one suit 'twere well to lay side :
    This I pray him, both to-day and ever,
Such it is, it needs must be denied.'
    ' Lady, words like these are ill.
He says : " What she would have, all that do I fulfil."

" ' Fellow, hath he ever plighted
Knightly faith to sing his lay no more,
    Save it were by my own lips invited ?
' Lady, when we parted, thus he swore,—
    Surely you have heard the tale.'
' Alas ! If I entreat him, that may be our bale,

> " ' Yet to leave him in his madness
> Were to lose my joy in him, and worse ;
>   Since, for spoiling earth of gladness,
> All the folk would load me with their curse.
>   Only now begins my care ;
> I know not which is best, to do or to forbear.

> " ' Sad we women, friends we gain not,
> Save who further grace than words would know.
>   Love of mine shall he obtain not,
> Unfaith works a faithful woman woe.
>   Were I false—as I am not—
> Then him I might forget, to be of him forgot.' "

While in these varieties the moods of love were explained by the descriptions of a second and third party, another series had set about the same thing by the different method of bringing the lover's life into relation with that of nature. Many of the songs are distinguished by their reference to a season : above all, into the two great classes of spring lays and autumn lays. Heine sings how, in the marvellous month of May, the buds burst open, and love, too, opened in his heart. This is the central idea of all those spring lays. The flowers come back, the bare trees bear tender sprouts, the sun shines again on the plashing grass, the birds are heard once more,—" they sing their young a lullaby," says Wolfram, " all through the month of May." Nature calls the poet to the field ; as Chaucer goes out " one May morning " to gather daisies, so he searches for the best flowers, red and white ; he thinks on the lady that looked from the window—he binds a wreath to offer her; he knows the fairest meadows—will she not join him there? When the world is glad from dawn to dark will she alone refuse to smile? In like manner the autumn lays tell of the lost glory of the summer and the misery of the earth; the dark nights grow longer, the cold winter is nigh, the fountain of his lady's grace is frozen. One of the earliest spring songs is written by Meinloh von Sevelingen, and, though not the most poetical, is among the most characteristic :—

> " The harbingers of summer I see, even blossoms bright.
> Thou knowest, fairest lady, the prayer of thy knight ;
> His secret suit he tenders, of nought he is so fain,
> Since last he parted from thee, at heart he still hath suffered pain :
> Now hearten thou his spirit for this blithe summertide ;
> At rest he never can be, until thine arms have held him, and
> clasped him closely to thy side."

As a specimen of the autumn song we may select a stanza by Heinrich von Veldeke, one of the earliest minnesingers who write under conspicuously French influence. He has said that without Tristram's draught he has Tristram's constancy, even in view of favour withheld; and then proceeds :—

> " See the glorious sun on high
>   For the cold its light concealing,
> Hear the anthems fall and die
>   Which the little birds were pealing.
> Sorrowful at heart am I
> For the winter draweth nigh.

> First his cruel might revealing
>> On the flowers left desolate,
> All their gayness
> Changed to grayness.
>> Thus they bode my fate
>> Joyless, full of hate."

Sometimes the connection with the season is less direct, and the treatment is freer and more elaborate. Here, for example, is a spring song by Walter von der Vogelweide, which more properly is a parallelism between women and flowers :—

> " When the flowers from out the grass are springing,
>> As with laughter for the sunshine o'er us,
> On some May morning ere the day is high
> And the little birds o'erhead are singing
>> In their sweetest and their subtlest chorus,
> What gladness else may with this gladness vie ?
>> 'Tis half the worth of heaven to share it.
>> Would you ask with what we can compare it,
>> For me, one only thing I trow
> Hath more rejoiced mine eyes, and seen again would more rejoice
>> them now.

> " Know you ought of woman's queenly presence
>> When well chapleted, apparelled fairly,
> With goodly following and with gracious cheer,
>> Gone amidst the people for her pleasance ;
>> Round she looks, but neither long nor rarely,
> As the sun the stars might overpeer ?
>> Let May have marvels out of measure,
>> What hath he so winsome in his treasure
>> As her own body rare and good ?
> We straight forget the fairest flowers to gaze on her sweet woman-
>> hood.

> " Rise then, join me at the feast on Mayday,
>> Ye who will to know the matter truly,

> Where Spring is come arrayed in all his might.
> Look on him and look on some fair lady ;
> Tell me then if I have chosen duly
> And which excels the other in delight.
> If charge were laid on me, by choosing
> One to win myself, while one refusing,
> How easy were that choice of mine.
> Sir May, thou shouldst be March ere I would give my lady's
> charms for thine."

Thoughts like these recur in song after song, slightly modified and in new combinations. They begin the sentimental poetry of nature, which either suffuses the world in subjective feeling, or at most makes the scene the setting for the emotion. Such poetry, always a little wanting in body, readily becomes conventional. It does so among the minnesingers, who after a while treat song and bird, sunshine and frost, greenwood and meadow, as so many indispensable counters in the game of verse-making. Spring and autumn are the respective insignia of the hopeful and the despairing lover, just as in heraldry eight strawberry leaves are the emblem of a duke.

This degeneration into allegory was almost necessary, for man's inner life cannot be arranged according to the calendar. The third great group of minnesongs have no such artificial connection with their subject. They describe a situation, a crisis, an event full of emotional meaning. By far the most of them are the so-called day-songs or dawn-songs, undoubtedly the perfection of the minnesinger's art. They correspond to the Aubade, or Alba, of the South, and are supposed to have been introduced by Wolfram von Eschenbach ; but there are traces of them earlier in Walter von der Vogelweide, in Heinrich von Morungen, and even in a song which, if truly ascribed to Dietmar von Aist, must have preceded the French influence altogether. At daybreak a lady arouses her knight—

"Sleep'st thou, dear heart ? Alas ! we must waken, for a little sweet bird which has lighted on the linden bough."

"I had softly fallen asleep, and now, child, thou call'st: To arms ! Love may not be without sorrow. What thou wilt, that fulfil I, my sweet."

Then the lady fell aweeping. "Thou ridest hence and leavest me alone. When wilt thou to my side again ? Alas ! thou bear'st my joy away with thee."

Here, however, the speakers may be man and wife ; the day-songs proper have also their point of departure in the return of the sun to wake the earth, but the circumstances are now more definitely marked and the persons are lovers *par amour*. In the dark, the knight has stolen to his lady's window, the sun rises and they must part. Heinrich von Morungen has written a poem of this description which, if not exactly a day-song, fulfils all the conditions but one. It is a

series of alternate recollections and not a dialogue, but
otherwise it is almost the finest in this branch :—

> " ' Alas ! and when again shall I
>   See flashing through the night
> Her shape made wondrously
>   And as the snowflake white ?
>   It did deceive mine eyes ;
>   I thought : The moon doth rise
>   To lighten all the skies.
>   And then it dawned.'
>
> " ' Alas ! and when again shall he
>   Await the morning here ?
> While night so fast doth flee
>   We give no thought to fear ;
>   Ah, soon returns the day !
>   When erewhile here he lay,
>   And all his grief would say,
>   Even then it dawned.'
>
> " ' Alas ! again and yet again
>   She kissed me while I slept :
> Her tears ran down like rain,
>   So bitterly she wept.
>   I soothed her sore distress,
>   Her sobs grew less and less,
>   She neared me to caress,
>   And then it dawned.'
>
> " ' Alas ! he would not be denied
>   To gaze on my poor charms :
> The veil he laid aside
>   And needs would see my arms
>   All disarrayed and bare.
>   It was a wonder rare
>   For such a sight to care,
>   But then it dawned.' "

These two songs give the chief motives of their

class, though some of the others are more fervid and impassioned. The morning light or the morning bird wakes the lovers and warns them they must part. They have been too much lost in each other to mark the flight of time, and now they will not understand that it is really day; they make believe that the sun is the moon, that the lark is the nightingale. The lady cannot bring herself to dismiss the knight; the knight is ready to stay if that be her good pleasure; at length in terror of the broadening light she hastens him away. The great scene in " Romeo and Juliet," rather than any translation, will give English readers an idea of these songs in their intensity of emotion. Feeling and feeling mingle and conflict; love and fear, the need of immediate parting and the sense that parting is impossible, the anguish of leave-taking and the hope of reunion all meet and crowd each other in the lines; and as a background we see the old castle on its hill, and the still dawn filling the valleys with light.

A further modification of Wolfram's, adopted by later minnesingers, was to make the castle watchman a confederate. He announces the daybreak in friendly words, interposes to counsel an instant separation, and with his cool sober sense presents a new foil to the distraught and passionate lovers. The whole, complete in a few stanzas, is like nothing so much as one

of Browning's dramatic lyrics. The following is a
version, not of the best, but (for Wolfram is a virtuoso
in metres) of the easiest :—

"'Behold! the daylight
Mounts aloft in all its strength
And rends the clouds with claws of flame.
I see the grey light
Broaden out : the sun at length
Will send him forth who lately came
To tryst of love—the valiant man—
And entered in with careful heed.
Hence shall I bring him if I can ;
His wealth of worth has claim to help at need.'

"'Watchman, thou singest
Songs that swell my sorrow still,
And steal me all my joy away.
News thou bringest—
That, alas! I like but ill—
Every morn at break of day.
Such thou oughtest rather hide :
And this I charge thee on thy troth,
Reward thou'lt have whate'er betide,
But leave in peace me and my lover both.'

"'Oh God! delay not!
He must hence while yet we speak ;
My sweetest lady, bid him go.
Thy knight will stay not
Soon again your love to seek
With life and fame unhurt of foe.
My sacred faith he bade me plight
To bring him forth when day was come ;
And now 'tis day : it yet was night
When you with kiss and clasp received him home.'

"'What suits thy pleasure,
Watchman, sing, but leave him here

> Who brought me love for love of mine.
>   'Tis thy false measure
>   Oft doth rouse us both in fear
> While yet no morning star doth shine
>   On him who came for love's delight;
> While yet no morning meteors dart,
>   'Tis thou dost ever snatch my knight
> From my white arms, but not from out my heart.'

>   " Here through the casement
> Glimmering beams began to glide.
> At this, and at the warder's hest,
>   In sore amazement
> For him who rested at her side,
> Her bosom close to his she pressed.
> He thought upon his nobleness
> (The watchman's song was in his mind);
>   He tore him from the close embrace,
> The meed of love—and left his joy behind."

Notice the daring description of the sunrise as a
bird that strikes fiery talons through the clouds. It
is almost as fine as Shelley's—

> " Sanguine sunrise with his meteor eyes,
>   And his burning plumes outspread."

But for all that, the beauty of these poems—and in
the original they are very beautiful—need not blind
us to their essential immorality. Indeed we shall
not see the one unless we see the other, for an appreciation of both depends on our thoroughly realizing
the situation. However the passion may be idealized,
however the adjuncts may be glorified, the underlying
fact is one which only a particular class of modern

novels would treat so lovingly. Of course it would be as unjust to judge it by the modern ethical formulæ as it would be to estimate the good Samaritan's charity by the present purchasing power of twopence; for moral standards change no less than those of finance. But it may at least be fairly said that in these poems much of the haze of feeling has lifted from the goal of the service of woman, and that henceforth either the reverence of love will be greatly diminished, or it will be retained by artificial means.

And this, in fact, strikes us about the remaining types of minnesong. Niethart, a younger contemporary of Walter and Wolfram, introduced a new song of situation, or, more strictly, bent an older one into quite a new shape. The minnesingers had long distinguished between the songs which were merely to be sung and those which should accompany the dance. Many of the latter introduce, as it were, an invitation to dance, and in these Niethart has his point of departure. But he loves to treat the merry-making as the subject of conversation between some peasant woman and her daughter, and always hints intelligibly enough that his gallantry and minstrelsy form the chief attraction, but also the chief danger, of the rustic festival. All this may be, and very often is, bright and clever; but one is conscious of a great descent from the tone of the old days when the knights did

not deign to sing of village amours, and when their
hearts beat high as their ladies approached the scene
of revel. Here is a dancing song of Walter's, not so
respectful as some others, for in the last stanza he
fears he has been too sentimental, and hastens to finish
up with a comic and impudent touch :—

> " ' This wreath, fair maiden, take ! '
> To a lovely lady thus I made request,
>   ' The dance for thy sweet sake,
> Will in fairness then of fairest flowers be dressed.
> Were mine a wealth of noble stones
>   All were on thy brow ;
>   Oh believe me now,—
> Is truth not breathing in these tones ?
>
>   ' You are so beautiful
> Blithe am I my chaplet in your hands to yield,
>   The best that I can cull ;
> Know I where are red and white flowers of the field ;
> In yonder heathland hid from view
>   Fairly are they springing,
>   And the birds are singing,—
> There shall we pluck them, I and you ? '
>
>   " She took my offering,
> So a child might take a gift half fearfully.
>   Her cheeks were reddening
> As the rose that standeth by the white lily :
> Then, as in shame, her bright eyes fell :
>   A fair reverence
>   Was my recompense,—
> If aught beside, I must not tell.
>
>   " Meseemèd that I never
> Gladness of the heart like this in life had found ;
>   The flowers were falling ever
> From the boughs above us down upon the ground,

And, look you, for sheer joy I broke
Into laughter there,
Dreamland was so fair,—
It dawned, and needs must that I woke.

"And hence is come my case,
All the summer through that every maid I see
I gaze into her face :
Found I her I seek, of pain I then were free :
Haply to dance she cometh now :—
Ladies, deign to throw
Back your bonnets low ! *
Oh, might I meet her, wreath on brow! "

Now here is a dancing song of Niethart's, not the most characteristic, but one of the most suitable for quotation :—

"An ancient dame steps forward now,
A thousand wrinkles on her brow ;
' Daughter, keep the house for me
While I dance for very glee.'

" ' Mother, what has taken you ?
Have your wits forsaken you ?
Fifty years have passed away
Since the time your hair grew gray.'

" Up she starts like bird from twig :
' Yet to-day I'll have my jig.
See, my joints are not worn out,
But good for many a merry bout.

" ' Daughter, thou the house must guard,
While I foot it on the sward.
Quick and stealthily, look there,—
Yonder youth with yellow hair !'

---

* An allusion to the low broad Austrian hats of the day.

> " ' Mother, I can go instead :
> The gallant asked me ; " Yes," I said.
> He keeps the time from being long.'
>   Herr Niethart wrote this dancing song."

It will not be disputed that if Niethart's production is nearer real life, Walter's has the finer aroma of feeling.

But those who tried to preserve the forms of feeling when the life was gone, became mere pullers of wire-drawn verse and arrangers of meaningless phrases. Passion yields to word-play, and reverie to conceit, and at last we find Frauenlob introduce for the first time into Germany, the tenso of the Provençals. This kind of verse argument became in his hands the very product and shrine of the formal understanding. In one of these, he maintains against Walter von der Vogelweide that *lady* is a nobler name than *woman*. But the shallowness of his purpose appears when we find that he fastens a quarrel on his great adversary only by arbitrarily restricting the word *lady* to married women. On turning back to the poem of Walter's which Frauenlob attacks, we discover that they are perfectly agreed. So, on this side, the minnesong degenerates into wordy sophistries.

These remarks on the form of the minnesong already suggest the history of its spirit. A Chaucerian poem on the praise of women sketches the course of the service of love in the case of certain *mauvais sujets* at the English court. They swear that they never before knew Love nor his dreadful observance, but now they feel how sorely he can wound. And with that they draw to bed, and complain that their lady has given them such pain with a dangerous look of her eyes, that they must needs go to their death. And then they sigh as though their heart would burst in two, and call her their "lady" and their "hertes queene," but if for ruth she give comfort in any wise, "than wolle these janglers deme of her full ille."

The career of the service of love as a general principle of the age is not dissimilar, if we only add that the later generations often went on tagging the fantastic devotion which the real life of the times had outgrown. We may, perhaps, roughly distinguish three periods of the art which mediæval love called forth, each with its prevailing tone, and each with its typical authors as characterized by history, or legend, or inference.

In the first, the lays approach nearly in form and substance to the floating popular songs which seem in all lands to grow up spontaneously without definite authorship. No name is attached to the earliest specimens of the minnesong; and when we come to the collection by "him of Kürnberg," we feel that this name, if it can be called one, is literally "attached" to a number of the pieces. A peculiar literary theory illustrates their position, and indeed that of most of the love-lyrics of this group. It was observed that the Kürnberger's stanza was the same as is employed in the "Niebelungen Lied," and the conjecture was started that he might be the author of that poem. But this similarity rather cuts the other way. For the " Niebelungen " stanza seems to have developed from the older native verse, and thus the lays of the Kürnberger run a chance of being considered rather public than private property. Be that as it may, there can be no question that in this period the inspiration is almost entirely native; that few measures have been adopted from without; and that the tone, save in depth and in increasing depth of respect, is more popular than in the lyrics of the second period.

In this, though the ownership of individual songs may still be doubtful, there is no further difficulty in pointing to the authors as a class, and in indicating the names of most of them. They are all of knightly, some of princely rank, and even imperial minnesingers are not unknown. This circumstance speaks for itself. We have here to do with a class which, in those days at least, had more culture, and, with that, more openness to foreign ideas, and more impulse to introspection than the masses of the people. Thus, as we might expect, the influences from Provence on metre and sentiment are now undisguised. The depths of German feeling are stirred by the breath from the sweet south, and break into ripples of liquid music. These songs have, indeed, the freshness, the sweet monotony, and the countless fine diversities of summer waves. The singers live, and dream, and have their being in the emotion of youthful love. They explore its reaches and sound its depths. They detect its lightest murmurs, its most inarticulate vibrations, and have trained their verse to reproduce each, as an Indian imitates the cries of his native forest. In other respects their careers were often noble and notable. Take three conspicuous instances : Friedrich von Hausen, whose songs are like old memories in their plaintive sweetness, for he has read the heart of youth, was a chivalrous crusader, a follower of the serious Barbarossa in his ill-fated march to the Holy City, and perished at the battle of Philomelium in the last triumphant charge. The army forgot its victory in mourning for his death. Walter von der Vogelweide, the greatest of the minnesingers, who meditates every impression, drinks in all beauty, masters each mood of love, is driven by his ponderings to themes beyond. In the struggle between rival emperors, he chooses his part with a view to the weal of Germany, and maintains it as he may. In the feud between emperor and pope, he assails the latter with his songs, for his faith is fixed mystically on the Almighty One, who is " too long and too broad," "too great and too small " for us to know. And Wolfram von Eschenbach, who rejects all that might be conventional, pierces the husk of sentiment, and in his burning day-songs crowns the period, is better known for a higher achievement. He is the author of " Parzival," the great mystical poem that tries to thread the maze of man's spiritual life; yet he would rather have fame as a good knight than as the best singer on earth.

Men like these, even if the fashionable view of love leads them into slippery places, do not care to dwell on its seamy and sordid side. If sometimes antimoral, they are never vulgar or brutal. It was at this time that they were compared with nightingales, and even in their sensual strains they somehow seem to rise above the earth into the element of air. They are bird-like in all their tones, whether they are tremulously tender like Friedrich, full and clear like Walter, or throbbing with passion like Wolfram. This, perhaps, as much as the name Vogelweide, or pasture of birds, suggested the beautiful old legend of Walter, and this was felt by the modern poet who repeats it. To repay the lessons they taught him, the minstrel is said to have left a legacy to feed the birds on his grave from day to day. And this was done till the monks of the abbey appropriated the bequest to the "fasting brotherhood." "Time," says Longfellow—

> "Time has long effaced the inscriptions
> On the cloister's funeral stones,
> And tradition only tells us
> Where repose the poet's bones.
> But around the vast cathedral
> By sweet echoes multiplied;
> Still the birds repeat the story
> And the name of Vogelweid."

But the minnesingers are fond of telling us how summer joys pass, and the birds are silent as the winter draws nigh. Winter, too, came for them, and they all became mute save some few who were either barn-door fowls or well-taught parrots. The bloom of the minnesong was too evanescent to last. The service of love was too unpractical, too much in conflict with the claims of the world, long to hold its place when its real nature was discovered. And in Germany, owing to that very meditative trait which is its chief charm, it was doubly exposed to a double danger. The practice of introspection would either disclose its real issue without disguise, or would become a mere pastime for the idle. Some later minnesingers are so unfortunate as to go astray in both directions at once, like that Ulrich von Lichtenstein, who, in his book styled the "Service of Women," unwittingly parodies what he writes about by his mere extravagance, yet is so insincere in his devotion that he creates an impression approaching disgust. But generally in South Germany the former alternative was chosen, and the songs became frivolous; while in the North the latter course was preferred, and they became artificial.

In form and tone the later lyrics of the first class tend, but with more lubricity, towards the type of the popular songs. Their verse is often simple, their personages are often peasants, and their scenes in the country. Sometimes there is a *naïf* humour about them, which indeed is their best quality. Thus Gottfried von Nifen tells us, in a dialogue, how he has the ill-luck to break a girl's pitcher, and charmed with her good-natured way of taking the mishap, asks her to run off with him. "No," says she, "I should lose my lady's favour; and, besides, she owes me a shilling and a shirt. Wait till I have these, then perhaps I may listen." This may be a caricature of the refusals which ladies used to give their knights, or it may be a genuine popular touch.

And this return to the folk-song was not without its reason. The later minnesingers in Austria were often poor knights, who were glad to go round the festivals of the well-to-do peasant, furnish music for the dances, and for guerdon enjoy, with other more innocent rewards, certain easy triumphs among the village belles. The chief of them is Niethart, who, for some unexplained reason, probably a discreditable one, had to make off from his native Bavaria. He was so notorious for his rustic adventures, that he earned the name of *Peasants'-foe*, and one is glad to think he came in for one of those drubbings which he has drastically described with a humour like that of "Peblis to the Play."

In its other current, the art spreads beyond the knightly class altogether, and runs into the later master-song, the mechanical exercise of well-meaning burghers; nay, we find a Jew among its votaries. The metres become over complex, the experiments in rhymes and arrangement more hazardous; till they can no longer be followed by the ear, but only by the eye if they are read with one's pencil ready, and with frequent back references. In substance they contain, at their best, prosaic apothegms, at their worst, verbal quibbles and tame conceits. The most talented offender is Frauenlob, *Anglicè* Ladies'-praise, whose name looks as if he himself had invented it in one of his brighter moments, but is nevertheless his true family addition. Pity that Mr. Walter Shandy knew not of this, when maintaining the influence of names on character. He would have forgotten Aunt Dinah for Frauenlob, for the latter did as much for the praise, as the former for the dispraise of the sex. Two circumstances may perhaps serve to characterize him. By way of sublimity, he addresses the Deity as Tetragrammaton, much as the Romans called a thief a man of three letters. And at his funeral, the maidens and matrons, as we are told, poured wine and tears into his grave, till a stream rippled round it, and flowed out from the churchyard. This, like his name, reads as if one of his conceits had been done into real life.

The relations of the two tendencies may be further illustrated by two traditions.

Tannhäuser, who wrote in the style of Niethart, becomes in legend the guest of Venus in her subterranean grotto, the votary and victim of infernal pleasures, the accursed of man and God; but the master-singers thought that Frauenlob had taken orders, and was doctor of divinity.

The verses of the men furnish some excuse for both these inventions, and it is just this that shows how the minnesong has fallen into decay. What a gulf between them and the legend that arose about Walter von der Vogelweide! We can linger with him and his fellows in many a vacant hour; we are lured back to them by their "native woodnotes wild," as *they* were drawn by springtime to the fields. But who cares to pursue the stagnating river till it is lost in the sands? The birds may give us hints for our best music, but we do not go for our best poetry either to the halls of theologians or to the underground caverns of Venus.

THE DON QUIXOTE OF GERMANY.

[Lichtenstein's works have been edited by Karajan and Lachmann. His life is given in Hagin's " Minnesünger," bd. iv.]

THERE are few stranger figures in the Middle Ages than Ulrich von Lichtenstein, and few stranger books than his "Vrouwen Dienest." * His vagaries make him an interesting monster; but that is not his only or his chief claim on our attention: he has a place in the history of culture. He is sometimes called the Don Quixote of Germany, and though the analogy is by no means exact, he does represent the decay of chivalry on its grotesquer side.

This extraordinary phase of life, the fantastical mixture of clerical and lay ideals, was already past its prime in Germany. In literature it had produced its best. It had found its most perfect expression in the Arthurian romances, and these their most genial poets in Hartmann, Wolfram, and Gottfried. In the

---

* *Frauendienst,* " Service of Women."

lyric, too, the minnesong had outlived its springtime. Even Walter von der Vogelweide did not in his later poems equal the freshness of his youth. The "service of women" was no longer quite heartfelt, the old completeness of feeling was broken up. Chivalry had reached that stage which comes in the history of every imperfect theory, when its extreme partisans only show its weakness, and by their very consistency make it ridiculous. Such an extreme partisan was Ulrich von Lichtenstein. Chivalry had attempted to unite the secular and clerical conceptions of life; it had done this by a mere compromise, and therefore only for the time. The elements soon fell apart. A religious and a worldly order of knighthood arose within chivalry itself. To the original Arthurian group were added on the one hand the legend of the Grale, on the other the romance of Tristram. On the one line by degrees the tone became more purely mystical, the subjects more purely legendary. The other ended in frivolity and coarseness, though these were for long concealed behind an excess of courtly forms. Ulrich belongs to this latter direction. He is fond of saying that for his lady's favour he would give the grale which Sir Percivale won with such knightly labour and pains. The "Service of Women" is the name of his book and the thought of his life: but it has undergone a change—there is none of the old *naïf* reverence about it. The flourish of knightly extravagance heightens rather than hides the background of vulgarity. The incongruity is all the greater that its satire is unconscious. The "Vrouwen Dienest" is Ulrich's autobiography; he regards himself as *preux chevalier;* his life is the fitting theme for an epic—which accordingly he writes in stately eight-lined stanzas interspersed with his songs. Of course in such an account, which is both "Dichtung und Wahrheit," the latter is a little apt to suffer. Still, on the whole, Ulrich is trustworthy. Some of his wildest freaks have external evidence for them, and others are told with a simplicity of detail which looks like truth. Again, he frankly confesses points which, were he elaborating, he would rather conceal. And, finally, if he altered at all, he would alter to improve himself, to make himself what he would fain be like, to give his life at his own valuation. His book would thus be a true description of his ideal, even if the facts should be a little twisted. And probably there is no serious misstatement even of them. The following sketch taken, save in its last scene, from his own account, and retaining where possible his own words, is a true picture probably of his life, certainly of his times.

Ulrich was born, in the beginning of the thirteenth century, of a noble and wealthy house. He himself was afterwards lord of three castles—Lichtenstein, Murau, and Frauenberg ; and his father seems to have kept some state and to have opened his halls to the minnesingers and minstrels. Their praise of chivalry and love the young Ulrich heard while he was yet a child riding round the room on a stick. And he thought, "When I am a man I will give my possessions and strength and life itself to women, and serve them as best as I can." When eleven years old he was sent to be page in the court of a neighbouring prince, whose name he is discreet enough not to mention. Here the little monkey, his mind on fire with the lays he had heard, looked about for a lady to whom he might offer his adoration. He modestly fixed on the wife of his prince. There was only one objection—she was of higher rank than he. But Ulrich was hopeful of overcoming that difficulty by faithful service. He began at once, so far as a child could, to pay his *devoir* early and late. In summer he plucked her flowers, and was overjoyed when they were accepted ; he thought, " Thou art touching them even as I have touched." His next proof of devotion is rather more wonderful. In those days knives and forks were not much used at table, so it was all the more necessary that the hands should be clean. As a precautionary measure water was presented to the guests before meat, and it would be the duty of

Ulrich as page to serve his lady with a silver ewer. When she was ready, he stealthily bore it away into a corner, and—*drank* the water. After waiting on the princess for five years, he was removed to the household of Henry, brother to the Duke of Austria; that is to say, his body was removed; his heart, he is careful to tell us, remained with his lady. But his new lord taught him all courteous manners and chivalry, how to serve women and how to sing the minnesong. With Henry he remained four years; then his father died, and he returned to Lichtenstein. At home he practised tilting and jousting; and three years later he was able to join in a great tournament at Vienna, on the occasion of the marriage of Leopold's daughter with a Saxon prince. Two hundred and fifty pages were knighted at this time, and among them was Ulrich. To add to his happiness, he saw from afar the lustre of his joy, his pure sweet lady; but on account of spies he did not venture to speak to her. However, he heard at second hand, and that was some satisfaction, that she approved of his knighthood. Under these good auspices he withdrew from Vienna, sought out tournaments all the summer through, and was everywhere successful; for which he thanked his lady in his heart.

But in winter matters were not so pleasant. He had nothing to do, and was sick for love. Fortunately, he found that a favourite cousin knew the princess, and through this good-natured young lady was able to transmit messages and a song. The princess was astonished at his presumption. No doubt the song was good, but she could never accept the service of an inferior. Besides, she objected to Ulrich's personal appearance. "It must always be a vexation to a woman," she said, "to look on his ugly mouth." Of this deformity Ulrich himself gives a fuller account. He describes himself as having three lips, whatever that may mean—certainly not a formation that would recommend him as a gallant. But as soon as he heard this criticism of his princess, he determined to get rid of the superfluous member. He rode off to Graez, where there was a famous surgeon. One of his lady's men, whom he chanced to meet, accompanied him to see the performance. The surgeon wanted to bind Ulrich, but to this he objected: he would bear the pain without flinching for the sake of a certain lady. The instruments were brought, and the operation was soon over, both parties having acquitted themselves with honour. As Ulrich tersely remarks, "The doctor cuts like a master, and I endured like a man." The spectator was deeply affected. "If only you recover," he said, "I am glad to have been here." For five and a half weeks Ulrich remained under treatment, which he describes in great detail. He

could not eat for the great pain in his mouth and
teeth; he feelingly alludes to his agonies of hunger
and thirst, and especially to the evil odour of a salve,
green as grass, with which his wound was anointed.
But all the while he consoled himself by composing
a song, and, when he was once more going about,
rode with it to his cousin. She was delighted with
his appearance, assured him that none could now take
exception to his mouth, and forwarded his poem in
a letter which told of the marvel that had happened.
The princess was really curious to see the transformed
Ulrich, and in a prose reply. mentioned where she
would be on the next Monday. Of course Ulrich was
there to meet her; but at the goal of his hopes he was
doomed to disappointment. Thrice he rode to where
she stood; but love deprived him of utterance, and
thrice he had to retire without saying a word. A jest
of hers completed his misery, and sent him home to
bed so wretched that his friends thought he was going
to die. The next morning, when they were fetching a
doctor, Ulrich sprang to his feet, leaped on his horse
and galloped through the streets. He met his lady,
and with the courage of despair told his whole story.
She called him a child, remarked very decorously that
it did not beseem a lady to ride alone with a knight,
and summoned a second cavalier to her side. Ulrich
withdrew, glad at least to have spoken with her.

When winter came, he composed a new song, and what was called a "Büchlein," a sort of love-letter in verse, and sent them to the lady. They were returned, but he saw that more was written on them now than when they left his hands. And here he makes a curious revelation. It was ten days before he learned the purport of the message, for his secretary was from home, and he himself could neither read nor write. When at length the mystery was declared, it did not greatly edify him. It concluded with the warning, repeated thrice: "Who wishes what he must not get, denies himself."

Ulrich was rather depressed at this response, but next spring was again ready for the lists. He took part in a great tournament at Frisach, and acquitted himself creditably. "What I myself did," he says, "on that day, and before, and often since, that for my breeding's sake I shall conceal. But one thing I will tell you, and my mouth speaks truly: there I was not the best, neither was I the worst." However, his cousin had heard that he *was* the best, and told the princess so when she sent his next poem. This song is a good specimen of Ulrich's lyrical style, so I quote the first stanza.

> " In the wild wood there are singing
> Little birds their gladsome lay,
> On the heathland there are springing
> Fairest flowers in shining May.

> Thus my valour blooms, I wis,
>   When on *her* sweet grace I ponder
>   Who on me doth gladness squander
> As dreams give the poor their bliss."

So far, however, was she from squandering any gladness on him just now, that she wrote back to his cousin, "*You* praise your kinsman from kinship; others praise him not." These words quite overwhelmed poor Lichtenstein. To make matters worse, the great lady forbade any further intercourse through the agency of the cousin, so his resources were exhausted. He spent the summer in jousting, then wrote laments on the lost glories of the earth; and in winter according to his own confession, rode into the country to seek out pretty ladies. More than once we find him consoling himself in this way when he should have been sitting in sackcloth and ashes.

Next summer he went tourneying again, and came to a great passage of arms at Brixen. There he met with an accident to which mediæval champions were continually exposed. He had a finger broken off so that it hung from the hand only by a shred—by the vein, Ulrich says. His friends were greatly concerned, but he bade them be still; it moved him right little, it had chanced to him in a woman's cause. A doctor bound it up, promising to make Ulrich whole again. But on the sixth day, when the bandages were removed, the finger was so black and discoloured that both patient and physician were horror-stricken. Ulrich chased his adviser from the room, and set out for Botzen, where a celebrated doctor lived. He lay for seven days under his treatment; and during his illness a strange lady sent him, first, four books for his entertainment, then a foreign melody to do into German, and lastly a little dog to reward the masterly execution of this commission. Ulrich, now partly recovered, began to search for a messenger to supply his cousin's place. For long he was unsuccessful; but at length met a page, a courteous boy, who was his friend. When this page, without being told, guessed who the lady was, Ulrich swooned with terror; could he have been indiscreet? Reassured on this point, he commissioned the youth to tell the adventure with the finger and deliver sundry songs. The lady's reply only expressed astonishment at his impertinence, though, she confessed, his service was true and his songs were lovely. The messenger, however, assured Ulrich that despite these words she was not ill disposed towards him; and often before he had received a similar consolation from his cousin. Their opinion will strike us as probably the correct one. The lady's subsequent behaviour shows that she was very well pleased to have as one of her admirers this clever young poet rising into notice, who was at the same time rich and well born, and able to hold his own in the lists.

Ulrich at any rate did not take his repulse as final. After a short absence in Rome, he sent new songs and greetings to the lady. But this time she received the messenger with more asperity than ever. She complained that Ulrich had betrayed her. She had been led to believe that he had lost his finger on her account; but in point of fact, as she hears, he had *not* lost it. The page had to admit that her information was correct. In vain did he urge that the finger was now crooked and of little worth. She was not to be propitiated. On receiving those tidings, poor Lichtenstein's resolution was soon taken. He summoned his friend, Ulrich von Hasendorf, and bade him strike off the offending finger. Hasendorf at first refused, but Lichtenstein was firm. He gives a very circumstantial account of this operation too—still in heroic measure. He placed his hand on the table, and a knife on the finger, and cried out, "Now, smite away, honest friend." His friend smote, and the little finger, as Ulrich puts it, "sprang away."

He then wrote a "Büchlein," wrapped it in green samite, and enclosed it and the finger within two golden boards, specially prepared by the goldsmith and clasped with two little golden hands. This he sent in a neat parcel to his lady. When she opened it, she very sensibly exclaimed, "Alack! I could never have believed such folly of any sane man!"

At the same time she melted so far as to say she regretted this, not from any regard for Ulrich, but from its having happened on her account. Moreover, she promised to place it where she could see it every day!

Ulrich was now jubilant, and received her sanction to a new undertaking which he always regarded as the crowning achievement of his life. This was his famous "Progress of Venus." He departed secretly, disguised as a pilgrim with staff and scrip, as though he would go to Rome. But he turned aside at Venice, where he hired a remote lodging. There he lived during the winter, and had women's clothes made to his order. The articles he mentions are twelve gowns, thirty sleeves, three white mantles with hoods, two beautiful long brown braided tresses interwoven with pearls; the last, he tells us, a kind of merchandise which was very plentiful. His saddle, shield, and helmet were all silver white, as were a hundred spears specially prepared for him. His page's clothing and his horse-cloths were also white. When all his preparations were completed, he issued the following prose proclamation, which he quotes in full: "The worthy Queen Venus, Goddess of Love, to all the Knights who dwell in Lombardy and Friuli and Karinthia and Styria and Austria, even to Bohemia, offers her grace and greeting, and makes known to them that she of her good pleasure will visit them, and teach them in what manner they should deserve and obtain the love of worthy ladies. She gives them to know that she will rise from the sea at Mestre the day after St. George's Day, and will journey to Bohemia in such wise. And whatso knight will come up against her and break a spear upon her, to him will she give for guerdon a golden ring : that let him send to the woman whom he loves best. The ring has such virtue that to whatsoever woman it is sent, she must ever seem the fairer, and love without deceit him who has sent it. If my lady Venus overthrow a knight, he must bow to the four ends of the world in honour of a certain woman ; but if any knight overthrow her, he shall have all the horses that she leads by her." Then follows the itinerary of my lady Venus, describing in detail the route she will take, and on what particular days she will be at the various halting-places. The progress is to last twenty-nine days, and on the eighth day after its termination she will hold a tournament at Neuenburg. During all that time she will not uncover her face or hands before strangers, nor will they hear her voice. The missive concludes by placing in the ban of love, and in the ban of all good women, whoso hears and comes not up against her. Therefore has she given her route that all may know when and where to meet her.

This proclamation was made by Ulrich (for he, of course, was the goddess Venus) thirty days before he should begin his progress, and it was repeated at each of the stations exactly thirty days before his arrival. By this means a great concourse was gathered together early on the day after St. George's, to behold ascending from the sea this new—

"Idalian Aphrodite, ocean-born."

This occurred on Sunday, April 25, 1227. Ulrich at once made himself ready for the road, and now describes his order of march with obvious pleasure in his own magnificence. First rode his marshal and his cook ; then came two trumpeters ; between them Ulrich's banner, white as any swan ; next followed three sumpter-horses with three boys running at their side. Then came three spare chargers, covered, under the care of three more pages. They carried Ulrich's silver shield and silver helm, and his silver saddle was always ready on the back of one of the horses. After them came a flutist, who also beat the drum ; then four other pages, each bearing a sheaf of three great spears. Here followed two handsome maidens dressed in white, or, as is probably more accurate, two boys costumed as maidens. Then came two fiddlers, who played a merry march ; and last of all Lichtenstein himself, decked out in his woman's attire, not unmindful of his hat trimmed with pearls, his silk gloves, his golden girdle of three fingers' breadth, and the costly brooch on his bosom. In this style they proceeded to Treviso; but here Ulrich met with a vexation which he had not foreseen. The " potestat," the magistrate of the place, interfered to forbid any jousting, and called the whole thing a foolery. The people thought they were to be disappointed of their amusement; Frau Venus and the knights she had summoned gave up hopes of an encounter. Fortunately the potestat was a man of gallantry, and a number of ladies had flocked to see the spectacle; at their petition he agreed to permit the exhibition. But now the press was so great that a bridge had to serve the combatants for lists. Here Venus broke her first lance, and after the battle gave away two rings, for which "many a rosy red mouth blessed her."

The history of Ulrich's twenty-nine days' progress is in the main uninteresting. It is a chronicle of tiltings and joustings, which are all very similar. Some of the incidents, however, that sprung from his feminine disguise are rather amusing, especially as Ulrich has no idea of their comic side. Thus on the second morning he slept rather long. A page rushed in and exclaimed (not "Sir," for even with his own retinue must the fiction be maintained, but) "Dearest Lady, noble Queen,—two hundred women have come to visit you." Ulrich put on his morning gown and received them. After a while they set out for church, heard mass, and went through the ceremony of giving the " pax," that is, the kiss of peace, which was still part of the ritual of the communion in the Western Church. Ulrich's experiences in this matter were dissimilar. As Venus, he always went to the women's side of the church; and in Italy, he says, there was invariably a crowd about him, while in Germany he could not get any one to accept his salutation.

But everywhere he was regarded with great favour by the ladies, who looked on his garb as a compliment to their sex. Once he had occasion to give four gowns to the wash; an unknown admirer ascertained this, and, when they were sent back, placed among them a fifth, containing a letter, a girdle, and a chaplet. It escaped the marshal's notice. Not till four days later, when he was looking over his wardrobe, did Ulrich discover the addition. He feared he might be charged with unfaithfulness, and was more grieved than pleased. He stormed at the marshal, who knew nothing about it. All that was ever ascertained was the statement of the note, "These trifles are sent you, because in wearing woman's dress, you honour all women." The reasoning is perhaps a little obscure.

Ulrich received another donation of this kind under more laughable circumstances. He was having a bath outside the city, in the greenwood, and had been left alone by his attendants. A strange page appeared, and, spreading a carpet on the sward, proceeded, despite Ulrich's remonstrances, to lay on it female apparel, which, he indicated, was the gift of a lady. Ulrich was furious; but the page, nothing abashed, fetched heaps of roses from two companions, and scattered them on Ulrich and his bath till both were completely buried. And in this condition the astonished chamberlain shortly afterwards discovered his master. The picture of the irate paladin in his tub, vociferating vengeance but afraid to move, and pelted with roses as a delicate attention, is one of the most amusing in the book, and of course is recorded with all tragic seriousness.

But though thus honoured, Ulrich was not the only knight " in character." He tells us of two other masqueraders whom he encountered. The first was got up as a monk, and this Ulrich took as a personal insult. Either for that reason, or because he did not choose to attack the cloth, he for long refused to fight him; and when, at the prayer of common friends, he at length consented, he punished the reverend gentleman rather severely.

The other masquerader was dressed, like Ulrich himself, as a woman, with earrings and yellow ringlets. When invited to this encounter, Ulrich offered to come merely in his robes, without harness, if his adversary were really a woman. From this, therefore, we see that underneath his silks he wore his mail coat—a precaution with which he has not always been credited.

And now follows an extraordinary passage. At Glokeniz, after jousting all day long, he secured the door of his lodging, and prepared for a secret expedition. He stole away with one trusty page and "rode joyfully to his darling wife, whom he *could not* love better!" Now this is the first time we hear that he is married. He has said much of his lady, but nothing of his wife. And in all likelihood he had children at this time. Moreover, he was comfortable in his home. His wife gave him a glad welcome, and he spent a happy day with her. Nothing shows more clearly the unreal, artificial character of the Service of Love.

But to this service Ulrich was sworn, and he soon rode off to resume his duties. On the way he met his messenger, and, following him into a field, demanded news. The messenger, with a glad face, refused to give them unless Ulrich should kneel. Ulrich was immediately on his knees, "as at prayers," he adds ; and was now informed that his lady, well pleased with his prowess, had sent him a ring. This threw him into ecstasies, and he went back to work with new vigour. At the end of his progress he had distributed two hundred and seventy-five rings and thrown four knights, without ever being thrown himself.. These figures show how his expedition commanded the sympathies of his class. His freaks were the freaks not only of the individual but of the age.

And now the day arrived for the final tournament at Neuenburg. On the morning of this event Ulrich had another message from his princess; this time not so favourable. She accused him of treason, of showing attentions to another lady, and demanded back her ring. Poor Ulrich, who was quite innocent of the offence, was so deeply hurt that he wept like a child, and only on compulsion rode to the lists. But there he fought like a good knight and true. When all was over, he sent off a pitiful message to his lady, while of himself he says, "I rode hence in sorrow to a place where I found comfort—to my darling wife. She could not be dearer to me, though another woman was mistress of my life!"

He heard nothing further for ten days. At length, as he was riding through the fields, a new message was brought him, which again he must kneel to receive. Secret emissaries of his lady had watched his behaviour at the tournament; they had satisfied her that he was true, and she now restored him to favour. More-over, she would grant him an interview, if on Sunday

morning he could be at her castle, disguised as a leper.
It was already Friday evening, so there was no time
to lose. Ulrich rode off in hot haste, without even
going home or sending word to his people. On the
Saturday night he procured porringer and clothing
such as lepers used, and next morning joined the crowd
of diseased beggars who sat before the castle waiting
for alms. When getting his share, Ulrich was told to
remain within reach till he received further instruc-
tions. This command he obeyed to the uttermost; and,
to disarm suspicion, actually took his food with the
lepers, not without shuddering. His hair rose to a hill
for their foul breath and at the sight of fingers "which
might have been a dead man's laid in his grave for a
hundred days." Ulrich now answers the possible
objection, how was not he discovered to be a healthy
man. "I knew then," he says, "and still know, a
herb, which, if taken into the mouth, produces swelling
and discolouration. This herb I then had, and had
dyed my hair grey." For his lady's sake, he spent the
rest of the day in asking alms from door to door, and
at night he slept in the corn. The rain poured down,
the wind blew, a bitter frost came; and what with
these and the stony ground, Ulrich was very miserable.
But another day brought him recompense. The
princess, surrounded by all her ladies-in-waiting and
attendants, granted him an audience, and praised his

devotion. And everything was managed just as the romantic Ulrich would have wished.

The interview took place at dead of night. He skulked among the bushes all the evening till a sheet was lowered for him. Unfortunately during all his years of service he had grown older and heavier than he once was, and the ladies' strength could not lift him very far. In this difficulty he substituted his page for himself. The youth was easily lifted, and Ulrich had the annoyance of seeing him greeted with a kiss which was meant for himself. But now, with the page's help, he was safely hoisted up. The interview did not remain very amicable, however, and Ulrich was suddenly dismissed. In letting him down, too, the ladies played him a trick: he fell headlong, crying, "Alack, alack, and ever alack!" and scaring the watchman out of his wits, who thought it was the devil in the flesh. Ulrich would have drowned himself in despair, but his page brought him a cushion, and said it was from the lady, again turned gracious. This, however, was not true. On the contrary, she was highly indignant at the noise he had made in falling, and imposed on him as punishment a pilgrimage over the sea. This Ulrich readily undertook, and meanwhile rode through the land, looking at the ladies, and by his own account finding many that were fair. The pilgrimage never took place. The lady excused him; and, besides, Ulrich, perhaps from the memory of his night among the corn, had gradually become less enthusiastic about her, till in 1231 he renounced her service altogether. "She did me a deed," he says, "which would make all honest men lament, could I for my breeding's sake disclose it." It is rather a pleasing feature in the shatter-brained Ulrich that he never betrays the secret of his lady's name or of her misdemeanour. But now he could not refrain from writing angry songs about her. Another lady remonstrated with him for this, and he gave it up. He set himself to find out a new empress, and discovered one "fair and gentle, who crowned her beauty with good bearing and soft manners, and there-with was pure and *suitably old.*" This last excellence would recommend her to Ulrich, who was himself no longer a youth. Possibly, too, this second lady was the same who stopped his attacks on the first.* In her honour he began a new progress: this time as Arthur, who had returned from Paradise to restore the Round Table. Nothing shows more graphically how the Arthurian romances had sunk into the lives of the court circles. A number of knights flocked to Ulrich, and named themselves, after the celebrities of the Round Table, Ywan, Parzival, Segremors, and the like. But they kept their native German desig-

* Comp., however, pp. 431 and 439, Lachmann's edition.

nature so far as their estates were concerned; and
we have thus such odd combinations as Tristram of
Lebenberg, Lancelot of Spiegelberg; "his right name
was Henry," naïvely adds Ulrich of the latter. On
the whole, however, this second expedition is rather
tedious, and henceforth such is the character of the
book.

One other incident deserves to be recorded. In
1246 Duke Frederick of Austria perished in his war
with the Hungarians; and two years later Ulrich
was surprised by two friends—Weinhold and Pilgerin
—who imprisoned him for a year and three days in
his own castle of Frauenburg. By imperial command
he was at length restored to freedom, but for some
time his two sons and his castle were held as pledges.
During his captivity the inveterate old beau, now
nearly fifty, had consoled himself by writing love-
poems. Indeed, the rest of his book is made up for
the most part of minnesongs and the praises of love.
Some of these are musical and graceful enough, and
read with a certain swing. Ulrich is fully alive to
his merits as lyric poet. He is fond of remarking at
the end of his verses: "This song was universally
sung," "This song pleased the fiddlers," "This song
was not understood by the simple, but was praised by
all who knew," "This song men thought good, *and
they were right.*" After one he exclaims, "These

verses were composed wonderfully, the rhymes set in a masterly fashion, the melody *could not be better!*"

On the other side, however, Ulrich has now to register a series of laments and rebukes. He sees the youth growing up destitute of courteous manners, the people living miserably, the men rejoicing more in hunting and drinking than in knightly service, and the women no longer inciting them to noble deeds. Probably to the same period belongs Ulrich's other work, " Der Vrouwen Buoch," which is one long indictment of the age for its corruption and degeneracy. In it a knight and a lady accuse respectively the women and the men as guilty of all the evil, till Ulrich himself enters and settles the dispute. The last pages of the " Vrouwen Dienest" breathe exactly the same spirit, and Ulrich's one resource amidst the growing barbarism is to cling more closely to his own service. His last statement is that his lady's behest has moved him to write this biography, and hence its name, " The Service of Women."

From these closing remarks we see that Ulrich eventually lost *rapport* with his age. When a system landed men in such extravagances as he has described, we cannot wonder that the majority should contemptuously reject it. Chivalry had been weighed in the balance and found wanting. In Lichtenstein himself we find much that shocks; even knights such as he were not free from the prevailing rudeness. The rudeness, indeed, as we saw, inevitably resulted in the inevitable disruption of chivalry.

What we notice here, therefore, is a contest between old and new, in which each side must have our sympathy. Chivalry, just in such adherents as Lichtenstein, had showed its insufficiency. It was thrown aside; but in the struggle to a new principle much lawlessness, much coarseness, much folly, were necessarily present. So it was natural that men of the old *régime* should remain true to it, and see in all the anarchy and change no new life, but only death.

The last incident known of Ulrich's career picturesquely illustrates this opposition between the old and the new. At a banquet in Breslau he, with some other nobles, was accused of high treason. The veteran jouster claimed the knightly trial by combat. But the world was grown prosaic. His appeal was disregarded; he was thrown into prison, and, when released, his castles were confiscated. This happened in 1268. He survived a few years, being alive in 1274 and dead in 1277; but the glory of his life had departed, like the glory of the order to which he belonged.

When we now take leave of the poor old knight, it is obvious where his resemblance to his Spanish brother breaks down. In truth, from one point of

view he is neither Don Quixote nor Cervantes.   Not
Don Quixote, for he is no isolated specimen; during
the greater part of his life his absurdities were the
fashion, though he may have carried them further
than usual.   Not Cervantes, for his satire is unconscious; he never guesses that he is describing
anything but the most rational mode of life.   In so
far, however, as he reduces chivalry to a burlesque, in
so far as the irony of history becomes incarnate in
him, in so far as his exit with the old order is partly
comic and partly pathetic, we have a right to call him
the Don Quixote of Germany.

HANS SACHS AND THE MASTERSONG.

[A good selection of Hans Sachs's works is given by Goedeke and Tittmann, " Deutsche Dichter des 16th Jahrhunderts," with literary an l biographical introductions. See, too, Gervinus's " Deutsche Dichtung," bd. ii. ; J. Grimm, " Ueber den Meistersang; " Goedeke, " Zur Geschichte des Meistergesangs, Germ.," 15,197.]

"Not thy councils, not thy Kaisers, win for thee the world's regard,
  But thy painter, Albrecht Dürer, and *Hans Sachs*, thy cobbler
    bard."

SUCH are Longfellow's words to the old merchant town of Nuremberg as he paces its streets and court-yards and dreams over its busy past. The memories of old Nurembergers crowd upon him, their fame is the fame of their city ; yet many of us know Hans Sachs only through this very poem. Such knowledge must be nebulous, but need not be incorrect. To associate his name with Albrecht Dürer, to recognize in him a Nuremberg burgher of the sixteenth century, the poet of its toil and traffic, is to find the right stand-point from which to judge him. For Hans is essentially the poet of handworkers and traders; he has the honesty and humour and good sense of the thriving *bourgeois*. He does not detect the passing shadows and delicate tints of life; its crimes and sorrows have for him no mystery, they have a moral; but he sees the world "as Albrecht Dürer saw it—its firm life and manliness, its inner force and steadfastness." *

This plain unromantic way of looking at things was very characteristic of the Reformation. Great pleasure and interest in daily life were accompanied by a certain dulness to its problems. After all, the liberty which Luther claimed was in the main a practical one. In his famous doggrel he rejects the cant of his cloister, "Who loves not woman, wine, and song, remains a fool his whole life long." But he would not permit much speculative liberty. The suspension of judgment on which modern science insists he would have denounced as doubt, as a temptation of the Devil. The obstinate questionings of unseen things which make Shakespeare's plays so free and human, never sounded in his ears, or if they did, were dismissed with a text from Scripture. He occupied a sort of double position. On the one hand, his appeal to private judgment and his joy in the world could not rest within the limits he prescribed, and on the other his resumption of a whole body of Divinity

* Goethe's "Hans Sachsen's Poetische Sendung."

could not harmonize with his other principles.   Thus we have in the sequel theologians more Lutheran than Luther condemning pleasure, condemning reason; and we have as his true followers those who face the problems of thought and existence, even should.they sink under them in despair.   Meanwhile the phenomenon at the Reformation was a hearty acceptance of the facts of life, and a hearty acceptance of a theological system.   That is what we find in Hans Sachs, and in this aspect he is the poet of the Reformation no less than the poet of the guilds.

Not that he was the first whom those influences inspired.   The spirit of reform was working in all the towns, rousing the ablest citizens (*e.g.* Sebastian Brandt) to satirize old abuses and inculcate a sober, practical morality.   And not only did a few such writers arise whose vigour and talent won them fame in other lands; there was a general literary fermentation among the labouring classes.   Never before or since did so many workmen devote their time to music and verse-making; indeed those were in the minority who could not rhyme.   They formed societies, modelled on their trades guilds, with statutes, penalties, and masters; and their authorized poetry was called the *Mastersong*.   This is the third great influence which moulded the mind of Hans Sachs, and as less familiar it must be described more in detail.

One of the official documents sets forth how " certain godless fellows go about the town screaming out shameless street-songs all night long." The staid burghers are much disturbed, perhaps in both senses of the word, by such misconduct, and take measures to suppress " these evil lays and give praises to God." Their remedy is the mastersong, which as a harmless and even edifying entertainment, is meant to supersede one more questionable. The hard-worked citizens were to find their needful relaxation and religious profit in the Mastersingers' Schools. These schools had a double function, an exoteric and an esoteric ; they had their public festivals for the uninitiated, and their private festivals, with the necessary rehearsals and practisings, for their associates. At the former any one might be present, and all could take part; the subjects of the songs were passages of Scripture, " fair maxims of ethics," or even stories from profane history, " provided always they be true and profitable." It was in its private meetings that the school showed itself as a school. In virtue of its religious and social character it was held in the town hall, or oftener in the church, and met on the holidays and the Sunday afternoons. Its songs must be religious, and indeed, after the Reformation, scriptural in subject. The rolls were rigidly kept, no member could absent himself without good excuse, and none but members were admitted. Entrance into the association was guarded, the applicant having to satisfy the board of his good character and birth in wedlock. When baptized into the fraternity his labours only commenced. The school was ranged in grades, and before passing from a lower to a higher he must undergo certain tests, for which he was prepared gratis by mastersingers of established fame. When taking his first lessons the associate was called a *scholar*, when he knew the technical rules by art he became a *school-friend*, when able to sing certain of the existing songs he was raised to the rank of a *singer*, after producing verses of his own in the recognized measures and to the recognized melodies he became a *poet*, and finally he was entitled *master-singer* only when he had invented a new *tone* or *wise* —terms which include both metre and music. He was called the father of his tone, and, choosing god-fathers, baptized it with some " befitting " name. Thus we have ruddy tones and green tones, long tones and high tones, tones named of dragons, of princes, of " strong nightingales," of " woman's honour." Wherein precisely the fitness consists the present writer is generally unskilled to say. No tone was considered original which encroached on another for more than four syllables, or was sanc-tioned without solemn deliberations. None was accepted if it violated oftener than seven times the rules of the art laid down in the *Tabulature*. This was the codex of the mastersong, a table of definitions, injunctions, and warnings. It fixes that the strophe must be of a threefold form, two like parts followed by one unlike, as we still see in the sonnet. It gives in its uncouth terminology a list of permissible rhymes and verses; a line containing only one syllable was called a *pause*, such as had none to rhyme with them were *orphans*, those which found their rhymes in the next stanza were *grains*. It enumerates the possible blunders, some artificial enough, others all too glaring; the common speech must have been barbarous indeed when it was necessary to point out the latter. The want of the connecting particle between words was condemned as a *blind meaning*, a false rhyme was a *vice*, the transposition of letters a *difference*, the compression of two syllables into one a *klebsylbe*, a lumped syllable. It is well known how much Luther did for the German language both by his theoretical researches and by the practical examples that he gave of a purer style. We can easily imagine what a god-send they would be to the mastersingers in their struggle with lawlessness and vulgarism. His translation of the Bible was adopted as their standard; idioms to be found in it were accepted, all others were condemned. And it was the final authority, as

for the expression so for the thought. We saw that
the mastersong was always religious and latterly
scriptural in subject. At the scrutiny of a new
piece the author had to cite chapter and verse, and
the official critic or *marker* who sat behind a screen
with a slate in his hands and a Bible on his desk,
jotted down not only the mistakes of form but the
false meanings, the variations from Scripture and the
wrong interpretations.

Besides the ordinary practisings, the school had
its solemn contests when the masters competed for
prizes ; these were chains and wreaths, often of considerable value. In Nuremberg the first prize, a
cord with three silver-gilt medals attached, was
called King David, after the Hebrew psalmist, who
was represented on the centre medal with crown
and harp. It was a great event for the master
and his friends when he gained a prize, and where
the school possessed many such decorations the prize-
takers were enjoined to wear them on all ceremonious
occasions. It was these prize-takers who initiated
the young apprentices into the mystery of the art,
who explained the tabulature and taught them the
more difficult measures, often sitting up late into the
night without expecting or receiving any fee. When
not busy in composing verse, instructing others, or
perfecting themselves, they spent their leisure in

copying out the standard songs. It is this unwearied devotion that strikes us so strange and admirable. No doubt the mastersong is on the whole without much merit. It attended only to the form and not to the matter, which it tortured into stubborn and unfitting moulds. Even in form it is scrupulous, laboured, and artificial, on the one hand; yet surprisingly rude and barbarous on the other. We must, of course, remember that we judge of it only by half, and may easily be one-sided; for of the accompanying music we know next to nothing, and if Gervinus's conjecture be rather rash, that with that before us we should see in the mastersongs the source of the oratorio, yet they may well be among its chief tributaries. But leaving this out of account, it seems a thing quite without parallel for wearied workmen, on leaving their tools and their booths, to devote themselves to a liberal art with, at lowest, the disinterestedness of artists. All their spare time they spent in teaching, practising, or chronicling what was to them their "benignant art."

Such then was the association of which Hans was the scholar and the teacher, which cherished his powers and grew with their growth. This fact must not be lost sight of in estimating his work. On the one hand it acted on him favourably, supplying

him with an appreciative audience; on the other,
it tied him down to a mechanical style. To understand his mastery over such tools and materials as
he had, the state in which he found them, and the
improvements which he made, we must know the
history of the mastersong.

Strange to say it is descended in direct line from
the minnesong, the old love lyric. Much indeed
is altered. The poets are no longer adventurous
knights, but cautious burghers; the meeting-place
is changed from the castle to the church; the worship of ladies has yielded to the praise of God.
Yet the connection is not hard to prove between
these later theologico-didactic rhymesters and the
dreamy minnesingers who sang like birds of love
and ladies and flowers. Even in these old days
when chivalrous poetry was in full vogue, the more
solid and instructive verse of the Renner and
Freidank had appealed to the citizens; and at the
break-up of chivalry, when the degenerate minstrels
were no longer received in the degenerate courts,
they found a welcome and a refuge in the large
towns. There they not only sang, but taught; for
after a time the burgher, from listening, began to
imitate. He attempted the measures of the court
poets, but their melody escaped him; their silken
network of sound was changed in his hands to

tangled yarn. And if the form was unlovely, the matter was barbarous; not prosaic, because unfit even for literary prose. Many subjects were treated, but naturally the religious interest preponderated, and the religion of the day could supply only subtle scholastic questions about the Trinity, the sacraments, the atonement. Where God was before the creation of the world; how He could be born by one of His own creatures; how the Holy Virgin could be the Holy Mother as well—on points like these the honest workmen dilate in stanzas which sometimes contain 120 lines. In such verse, then, did the minnesong issue when transplanted from the castle garden to the town green. The transition is proved beyond question. To some extent the ancient peculiarities of the verse, and notably the threefold divisions of the strophe, are still preserved; and among the twelve patriarchs from whom the legends of the master-song trace its descent, some are famous minnesingers. The story runs that these twelve reproved the shameless lives of the clergy, and were found guilty of heresy; but, on appeal, were acquitted and rewarded by the emperor, who is sometimes called Henry I., sometimes Otto the Great. This story is not historically true. With Frauenlob, chief of the twelve and the smith Regenbogen, both minnesingers of the decline, it associates others who lived long before;

but probably it contains a reminiscence of the real
origin of the mastersong.

The reverent regard in which these minnesingers
or twelve wise masters were held, shows no less the
divergence than the connection between the two
schools. In olden times it was considered plagiarism
to employ the stanza of another man, whether predecessor or contemporary. The originality of a poet
lay in his power of inventing new verse forms. But
the unskilled artisans dared not alter their models,
they feared to be original. Certain measures were
attributed to the twelve masters and called by their
names; to these their disciples were tied down, and
no new tone was admitted. Such, at least, was the
theory. In point of fact the perpetual recurrence
of the same leathern forms, and the same wiredrawn
subjects, proved too much for the most timorous
piety. From time to time new melodies were smug-
gled in; but they were at once labelled with old
names. In the middle of the thirteenth century
some such fraud was detected by the mastersingers
of Mainz, who seem to have been especially con-
servative, and the culprit was publicly censured.
But, meanwhile, the craftsmen had been working
hard at their new craft, and were ready to throw
up their indentures. The wiseacres of Mainz must
have stood aghast at the reception which their

verdict found in the neighbouring town of Worms. Hans Folz, a barber, broke a lance, or perhaps a razor, on behalf of the new art. He ridiculed the pretended enthusiasm for old melodies which were, in fact, chiefly new; he laughed at the pedantry and barbarous language of the schools; he extolled the teachings of nature, and maintained that the best masters were Spring, Summer, and Autumn.

These opinions were revolutionary in art, and in those days a literary quarrel had very practical consequences. Folz made the district too hot to hold him. He had to emigrate to Nuremberg, where, partly through his influence, a new period of the mastersong commenced. Artificial and wooden it remained to the last, but Folz at any rate vindicated a larger sphere to individual talent. Dogmatic riddles still remained the theme of his verse; but probably the new regulation dates from his time, which grants the name of master only to the maker of an original tone.

Few towns of the day were so ready to receive new ideas as Nuremberg. For generations it had steadily grown into mercantile importance, till in 1427 the inhabitants purchased city rights from the emperor. After this its development became more rapid. The fame of its manufactures, especially in hardware, spread far and near. In commerce it rivalled Augs-

berg as depôt for the drugs, silks, and spices of the
South, which poured in upon it by way of Venice.
The prosperity of the great Southern Republic brought
new wealth to Nuremberg, and the advantage of their
intercourse was not merely commercial—it fostered
the taste for gaiety, culture, and art. The streets
were always bright and tumultuous at the Carnival;
the processions were celebrated with a splendour
hitherto unknown; the wealthy burghers' sons had
their tilts and tournaments, and knew how to maintain their rights against the neighbouring nobles, who
disliked such sports among the commonalty. The
governing council was a little despotic and overbear-
ing to the plebs; but it had the interests of all at
heart, and the whole population shared in the muni-
cipal prosperity. Of great men the town had
nourished not a few. It could boast one alleged
inventor of gunpowder, one alleged discoverer of
America: Schwarz, in the thirteenth century, was
its citizen; Behem, in the fifteenth, was its son.
Less questionable were other of its claims. The
humanist Wilibald Pirckheimer, the friend of Hutten
and Erasmus, was a member of its council; Konrad
Baumann, the blind organist of St. Sebald's, had
a reputation throughout Germany and Italy. Its
churches, its fountains, its sculptures, bore witness to
the talents of Adam Krafft and the Fischers; and

now, at length, it had produced Albrecht Dürer, the genius of earnest and truthful work.

It was in this stirring town that Hans Sachs was born in 1494, when his great townsman was a youth of twenty-three. His father was a tailor, and seems to have succeeded fairly in his trade. But a modest competency did not save a man in those days from narrow alleys and close rooms, and Hans was born at once into the common trials of the time. The plague was raging in the city; both parents were struck down, but not fatally, and strangely enough the infant escaped altogether. In due season, at the age of seven, he went to school, and began a curriculum which quite appals us. Even in these days of higher education what schoolboy but would tremble at the programme :—Grammar, rhetoric, music, logic, arithmetic, astronomy, geography, astrology, philosophy, poetry, and the "science of many creatures in air, water, earth and *fire.*" Later, he confesses that he has forgotten it all, perhaps fortunately for his readers; but, in the first place, it cost him ten years to acquire. This period deserves attention, and if the usual one is a credit to his age and his class. For, despite his formidable row of accomplishments, Hans was not to follow any of the learned professions, which, if we may trust Hutten, were all three gigantic swindling societies. Hans was to be useful at any rate, and he turned his philosophy, rhetoric, and astrology to account in making boots. We are apt to consider his ten years at school rather badly employed; but, after all, he learnt the best the age had to offer. And only when the sciences dwell among the people are they secured against useless flights, only when they become national property can there be a national development. Hans, and perhaps many like him, had a certain acquaintance with the technical world of the schools. They knew something of its ways, could judge roughly of its results, and were not simply puzzled in the controversies which were soon to arise. But, on the whole, the best thing that Hans learned was to speak his mother tongue "neatly, purely, and truly," to play on stringed instruments, and to sing. These lessons, at least, he did not forget amidst the new cares and duties of his trade. As shoemaker's apprentice he could join the mastersingers' school, and so have a right to instruction in their art. This he did, and was taught by Leonhard Nunnenbeck, "the weaver liberal in song." At the same time he did not neglect his business; he seems to have felt a kind of love for it, and did not shrink at a later day from singing the praises of pitch and leather, of bradawl and last.

Meanwhile, after an apprenticeship of two years he became journeyman, and entered on his *wanderjahre* or years of travel, working his way from place to place after the fashion of German artisans. This enlarged his circle of ideas, and by lifting him out of the Nuremberg world qualified him to become its exponent. For despite the fuller life of the town and its stimulating influences, the artisan may be as dull as the agricultural labourer. If the peasant is connected with no larger existence, the townsman is only a part of such; if the one is naturally a vegetable, the other may become a machine. The years of travel obviate this, and in contact with other principles and ways we get to know our own.

Hans was now brought into relation with the confused, restless life of the time which in Nuremberg he could only learn at second hand. The government there was, on the whole, just, enlightened, and autonomous. It was a shrewd, orderly trading city; but in less favoured districts what abuses, what ignorance, what superstition reigned supreme! Hans tramping the country learned the ways of the peasants, and the smart young tradesman was vastly amused with their simplicity and slowness. Later, when he could make verses, it was a favourite theme. Thus he tells of certain villagers whose whole wardrobe, like that of the future Bolivar, was a blanket with a hole in the middle; but Hans does not discuss it so profoundly as the philosophic Teufelsdröckh. A crab which a peasant has caught, and which incurs the displeasure of the township, is condemned to death *by drowning.* A country fellow finds a crossbow in the forest, and taking it for a cross, lifts it reverently to his lips; but the bow goes off, carrying away his nose, so he throws it to the ground, exclaiming, " You may lie there a whole year before I pick you up again." At another time, the peasants go to the wood to gather acorns. One slipping from a tree is decapitated by a forked branch and falls headless to the ground. By-and-by his friends find him, and debate whether he had his head with him, in the morning. They take him home and appeal to his wife, but she does not know; she is sure he had it on Saturday, but after that she cannot say. Hans, though often harping on the contrast between town and country life, knows that the advantage is only half with the former. In one of his adapted fables the gout meets a spider, and complains that he can't thrive or even live among the peasants. The spider replies that the town housewives won't leave her in peace. They exchange quarters, and the spider is never molested more; while the gout is comfortably housed and fed.

The poor peasants, indeed, were little exposed to such an ailment, harried as they were by all who were stronger or cleverer. They had their oppressors recognized and unrecognized, spiritual and temporal, but always irresistible. The nobles exacted their dues, the priests their tithes; the wandering soldiers robbed in the emperor's name during war, in their own during peace; the wandering magicians, embryo Fausts, and the resident witches extorted the rest by threats and promises. Much of this Hans, no doubt, would see; much more he would hear. For, despite their alleged stupidity, these peasants had their share of shrewd mother-wit. They told stories against themselves and their oppressors, stories that were in every mouth, but had no author. The French monarchy has been called a despotism tempered by epigram; their condition was misery solaced by anecdote. Such anecdotes Hans would lay up for future use; meanwhile misery needs no boots, and he went further. But to work one's way is a precarious method of travelling. Shoemaking seems to have been as superfluous in town as in country, and at Innsbruck we find Hans with trade changed, acting as forester to Kaiser Maximilian. At this he remained long enough to learn the rules of venery, of which he afterwards compiled a poetical code, and to gain some knowledge of the ways of the court where the emperor fostered the arts and sciences, the false and the true. But the independent tradesman could not long remain a servant among the great lords whom he loved to make fun of and ironically calls the " pious nobles." Perhaps, too, in his kindliness to all created things, he had a plebeian dislike to his work. By and by, at least, he describes a "wonderful vision, how sundry hares pursue, catch, and roast a huntsman," and his sympathies are evidently with the hares.

But with all his homely predilections and *bourgeois* morals, Hans was not of those for whom Bohemianism has no charms. He was urged by his companions and drawn by his own desires towards the careless life of the soldier. Only when Genius, " the God of Nature," showed him the smoking homesteads, the ruined churches, the empty schools, the idle workshops, the famine, violence, and shame which filled the country; only when he heard the ribald talk of the camp, saw the rags, debauchery, and slaughter of the soldiers, did he decide for a peaceful career. Revelry and luxury also tempted him, but even in his youth he was "stern with all folly." What then was he to do with his time when business did not engross nor common pleasures content him? In this perplexity he recurred to the " lovely art of the mastersong;" he found suddenly that he was called to be a poet; for hitherto, though unconsciously gathering materials, he had written nothing. Long afterwards, he described how he awoke to his vocation, and much true feeling shines through the conventional allegory of the narrative. Weighed down with heavy troubles, the falsehood of friends, the hatred of foes, the shame of love, he falls asleep by a rocky fountain among the flowers and the grass. The Goddesses of Art appear and call him to their service, in it he will find relief. Delighted, but doubtful, he hesitates to accept till they approach and reassure him with many gifts. It is worth while noting the list, for it shows what merits he attributed to himself. Characteristically he lays stress on " steadfast will, constant practice, wide experience ; " so far he seems to degrade poetry to a handicraft, but his remaining endowments are " joy in his work, a pleasant style, and daintily-leaping measures." Again, the aims set before him, " the glory of God, the praise of virtue, the blame of vice, the instruction of youth," are not exactly what we might expect from the Goddesses of Art, but they do not forget " the delight of sorrowful hearts." Thus Hans Sachs characterizes his own genius. Whatever else we may think, there is at least nothing affected or tumid about it. His muse is laborious, practical, didactic, but honest, pleasant, and kindly. She is no light-robed, light-limbed heathen nymph, but a homely German housewife who smiles over her work, and goes to church on Sunday. To this muse Hans henceforth surrendered himself with a devotion which no chance nor change could interrupt. At Braunau he composed his first tone, and was made a master. After this, whenever he halted in a city he joined its mastersingers' school, and became one of the office-bearers and teachers.

At the age of twenty-two he returned to settle in his native town. He had learned much in his travels, accustomed himself to other men and ways, and penetrated into the mysteries of his art. But Nuremberg was his home and had his first affection; he loves to sign himself Hans Sachs of Nuremberg. In one of his allegorical dreams he sees a well-hedged rose garden on a round hill. Through the tufted boughs are visible pomegranate and nutmeg, orange and vine, fruit-trees and spice-trees in plenty, and rows of sugar-cane. The dreamer takes it for paradise. On a rose-bush warbles a marvellous bird like an eagle, with coal-black feathers, one side decked with roses red and white. It gathers its young under its pinions, it feeds them and keeps them safe: it rests right little by day or night for evil birds and beasts that lie in wait to devour it. When they approach it fights manfully, it rends them with beak and claw, and four noble maidens stand by to succour it. The first in robe of white has a golden scroll in her hand; the second is clad in blue, and holds a sword and balance; the third in green bears the sun in her arms; and the fourth is harnessed from head to foot and armed with a great steel hammer. The hill is the site of Nuremberg, the stores of its gardens are the produce of the world, the eagle is emblem of the city and the other birds are its foes, the four maidens are its Wisdom, Justice, Truth, and Strength, which ensure its final triumph. When a man is so proud and glad in the civic life that surrounds him, his happiness is secure, and Hans was a happy man. In a little house, at first outside the gate and afterwards in Meal Alley, he plied his trade and resisted the solicitations of Jack Idle, Hal Headstrong, Lazy Lenz, Harry Restless, and other typical figures whom his poems immortalize. At this time he married Kunegund Kreuzer, with whom he lived for forty-one years. After her death she appeared in a dream to comfort him, and his account of this portent, in the main solemn and religious, reveals by one little realistic touch that their household was not invariably peaceful: "She was ever faithful, orderly, and frugal, but somewhat violent in her words to the servants." To more than the servants, if we may trust another account. Hans begins a poem on the " Bitter Sweet of Wedded Life," with the remark that all women have long clothes and short tempers, and proceeds to describe his wife in the same antithetical style. She is his paradise and his purgatory, his angel and his demon, his rosebud and his thunderbolt—in short, all his weal and all his woe.

With a wife who was thus *everything* to him, in a city that he loved, with good business and flourishing family, we see Hans a prosperous man. To crown all, he remained true to the benignant art. He found it sadly degenerated in Nuremberg, and set himself at once to teach the young apprentices, to heal the dissensions of the school, and to preserve its traditions. With what loving care he fulfilled his task may be seen from a manuscript of extreme beauty executed by him. It contains the songs of his predecessors, only at the end are a few of his own. There is nothing as yet to distinguish these from the ditties of Hans Folz or Nunnenbeck. The rhymes may be smoother, the style purer, but the subjects are still old dogmas, prayers to the saints, hymns to the Virgin. But now an event took place which influenced Hans profoundly in his life and his work. The time of the Reformation was come, and he left versifying for a season to study the new doctrines. In 1521 he had by him forty-one tracts by Luther and his friends; in 1522 he was poring over the Testament; in 1523 he wrote his "Wittenberg Nightingale," the first fruits of his new style fittingly inscribed to Luther. In his "Morning Wise" he greets the dawn of the Reformation. "Wake up," he cries, "the dawn is nigh. I hear a joyous nightingale singing in the green hedge, it fills the hills and valleys with its voice. The night is stooping to the west, the day is rising from the east, the morning red is leaping from the clouds, the sun looks through. The moon quenches her light; now she is pale and wan, but erewhile with false glamour she dazzled all the sheep and turned them from their pasture lands and pastor. Both have they forsaken, they have followed the glistering moon through the forest into the wilderness. The lion, too, have they followed; they have harkened to his voice, craftily has he led them far astray into the waste. They have lost their sweet pasture, have eaten weeds and thistles and thorns; the lion has snared them, torn and devoured them; wolves and serpents have bitten them in every limb; therefore are the sheep withered and lean. But now they are roused by the nightingale's song, the sun reveals ravening foe and deceitful pasture. The lion and his brood, swine, goats, cats, snails, and other unclean beasts plot against the nightingale. 'What new thing is he singing ?' they ask; 'let him stir up no tumult among the sheep.' But he, secure in his hedge, sings ever the louder. The sheep hear and return, many are slaughtered on the way, but the sun shines on, and none can hide the sunlight."

Quaint and incongruous though it be, does not this suggest another new song to another new dawn? A

song like this that welcomes the melting of clouds
and dreams and the "stars that shone as sunbeams
on the night of death and sin." A song like this that
hails the morning, and cannot yet sing the glory of
the noon.

> "For the shades are about us that hover,
>   When darkness is half withdrawn,
> And the skirts of the dead night cover
>   The face of the live new dawn.
> For the past is not utterly past,
> Though the word on its lips be the last;
> And the time be gone by with its creed
> When men were as beasts that bleed."

We have quoted about a quarter of the "Wittenberg
Nightingale," sometimes epitomizing. The remaining
three-quarters contain an interpretation "that we
may understand more clearly," an interpretation
which destroys the poetical charm like a bad commentary, but is there with an object which it probably served. Few of us, perhaps, would compare
Luther to a singing bird; but he, it seems, is the
nightingale whose song brings back the wandering
sheep to the true fold. The unclean beasts are his
enemies; Emser and Dr. Eck are the goat and the
swine—their lives, says the poet, justify the comparison. The relevancy of other names lies in a pun:
Pope Leo X. is the lion; the snail is Cochlæus, the
theologian; the satirist Murner is the cat. The fading
moon is the papacy, the new risen sun the Evangel.

This poem, composed first as a mastersong and then in couplets, was received with delight, was read and re-read, and ran through many editions. The reform had begun among the theologians, but had soon reached the people, and now Hans Sachs, one of themselves, was found to carry on the work. He set himself to purge his early songs of the old leaven; they appeared in altered form, "christianly revised, evangelically corrected," *i.e.* with the saints' names expunged and the name of Christ in their stead. His new views inspired new efforts; he paraphrased the Bible in song after song, and his verses, sung in nearly all the master-schools of Germany, spread the Lutheran faith among the most earnest and energetic workmen of the towns. Moreover, in this he set the fashion; his example became law, and soon in all the great singing guilds nothing but the Scriptures could be heard.

But the mastersongs were confined to the initiated, and Hans wished to teach the nation at large. He took to writing dialogues on the great topics of the day—the right of private judgment, justification by faith, the union of the Churches, the new social duties which the new doctrines brought. These questions he discusses in seven tracts, which, says Goedeke, excel all the dialogues of the day, save, perhaps, Luther's; in artistic form (and, we may add, in temper) even Luther must yield the palm to Sachs. Earnest he always is, but never fanatical; keen, not cruel; enthusiastic, but placid. The monks dubbed him the "cursed cobbler;" he accepts the name with a smile, and Hans the shoemaker plays an important part in these colloquies.

The simplicity, force, and homely humour of these papers made them far more popular than the "blasts" of the theologians, who began to see in Hans an important ally. Andreas Osiander, the celebrated divine, at this time a pastor in Nuremberg, had discovered an old book of prophetic pictures, and determined to issue a facsimile with anti-papistical interpretations. He asked and obtained assistance from Hans, whose couplets and quatrains, printed below the plate, summed up all the heavier theological explanations of the opposite page. Luther, whom one of the pictures was altered to suit, disclaimed the compliment but praised the book; he himself (he wrote) would reissue these "hieroglyphica," and, indeed, there are two other editions in the same year. But the town council of Nuremberg did not share his satisfaction. This council, though ultimately deciding for his party, was very cautious and deliberate in its behaviour. It established the new religion, but the monks and nuns were left undisturbed. When an old hymn, "Salve Regina," was altered to "Salve Jesu

Christe," it forbade the tune altogether. The same tolerance which makes the controversial cobbler gentle as a dove, made the merchant princes wise as serpents. They considered this prophetic picture-book quite out of place, suppressed the edition, summoned, warned, and rebuked printer and authors, adding, in regard to Hans, that it was "not his place nor business to treat such matters, and the council strictly enjoin him to mind his handiwork and shoemaking, and henceforth refrain from publishing any rhyme or pamphlet whatever." Poor Hans, commended by Luther, the truest poet of his age, must "refrain" from doing what he can best do, as "it is no business of his." Strange how Dogberry in all ages insists with clamour that you write him down an ass.

Hans, however, in the midst of his family, in the midst of his township, could not disobey; probably he was too loyal to think of such a thing. His songs, printed separately on loose leaves, become rare during the following years; perhaps along with this public prohibition he may at this time have been paralyzed by a private trouble. What exactly it was we do not know, for he alludes to it vaguely. He describes himself as puffed up with pride and success, walking like the hypocrite in the temple. Only through a sore temptation into which he fell was he taught humility, only through agonies of despair was he restored to his right mind. "God," he says, "drew me to Him by the hair of my head." We need not take all this self-reproof too literally. Hans, we may be sure, never swerved very far from decent citizendom; it is easier to believe him unjust to himself than untrue to his principles. But, if great prosperity endangered him, he was soon to be safe. His business went wrong, his seven children died one after the other, and last of all he lost his wife. It is touching to hear him tell us in his simple way how he did not feel his loss till he got home and saw the empty rooms, the unused clothes, or how he forgot that she was dead, and kept thinking that she must be with some neighbour, or was late with her marketing.

Meanwhile, from private distress, whether temptation or adversity, Hans found refuge in working all the harder for his people. His political poems become more frequent. He exhorts the nation to unity; attacks the hostile powers of France and Turkey; insists that every selfish man is a public enemy. He feels the importance, the vital necessity, of the citizens having the civic virtues; and it is now, as Gervinus shows, that the classical literature becomes to him a living power, which he studies and partly understands. To his amazement he finds in it exactly what he wants—the ideal citizen. He wonders over the old stores; hunts after new translations; cannot leave the book he has once begun. He throws himself on this study with the same *abandon* as formerly on the Bible. He had paraphrased its stories, and set others to the work; now he will do as much for the classics. Anecdote, history, apologue, dream—inspired by some old maxim—borrowed from some old author—flow without stint from his pen, and all are animated by the same pædagogic intention. Gradually the anecdotes predominate; the didactic moral, though not abandoned, is curtailed; the range of the sources is widened. He returns to Boccaccio, whom he had read as a youth; he dives into chronicles, history, folksbooks; he studies native poetry, and listens to native humour. In his old age he turned his attention to the drama, and produced tragedies, comedies, and farces with the same marvellous fertility. Whatever we may think of them now, they were popular at the time. They were in request for representation in public and in the houses of wealthy citizens; for apparently the local magnates resented the shoemaker's fluency only while they disagreed with him. Hans now entered on a new period of prosperity. He married again, and lived happily with his second wife for fifteen years. A publisher, with his sanction, began a collected edition of his works—a rare honour for an author in those days, and the congenial labour of revising, arranging, and registering occupied Hans in his declining years. Besides this general popularity he was chief of the mastersingers, acknowledged as such in his own and other schools, and surrounded by young disciples in whose measures he would still occasionally compose. One of these admirers, Adam Puschmann, gives a pleasing, but rather suspicious account of his old age. He dreams of a little house in the garden of a merry city, where an old bearded man, grey and white like a pigeon, sits poring over his books. When strangers enter and greet him he gazes on them and nods gently, without speaking; his senses begin to fail him.

Authentic or not, this is a likely picture of poor old Hans, and we may without scruple think of him thus in his last days; for he lived to a great age, and we may be sure would never leave his beloved books. When he died in 1576, in his eighty-third year, he had written more than four thousand mastersongs, more than two hundred plays, and nearly two thousand other poems.

How are we to estimate this German Lope de Vega? Many of his works are in manuscript, many are practically inaccessible; but the ordinary editions contain quite enough to overwhelm us. Perhaps the very quantity suggests the first characteristic. Hans must have turned out a new poem almost every day—we were near writing, almost every hour. He does not think long over his work, or wait for inspiration ; he does not investigate causes or harmonize motives—he takes his subject very much as he finds it. He is not a shallow writer, but his depth lies more in his temper than in his treatment. He has marvellous facility in rhyme, marvellous power of making pictures; with him everything has definite external features. He is a good storyteller. He is like a man who at his quiet family dinner gives the daily bulletin of news, retailing all that he has heard, or read, or seen. Hans has such a daily bulletin of poetry. Of course he must make considerable loans; but all is done in good faith, and he seldom omits chapter and page of his authority. Sometimes he develops these materials and works them up; sometimes he translates almost literally, adding here and there a happy phrase, or shifting time and place into contemporary Germany.

With all his borrowings, Hans had little understanding of past times or a foreign spirit. This is not strange. All his poems show him content with the present—inspired, not troubled by it. Such unquestioning absorption in his time gives him fluency at the expense of passion and thought; it also disguises the distant and the past, which are in his eyes only another—perhaps in some points a better—present. He has no feeling for tradition. If he tries something in the style of the old minnesingers he breaks down.

Thus among his mastersongs there is an imitation of their *aubades*, in which the watchman warns the lady and her lover that the sun is up, and the lord of the castle will soon awake. We are astonished to hear such things from moral Hans; but he hastens to explain: the lady is the soul, the strange knight is the flesh, the watchman is conscience, and the unfortunate husband is—we dare not finish lest we seem profane. In the same fashion he approaches foreign authors; he wants above all to make them edifying. One of his most important functions is translation: like that "grant translateur, noble Geoffroi Chaucier," he familiarized his people with the treasures of other tongues. In many cases the sources of the two poets are the same, but how different in their treatment! Thus, in the story of Griselda, Chaucer tones down the improbable by humanizing touches and sly sarcasms; but Hans takes it all for gospel, and sees nothing in it to laugh at. According to him the story teaches that "the husband, as saith St. Paul, is the head of the wife," a moral which the playful "Envoye de Chaucer" distinctly rejects :—

> "O noble wyves, ful of heigh prudence,
>   Let noon humilite *your* tonges nayle,
>   Ne lat no clerk have cause or diligence
>   To write of *yow* a story of such mervayle."

Or, again, the history of Isabella's sorrows, which Keats concludes with the wail—

> " Oh, cruelty!
> To steal my basil-pot away from me,"

contains for Hans two important lessons: (1) that love and (2) that murder will out. It is the same with his translations from the classics. He does not care for the acknowledged masterpieces. Homer and Virgil leave him cold. He loves little gossiping stories, like those about the death of Æschylus or the birth of Augustus, and he never fails to extract from them the inevitable moral. In this branch his versions of Scripture are probably the least interesting nowadays, but they are also the best. Here he has thorough sympathy with the foreign spirit, or rather the spirit was not foreign, Luther had naturalized it—it was the spirit of the age.

And whenever Hans is inspired by the feelings of the day, by the daily life of the time, he ceases to bungle. He is no longer an imitator, but a true, original poet; his words are instinct with life—they may be homely, but they are always fresh. He has left us a gallery of pictures, grave and gay, of feelings, customs, and men, which the historian has certainly not exhausted. His "Wittenberg Nightingale" and "Lament for Luther" are masterpieces in their way, and there are many such among his religious, his political, and, above all, his social poems. We mention only "Why art thou cast down, O my soul?"—"All the works of God are good "—" The Council of the Gods." Perhaps the quaintest and most pathetic is his " Vision of the Wild Army." It overtakes him at nightfall in a forest, he shrinks aside and sees it whirl by—a route of ghastly, famished wretches; the last one stops and hails him grimly. These are the petty criminals, the little thieves, robbers of henroosts and the like, who have been hanged on earth, and now they prick and spur to and fro, hunting for justice. *They* are not guiltless; but why do the guiltiest, the great thieves, the usurers, the oppressors of the poor, still live at ease, in peace and plenty? Justice they shall find—on the day of judgment. This fancy is typical of Hans Sachs. The progress of the gods has ceased to impose, the demon host to appal; we see instead a crowd of wretched men whose miseries call for pity and redress.

Equally good are his pictures of comic life. Alchemist and witch, priest and lawyer, shrewish wife and henpecked husband, none escape him; and the peasantry, as we mentioned, have the lion's share of his satire. He is at his best when his humour has a purpose, when his love of teaching and his love of laughter become indistinguishable. He warns those who consort with Hans Idle that soon their only cattle will be their cat; he pictures the Good Monday, a day on which workmen would not work, as a hideous beast, seven-legged, pot-bellied, with sharp teeth, and a bald head; it crawls fawning to his bedside when he lies too late—a nightmare that might rouse the laziest dreamer. In his " Schlauraffen-land," or lubber's paradise, the German Land of Cockayne, roasted pigs run about with knives and forks in their backs; the ponds are full of nicely boiled fish, and birds cooked to a turn fly into one's mouth ; the trees grow pheasants, and the horses lay eggs. Men are paid twopence an hour for sleeping; if they gamble their money away, it is restored them double ; if they cannot clear their debts, the creditor hands them the amount. The archer who shoots widest of the mark, the runner who is last in the race, receives the prize ; the laziest is king, and the honest man is a rogue and a vagabond.

Hans teaches without tediousness and laughs without guile. To modern readers he may sometimes seem profane ; but no judgment could be more unjust. A refined man will treat every subject with delicacy, and a subtle man with subtlety ; in the same way a humourist will always be humourous—and Hans is emphatically a humourist. With the gravest subject, with the most serious intention, he cannot suppress his genial smile; and because we feel that it is not quite in keeping, it makes us laugh outright. Thus it seems odd for a strict Lutheran to make fun of the

devil, and the devil is Han's favourite butt. When
the Prince of Darkness is represented as a gay wooer,
as a hen-pecked and then a runaway husband, as the
dupe of an old witch, as rather stupid but perfectly
good-humoured and harmless, it is impossible to keep
one's gravity. On one occasion he hears the *Landsknechte* mentioned as people after his own heart, and
sends "Belzebock" up to earth to fetch him one.
These Landsknechte were fellows who took to soldier-
ing, hired themselves to the largest bidder, and went
about robbing the country—obviously a set of men
whom tradesman Hans would particularly dislike.
Belzebock goes to a tavern where some of them are
drinking, and hides behind the stove to wait his
opportunity. But their talk fills even him with
horror; his hair stands on end at their stories, and he
is afraid to touch them. At last one fellow who had
stolen a cock and hung it up where Belzebock has hid,
cries to the host, "Landlord, pluck the poor devil
behind the stove and roast him for supper." This
command completes Belzebock's dismay; he flies for
dear life, and when once more among his friends
implores the devil to give up thoughts of these people,
and content himself, as hitherto, with monks and
nuns.

A second story of these Landsknechte introduces us
to St. Peter, the other comic personage in whom Hans

chiefly delights. This rather extraordinary selection is a new sign of his evangelicism. The Devil whom Luther can frighten with an inkbottle, and who is considered the chief emissary of Rome, is clearly fair game for all good Protestants. In the same way St. Peter, chief of the Roman Hierarchy, has no great hold on their reverence. He is portrayed as a self-opinioned critic of the Divine Government which he wishes to reform. One day he is allowed to try his hand : the first prayer that he hears is from an old woman to look after her goat; the weather is hot, the goat is active, red and breathless Peter must chase it up and down; he has no time for anything else, and at length, in a copious perspiration, is thankful to resign office. So, too, in the story of the Landsknechte, the most amusing of which he is hero. A party of them appear before the gate of Heaven and demand admittance, but Peter has received strict injunctions not to let them in. At this they begin to swear, " Sacrament," " Body of Christ," and so on, till the porter's heart warms to them, for he thinks they are praying. " I never saw such pious people in all my life," he cries, and opens the door. But no sooner are they in than they fall to gambling and quarrelling, and when Peter remonstrates they hunt him through the streets with their naked swords. He escapes panting to the Deity, and asks what is to be done.

"I told you how it would be," is the answer. But the matter is not beyond remedy. An angel is sent to blow a trumpet outside the walls, the soldiers hear and think a new war must have broken out; they rush off to enlist, and the door is promptly closed behind them.

But Hans surpasses himself in the story of " Eve's Unlike Children," the best known and most delicious of all his productions. Adam and Eve, cast out of Paradise, sit wearied and depressed with their day's work.* Adam, trying to comfort his wife, mentions, in off-hand fashion, how an angel has just given him a piece of news. God will visit them to-morrow to hold high feast (*hohes fest*), and see how they are keeping house and bringing up the children. Therefore, let Eve sweep the rooms, spread the floors with sweet straw, wash the children, and dress them in their best. The first part of the injunction is easily obeyed, but not so the second. For Eve's children are sharply separated into two groups. Some are very good, pretty, and obedient ; the others are bad, dirty, unruly, and deformed. Abel and those like him are soon made tidy, but Cain and his fellows are playing and quarrelling in the gutter, and flatly refuse to let themselves be washed. When Abel announces who

* It was also a favourite subject with the author, who has made use of it four different times. In the following sketch I have borrowed traits from all the versions.

is coming, Cain replies, " I'd liefer He would stay away." When his father bids him prepare for the prayer, sacrifice, and sermon of the morrow, the wicked child wishes that "prayer, sermon and sacrifice had never been invented." At this, Eve loses her patience and exclaims, she will leave them the eyesores that they are, and God will find them a dirty rabble foul as pigs; but in one version she relents, and stows them away in the loft, under the straw, in the chimney. Next day the visitor comes as announced, and after a hospitable welcome asks to see the children. Those who are dressed, with Abel at their head, advance singing a psalm, and shake hands with the guest. He asks them questions out of Luther's Catechism on the Lord's Prayer, the Creed, the meaning of Amen, the Commandments, with what they forbid or require, and the children come off with flying colours. Reassured by their success, Eve ventures to produce the other lot; but when they come tumbling in dirty, naked, shapeless, unkempt, God cannot keep from laughing (*der Her tet des rostigen haufens lachen*). They offer Him their left hands, make a frightful mess of the Catechism, and excuse themselves on the plea that they don't see the use of it, that they can't remember it, that they did not know He was coming. The examiner is much displeased and determines to punish them; they and their seed shall be mechanics, fishermen and peasants, but Abel and the good children shall be kings, nobles, rich merchants and scholars. Eve in pity for her offspring offers objections, but is told that all is for the best, only in this way can there be order in the world.

Even here, then, Hans writes with an object, and with the very Lutheran one of justifying the existence of ranks. In this sense Melanchthon tells the story in another version, and to any who have found it irreverent, we may say with Hans himself, that he has it from the Latin of Melanchthon. But such an excuse is unnecessary. Even the figure of the Deity is not irreverent, but only quaint, and at heart truly Protestant. Tieck characterizes him as a "strict but affable superintendent." Scotchmen will rather think of the old Presbyterian catechists who used to make the rounds of the outlying districts, stopping at the farms, and examining the whole household, parents, children, strangers and servants, on the Bible and Shorter Catechism.

After a lifetime of popularity, and two centuries of neglect, Hans Sachs attracted the affectionate admiration of Goethe. In his autobiography the greater poet describes how this study influenced his style, and in "The Poetical Vocation of Hans Sachs" pays a sympathetic tribute to our worthy mastersinger. In this

U

poem Goethe describes and explains an old wood-cut. Hans sits in his workshop on Sunday. The young damsel Honesty, the old crone History, and a merry-andrew crowd round offering him their stores. Pleased with his task, but at a loss for words, he looks up and meets the friendly gaze of the Muse. She vows him to herself, promises that his heart shall be ever "merry as a bud in dew," and shows him his wife waiting in the garden to cheer and hearten him in his work. An oak wreath floats above him in the clouds, and a frog-pond in the corner for carping critics completes the picture. "After this manifesto," says Hoffman, "Hans was safe. Few wish to be banished by Goethe into the frog-pond."

KLOPSTOCK.

[Klopstock's complete works were published in 1817, and Düntzer has edited his odes separately. Of the biographies the most convenient is Gruber's, and Strauss has given some interesting particulars in his " Kleine Schriften." Gervinus has given an admirable criticism of Klopstock's life and works—the best that I have seen—in his " Deutsche Dichtung," bd. iv., being here more in sympathy with his subject than he sometimes is; from it I have largely borrowed.

Klopstock was unfortunate in the quality though not in the quantity of his English translators, and his complaints about this formed one item in his famous conversation with Coleridge and Wordsworth. In Mrs. Meeke's version of the " Messiah," his diction ceases to be, what Herder called it, " a dance of syllables," and becomes rather a prance of syllables. In the following essay I have made use of Baskerville's unrhymed and of Nind's rhymed translations, the latter the best English renderings of Klopstock, but not quite faithful because they are rhymed.]

DURING the first half of the eighteenth century presages were not wanting in Germany of a coming literary revival. People acquired a sufficient interest in poetry to lose their tempers about it; they discussed it with zeal if not with knowledge; the rival leaders, Bodmer and Gottsched, had each a keen scent for the faults of the other, if not for his own.

But the direct results of all this controversy were very meagre. Neither party as yet had a genius in its ranks. The verses produced were commonplace prose chopped into defective metre, from which all the essential elements of poetry were carefully excluded.

The German writers of the time failed in three respects. They wanted first, the sense of form; second, independence and national character; but last and most, all contact with life. No doubt both Gottsched and Bodmer busied themselves with inquiries into language and style, but their methods were inadequate, and they were worshippers of false gods. Gottsched wrote in the French interest, but the French lightness of treatment and suggestive wit escaped him altogether, and the French wisdom of life which fulfils a Molière he never tried to acquire. In the same way Bodmer, who appealed to England, had not Shakespeare in his eye; and though he professed himself a disciple of Milton, it was only Milton's mistakes that he admired. The energy of plastic creation, the "planetary harmonies" of the English poet—for these he had no sense, and he placed him much on the same level with such respectable persons as Edward Young, author of the "Night Thoughts." Thus the two rivals got little more from their study of foreign models than inflated blank verse and monotonous Alexandrines. And they looked upon these measures as absolutely perfect: they applied them mechanically without understanding their principles; they did not know that the form of a work of art is prescribed from within by the spirit; that it is like the shape to which a flower grows, not like a mould into which metal is cast.

But perhaps a worse fault than having an imperfect ideal was having a foreign one. No doubt every nation, if it be wise, will learn from all its neighbours; no doubt it will absorb elements offered from without. That is a vastly different thing from accepting any foreign standard. We may import tea from China without importing its mandarins. But Bodmer and Gottsched thought differently. At war in all else, they agreed in this, that Germany could produce nothing of its own; that it must imitate the literature of more fortunate countries, and that such imitations would supply all native wants.

The reason for such preposterous opinions among men of talent lay in the separation which existed between poetry and life. People had no idea that a man's writings were connected with his character. The statement of Goethe that his poems are his confessions—the words he attributes to Tasso—

> " And if the human heart in silence break,
>   Mine is the God-given strength to *tell* my sorrow,"—

would have been applauded as amusing paradoxes.

Bodmer professed enthusiasm for Milton ; but when in later days Lessing repeated Milton's principle that to write a poem one must live a poem, that no one can sing what he has not felt, Bodmer made merry over this "monstrous idea."   "No, no, friend Lessing," he exclaimed; "it is not the man, it is only the poet, who loves and revels and weeps in his verses."   Of course these opinions could hold ground only while there was no one of poetical insight to contradict them.   As soon as men of real feeling and genius arose, their first task would be to restore literature to paths more human, more German, and more artistic.   The two writers who fulfilled this mission, though in very opposite ways, were Friedrich Gottlieb Klopstock and Christoph Martin Wieland.

Already in Klopstock's life we see that he was peculiarly fitted for the work of reform.   He was born in Quedlinburg in 1724, and like most German boys of his rank, grew up in an atmosphere of the strictest religion, but *un*like most of them, with plenty of active exercise and outdoor employment.   Both influences were due to his father, a man of somewhat excited pietistic notions, who believed in spectres, presages, and the bodily presence of the devil, but who was also keenly alive to the importance of muscular Christianity. The son was not behind in either direction.   One of his biographers would have us recognize in the child the ancient Cheruscan hardiness described by Tacitus, and dwells with especial delight on a swimming adventure which he undertook in spite of his parents' commands. Sent to school at Pforta, the other side of his character began to disclose itself. He threw himself on the study of Greek, broke loose from the pedantry of his masters, and read Homer, not as a grammatical exercise, but as the great epic of every nation and every age. The contrast of this with what in his own country were by courtesy called poems, filled him with burning shame. He vowed that if he lived he would wipe out the reproach of his fatherland; at night he could not sleep for thinking of his high career; and though his conscience accused him of worldly ambition, his heart beat high with hopes of immortality and fame. Among the rather puritanical circles in which he moved he came to be noted for a certain exuberance of life. He revelled in an excited feeling of friendship. Friendship, next to peace of conscience, was the supremest happiness of man. He was an enthusiast for field-sports. He drew up a code of laws for skating, which he afterwards celebrated in an ode. Goethe, too, was proficient in these matters, but the eternal riding, swimming, and boating of Klopstock and his school soon became a very nuisance to the more judicious poet. When Klopstock visited Zürich, Bodmer and all his pious friends were greatly shocked. They had expected a holy young prophet, and were prepared to shed tears with him over his religious poems. But the lion would not roar, or rather would not weep. He was in disgracefully high spirits, and deserted his tearful admirers to amuse the ladies of the company.

But like most men in whose character the emotional predominates, Klopstock could be as easily depressed as exalted. Some of his odes, inspired by a merely hypothetical lady, express the innermost languishing of love. In others, which, contrary to contemporary German usage, he addressed to a real lady, Fanny Schmidt, he is often hoarse with misery. With streaming eyes he entreats Bodmer to intercede for him, and Bodmer good-naturedly consents. He is jubilant at the welcome which in 1748 the first three books of his "Messiah" receive; but he is presently plunged in despair when he remembers that, tutor as he is, he cannot devote his whole soul to the under-taking. This grief was removed. Bernstorff, Prime Minister of Denmark, invited him with a pension to Copenhagen. Klopstock set out in his most expansive mood, and during the journey fell in love with Meta, or Margaretha Moller, whom he celebrated under the name of Cidli in several fine odes, and who three years later became his wife. This is the lady who, with no introduction but her admiration, struck up a correspondence with Richardson the novelist, and who, with her pleasant broken English, her talk of a " manly (*i.e.* male) Clarissa," and of " war, the great fiend of friendship," was at one time pretty generally known in this country. In these and other letters she appears to the full as gushing, as lachrymose, and, we may add, as high-souled as either Richardson or her husband. She returns to the days "when," to quote her own words, "I was only the single young girl." She writes of her first meeting with Klopstock : " I must confess that, though greatly pre-possessed of his qualities, I never thought him the amiable youth whom I found him. This made its effect." For though merely his friend to begin with, " at the least," she proceeds, " my thoughts were ever with him filled." It is perhaps cruel to make her furnish evidence that Klopstock was a sentimentalist and a bore, but after all the statement is now in print, and she gives it with an enthusiasm too innocent to pass by. On the anniversary of her marriage she writes to a friend, " Klopstock greeted me, ' Wife of my heart, best wife, rare Meta, thou angel, thou, my heart and soul.' Yes, he said all that and much more, and ah ! he has been saying it already the whole year through." Which certainly is exactly what we would expect of Klopstock, but few would add with his victim, " How happy I am ! "

After his marriage, Klopstock resided in Hamburg, where he lived a quite poetical life, idolized by his friends, his wife, and even by his wife's family. The "Messiah" was his dream by night and his work by day, and whilst he wrote, his wife prayed that he might have inspiration. Klopstock can describe the existence he now led only in the most superlative of superlatives. But it was soon to pass. After four years his wife died; his progress with his work was slow, twenty-five years elapsing between the publication of the first book and the last, and during the interval the German public gradually cooled in its enthusiasm till it grew quite severe. Klopstock consoled himself for these misfortunes as best he might. He tried his success in what he called *bardiettes*, imitations of what he fancied the poems of the bards must have been, and becoming the leader of the Patriotic School, formed a "society of bards," which met on Saturday afternoons. He also founded a Ladies' Poetical Club in Hamburg—of which Lessing's wife wrote, " I shall never be admitted : I am neither young nor pretty enough for Herr Klopstock,"—and by-and-by he married again, this time a widow lady named Winthem. For the defection of the public he comforted himself with the admiration of aristocratic friends, who granted him pensions, and paid him almost divine honours. " After the mother of the Messiah

himself," writes one, " comes the mother of Klopstock."
He lived to welcome, and then to denounce the
French Revolution, both in unmeasured terms, and
died in 1803.

From Klopstock's biography it seems pretty evident
that his gifts are chiefly lyric. There is no trace
with him of the measured, stately self-control that we
associate with great epic poets, with Virgil and Dante
and Milton. And still less does he possess that quick
wide sympathy with all types of character, all shades
of opinion which the dramatist requires. He once
pronounced it sin to love a freethinker. But his continual enthusiasm, his raptures of despair and delight,
would all find their vent in the intenser kinds of
lyrical composition.

It is noteworthy that Horace and Pindar were
his early favourites, and inspired his first poetical
attempts. With them he cultivated his sense of
form. As soon as he tried odes in German he found
that he must have a perfect control over his language,
a thorough insight into its spirit, a complete mastery
of its materials. He studied it in the light of his
Greek and Roman masters; he plunged into it, and
it bore him up; he felt he could compete with the
ancients in their own measures, and contemptuously
rejected what he called " the modern click-clack of
rhyme." He strove with might and main to reach

the old classical perfection of form, and not without success. "Klopstock," says Kolbe, applying the famous epigram on Dryden, "might boast as Augustus boasted of Rome, 'I found the German language brick, and left it marble.'" It is unfortunate, but it is characteristic of the man, that this formal perfection means nothing more to him than mastery in speech, metres, and the arrangement of sounds. But in these he almost always succeeds, at least where they are the vehicle of exalted feeling. No doubt he takes liberties in his treatment of German, he forces it to be sublime in spite of itself; what it gains in majesty, it loses in simplicity. A friend once told him that people did not understand his language: "Then they may learn it," was Klopstock's reply. In this he was too proud and uncompromising, he would not take a telling. He persevered in classical constructions, involved sentences, obscure allusions, which it requires some erudition to explain. To illustrate this it is usual to quote his verse—

"The pious monk's invention now resounds."

Perhaps few readers guess at once that he means "the gun is fired," and that "the pious monk's invention" is the powder. A smart but somewhat flippant critic greatly annoyed Klopstock by proposing to translate his odes into German. Often he seems to have constructed his periods like Chinese puzzles, that his reader may have the pleasure of taking them to pieces again. But, after condemning all these faults, we must remember that they are by no means universal with Klopstock, and that it is very easy to make too much of them. Take him at his best and he is one of the best ode-writers of the modern world, and worthy to stand beside Dryden and Collins. "Hence it comes that he has the ease and confidence of a master in all the primitive and original kinds of poetry. He seizes in its very essence the stormy ecstasy of the bards, the religious majesty of the Psalms, and once or twice the more human beauty of the Greek lyrics." It has been said that in his youthful odes we hear again Pindar and David and the Edda. These names suggest a rough threefold division, not only of those, but of all his poems, according to three principles, which exercised a powerful influence on his life and development. Some of the odes are simple and severe, and have a faint breath of Greek beauty. Others are abrupt, difficult, involved and obscure, composed after Northern models and intended to express the Ur-deutsch, the original native German. A third class are dithyrambic hymns of religious content, steeped in the spirit of David and Isaiah and St. John.

The Grecian inspiration, as we saw, was his first. In the classical world he learned the significance of form: Pindar and Horace taught him their measures and their style. All his odes may be considered as the direct or indirect outcome of these influences. "But in that alien pagan world as it was to him he could not long linger. Already when he left school he pitied Homer and Virgil for their religion's sake, and refused to follow in their steps." He placed the bard above the poet, the Christian above the heathen. "My heart," he cries, "demands tumult and storm and lofty flight, the audacious pictures of Northern song, countless, hot, and true." Thus we see him return from Greece to his own country, he is fired with the idea of independence; he will be a national poet and sing German strains; the scholar is merged in the patriot. This change it is not hard to explain. No man of sufficient poetical feeling really to appreciate the Greeks could fail to see that they were great by the inspiration of the life around them. The pulse of their people beat more quickly in their veins, and the aspirations of their people shone more brightly before their eyes. Will one produce Greek art, the sure way to fail is to imitate it: the only chance of success lies in making one's self the mouthpiece of one's own country and one's own time. This the young German felt. He began to search for a native hero and a native theme. He sought to revive the primitive German virtues. He wished to make his countrymen free and simple and hardy once more. This explains his passion for field-sports. "Had he been converting the heathen he could not have preached skating with greater unction." When Macpherson's "Ossian" appeared, Klopstock was in ecstasies. To call it a forgery was, in his eyes, blasphemous. Here was a poem original to the Western races, "which defied Homer and shamed Apollo." Besides, in those days the distinction was not very precisely drawn between Celt and Teuton, and Klopstock was disposed to claim Ossian as the champion of all Northern Europe. "Ossian was a Caledonian," says Gleim; "and therefore of German origin;" and Klopstock talks of his "Celtic or ancestral mythology." At a later day, when he composed his cumbrous allegory of the "German Republic of Letters," he described it as a sort of society of Druids. In like manner, considering the bards common to both races, he wrote strange hybrid poems, which he called *bardiettes*, and which celebrate the feats of Arminius, or Hermann, who had routed the legions of Rome. I may quote the following fragment to illustrate generally his treatment of these patriotic themes. The dialogue is between Hermann and his wife Thusnelda, when he returns from a victorious battle. The original antique metres are preserved in the translation :—

> "Lŏ ! wĭth swĕāt ŏn hĭs brŏw, wĭth Rŏman gŏre staīned,
> Wĭth thĕ dūst ŏf thĕ bāttlĕ dĕcked hĕ cŏmĕth,
>   Nĕ'ĕr wăs Hĕrmănn sŏ lŏvĕly,
> Thūs nĕvĕr flāshed hĭs brĭght eȳe.

"Come ! I tremble for joy ; give me the eagles
And thy sabre blood-reeking, come, breathe freely !
    Rest within my embraces
    After the terrible fight.

" Rest, that I from thy brow may wipe the sweat-drop,
And the blood from thy cheek, thy cheek how glowing !
    Hermann ! Hermann ! Thusnelda
    Never hath loved thee as now.

" Not even when in the forests' shades so wildly
Thou with sun-embrowned arm didst seize me, stopping
    I already beheld thee
    With immortality crowned.

" ' Wherefore twin'st thou my locks ?   Lies not our father
Silent, dead at our feet ? Oh had Augustus
    Led his hosts to the battle
    Gorier *he* would lie there.'

" Let me bind up thy waving hair, O Hermann,
That it may o'er thy wreath in ringlets threaten !
    Siegmar dwelleth in Heaven,
    Follow and weep not for him."

But it was not Hermann who first suggested himself as the great epical hero of Germany. Klopstock's earliest choice was the Saxon Emperor, Henry the Fowler, who had delivered his country from the Hungarian invaders. A little unrhymed ballad on this subject remains, which is a good specimen of Klopstock's simpler style :—

"Behold the foe ! the fight begins,
    Come on to Victory !
    The bravest hero leads us on
    In all our fatherland.

> "The sickness feels he not to-day,
>   There bear they him along,
>   Hail Henry, Hero brave and good
>   In fields of flashing steel!
>
> "His eyeball glows with honour's flame
>   And victory compels,
>   Around him are the nobles' helms
>   With hostile blood bedewed.
>
>   .   .   .   .   .
>
> "Oh welcome death for fatherland,
>   Whene'er our sinking head
>   With blood be decked, then will we die
>   With fame for fatherland.
>
> "When we before us see a plain,
>   And but the dead behold
>   Around us, conquer then will we
>   With fame for fatherland.
>
>   .   .   .   .   .
>
> "The fame we've won shall aye remain,
>   Yea, even when we are dead,
>   When we have for our fatherland
>   The death of honour died."

But though Klopstock at one time thought of Henry for his hero, he soon abandoned him. We instinctively think of Milton, who once, from a crowd of epical and dramatic studies, selected the history of Arthur for his life-work. But finally both poets followed the summons of the sacred muse, and probably they were right. In the ode "To my Fatherland," Klopstock exclaims:—

> "Thine was I from my boyhood, when my breast
>   Felt the first pulses of ambition spring.

> I chose from heroes of the lance and crest
>   Henry thy rescuer to sing.
> But I beheld the higher track of light,
>   And more than mere ambition fired my mind ;
> The pathway I preferred that leads from night
>   Up *to the Fatherland of all mankind.*
> That I pursue, but when the toil too much
>   O'erburdens this mortality,
> I turn aside, and, to the telyn's touch,
>   Sing, Fatherland, thy fame to thee."

" In this way," laments Gervinus, "he sacrificed Homer for Ossian and both for David." But this was really the best, indeed, the only thing he could do. How could he have sung a German heroic when Germany at the time did not exist? The Peace of Westphalia, only less disastrous than the war to which it made an end, had made any practical patriotism impossible. The little princelings had received sovereign powers which made them independent of their emperor on the one hand, and of their subjects on the other. Neither unity nor freedom existed; there was no German empire and no German people. Klopstock might feel that patriotic sentiment that burns itself out in an ode; but the love of country which is necessary to inspire a great effort, which springs from love and gratitude and complete self-surrender, how could he feel that for a land " where the subjects were lackeys and the sovereigns were brutes ? " For the monarch who laid the foundations of a new Germany, for Frederick the Great of Prussia, Klopstock on religious grounds had no sympathy; and indeed in his odes, though not in his life, all kings indiscriminately were "sots, albinoes, and ourang-outangs." In these circumstances what catholic interest remained on which he could feel strongly save the interest of religion? Discontented with his own fatherland he turned to the "Fatherland of all mankind." "I searched for a hero," he says, "and sank exhausted. Then suddenly him, whom as a Christian I loved, as a poet I saw with one swift triumphant glance." Whatever faults there may be in the choice of subject and in the execution, we have here at least the first essential condition fulfilled,—the poet feels what he is writing about. He will pour his life into this chalice, he will consecrate all his powers to this task. The fruit of his classical studies, the noble hexameters which few could wield as he, his exuberant and headlong diction, the inheritance from his Northern ancestry, these, he says, "I will now hallow by dedicating them to religion." He strove and struggled with himself to delay beginning his work till he was thirty years of age. But his subject possessed and overwhelmed him. It carried him away; he could not resist it, he *had* to begin. Feeling begets feeling: a poem which issued from such a state of mind must succeed: the first three cantos of the "Messiah" awoke an enthusiasm equal to the author's own. No doubt a reaction followed on both sides. Klopstock alternated between exaltation and ague, fever and depression. The public turned away from a work which dragged itself out for years till it lost all wholeness of feeling, and came to look like a string of lyrical fragments. But meanwhile the deed had been done, the stimulus given. Henceforth there could be no question that the Germans had in them poetry of their own. They could now advance to their new classical period. They could never return to the "masterpieces" which had disgraced the last two hundred years.

In his choice of a subject we must admit that Klopstock was wrong. When a poet treats a larger theme he is generally exposed to a twofold danger. On the one hand his tastes may be a little recondite, he may select what is neither well known nor popular. In this case he will fail to excite catholic sympathy, his work will not be national nor ever become household property. Or, again, he may choose what is too familiar, what is already sacred and hallowed in the minds of the people, so that no further artistic development is possible, and all change is regarded with suspicion. No one, out of France, is rash enough to write a new " Hamlet," and Klopstock was guilty of almost as much foolhardiness when he undertook to work up the simple stories of the Gospel into an elaborate epic poem.

And the very conditions which determined his choice made it impossible for him fully to succeed. It was his orthodoxy dashed with pietism that drew him to the subject. Now while his pietism filled him with devout brooding reverence for the figure of Christ, his orthodoxy forced him to view it only through the old dogmas. These prescribed a certain treatment and forbade a certain treatment. He could not piece together, reject, remodel, and humanize. We have seen this done in the prose of Renan and others with results at least far more artistic than came within the range of Klopstock's verse. Even the Evangelical theologian, Dr. Dorner, says of him, "He failed to perceive that the Divine, save when human, remains unrevealed, aud hovers in a sublime haziness, which may inspire inspiration and ecstasy, but never keen plastic contemplation." Klopstock conceives the Divine in what Dr. Dorner would call its unrevealed state. He seeks its expression, not in the workings of man's spirit, but in signs and wonders. So, instead of bringing his theme more fully and clearly within our consciousness, he shifts it further away. To this result his artistic concurred with his religious orthodoxy. He held the traditional tenet that an epic poem demands supernatural machinery. The whole apparatus, therefore, which he found ready to his hand seemed to require enlargement rather than dismantling. So he introduces a multitude of marvels, a crowd of persons, an enormous dæmonic apparatus, of which the Evangelists know nothing, and which every judicious reader must feel to be out of place. Samma, a convert, Philo, a Pharisee, play important parts, and Pilate's wife, Portia, with her dreams and presentiments, has nearly a whole canto to herself. Nicodemus, Joseph, Lazarus, are made the heroes of imaginary occurrences. Indeed all the minor characters of the Gospel, who are introduced casually, whose names are hardly mentioned, or are left unmentioned, become the centre of detailed and fantastical romances. Perhaps the most ridiculous example is the little love story of Semida and Cidli, the young man of Nain and the daughter of Jairus. Since both died and both were raised from the dead, Klopstock discovers that they were evidently intended for each other. Their connection is not indeed mentioned in Holy Writ, but it is the glory of the poet to remedy such omissions! So he conducts them through a long and tearful courtship, and at length unites them amid a company of glorified saints and prophets who visit the earth after the Crucifixion. Most of Klopstock's admirers would think this blasphemy, did it not occur in a religious poem.

Perhaps even more superfluous are the hosts of

angels, demons, and genii who are intended to help on the action, but who really impede it. Nothing happens save through their agency. Herder condemns this with rather an amusing illustration. The Evangelist in his story of the Crucifixion says, " Now it was about the sixth hour, and there was darkness over all the earth until the ninth hour." These simple words are intended to bring out the solemnity of the time, and do so completely. But in Klopstock, the seraph Uriel has been waiting for the proper moment, and then punctually signals to a star to place itself before the sun. In the same way no one can talk or think but it is by the prompting of an angel or a devil. " We get to know not men, but their guardian spirits," says Gervinus. This fashion of supernatural poetry became the bane of Germany, and Lessing proposed to write a satire upon it in which old Gottsched should ride out " to hunt the seraphim." Klopstock only once attempts to portray character, and that is in the case of the fallen Abadonna. Abadonna was penitent, and his fate excited great interest in Germany. It became one of the burning questions of the day. The Zürich society supplicated for him, and in Magdeburg his salvation was solemnly decreed. This is not without parallel in England. Prayers have been offered that little Dombey might not die, and—what is even more *à propos*—that Lovelace's soul might be saved. In Germany these pious efforts were crowned with success, and at the end of the poem, when Abadonna beseeches God to annihilate him, he is mercifully restored to his place in heaven.

He alone of all the spirits has definite features. The others are a shadowy host, distinguishable only by their names. Schiller says truly, "From all that he touches Klopstock withdraws the body." And yet despite that, he is grossly materialistic. He places the infernal regions in the centre of the earth, lighted by a sun of their own. He describes God as a visible figure in space. He conceives spirit as body that has somehow ceased to be solid. Coleridge rather unkindly translates his name "Clubstick," and certainly he has no great subtlety of discernment or fineness of thought.

This defect shows itself in the whole plan of the poem, or rather in its absence of plan. When the early cantos appeared, and every one was raving about the new epic, Lessing cautioned the people that their applause was premature. "You can't judge a work of art from the parts," he said, "but only as a whole." This warning was disregarded at the time, but every new canto proved more and more conclusively that Lessing's fears had been well founded. What an epic imperatively demands is unity of action, but the " Messiah " had in the first place no unity, and

in the second no action.   Christ is nailed on the Cross
at the beginning of the eighth book; angels, mortals,
saints, and devils gather round, sing and declaim
during his dying agonies; and at last he gives up the
ghost at the end of the tenth book.   Now, one would
think the story must draw to a close, the catastrophe
is passed, the goal is reached.   But in ten other cantos,
quite as long as the first ten, Klopstock, with choruses,
colloquies, and hymns, by a lavish use of celestial
armies and the spirits of just men made perfect, fills
up the interval between the Crucifixion and the
Ascension.   If this betrays a want of epical power,
there is much else that absolutely contradicts the idea
of a narrative poem.   Instead of deeds, we have long
debates : instead of acting, people talk.   If before we
were offended by Klopstock's interpolations, now we
must marvel at his omissions.   The procession to the
Cross, the threefold denial of Peter, the end of Judas,
should have been godsends to the poet; already there
are touches about them hardly to be found out of our
best old ballads.   But Klopstock does not know when
he is well off.   We see the spectacle on the Cross; of
the Via Dolorosa we hear no word.   Peter's treason
takes place in the background, and when all is over
he comes forward and "weeps himself" (*erweint sich*)
the martyr's crown.   At Judas' suicide, first the culprit makes a long speech, then his genus and a bad

angel discourse together, and finally the departed spirit joins in the talk with a fatal fluency that death has not impaired. Not only does everybody speak, but their words are broken with passion : they foam at the mouth, or if they do not lose their self-control it is because they are sublime. Everything is at the highest possible pitch. "For every feeling," says Lessing, " "we feel nothing." Klopstock exasperates his reader with continual interjections; he had to be reminded, "Not every one that crieth Lord! Lord! shall enter into the kingdom of poetry." The same phrases occur in wearisome iteration. Everybody wonders and weeps, and swoons and smiles and embraces everybody else, and dissolves in tears scalding or holy as the case may be. This last performance is specially Klopstockian. In almost every page one finds the expression " weeping eyes."

All these criticisms we must make if we take Klopstock at his word and regard the " Messiah " as an epic poem. But if we do this we are less than just. We shall gain a truer point of view if for a moment we contrast the " Messiah " and the " Paradise Lost." We will not echo Coleridge's biting answer to those who called Klopstock a German Milton. " Yes, a very German one ! " Rather we must decide that the two poets have as little as possible in common. With Milton everything has distinctness, firm outline, definite shape. Even his more hideous images have been compared by Winckelmann to beautifully painted gorgons. But no one in his senses would think of naming painting in the same breath with Klopstock. With him there is nothing fixed, nothing plastic; to use one of his own favourite formulas, "all things melt in feeling." Take even the following noble stanza on death :—

> " Again to bloom the seed the sower sows,
> The Lord of Harvest goes
> Gathering the sheaves,
> Death's sickle reaps and leaves ;
> Praise ye the Lord."

It is not too much to say that no pictorial thinker could have written this, for it labours under a radical confusion ; sowing and reaping, seed time and harvest, are both employed as types of death. It certainly is no picture, but does it not suggest another art ? Take now this poem, which he calls the "Rose Wreath :"—

> " I found her by a shady rill,
> I bound her with a wreath of rose,
> She felt it not, but slumbered still,
> looked at her, and on the spot
> My life with hers did blend and close.
> I felt it, but I knew it not.
>
> ' Some lisping broken words I spoke,
> And rustled light the wreath of rose,
> Then from her slumber she awoke ;
> She looked on me and from that hour
> Her life with mine did blend and close,
> And round us it was Eden's bower."

The presentiment, the dreaminess, the hush of feeling that mark these lines at least in the original, do they not come over the soul like a breath of melody? All poetry contains ideally the arts of painting and music. It is word-painting and word-music, though it is something more than their union. Klopstock's peculiarity lies in this, that with him the first element is more nearly wanting, and the second more fully present than with almost any other poet. One more quotation for the sake of one more comparison will serve to illustrate this. It is from his ode on skating :—

> " Sunk in the tomb of endless night
>   Is many a great inventor's name;
> Our torch we kindle at their light,
>   But where is their reward and fame ?
>
> " How name ye him who ocean crossed
>   First with tall mast and swelling sheet ?
> Nor would I that his name were lost,
>   Who added wings to flying feet :
>
> " For should not he immortal live
>   Whose art can health and joy enhance
> Such as no mettled steed can give,
>   Nor ever panteth in the dance ? . . . .
>
> " The scene is filled with vapoury light,
>   As when the winter morning's prime
> Looks on the lake; above it night
>   Scatters like stars the glittering rime.
>
> " How still and white is all around !
>   How rings the track with new-sparred frost !
> Far off the metal's cymbal sound
>   Betrays thee, for a moment lost.

> " Why to the isle dost list aloof ;
>   Unpractised skaters clamour there.
> The ice not yet will load and hoof
>   Above or net beneath it bear.
>
> " Ah, nought upon thine ear is lost,
>   There wailings loud the death crash makes.
> How different sounds it when the frost
>   Runs splitting miles along the lakes."

Now contrast this with what Wordsworth says about skating in his poem on the "Influence of Natural Objects." I regret that I cannot quote it in full :—

> " So through the darkness and the cold we flew,
> And not a voice was idle; with the din
> Smitten the precipices rang aloud,
> The leafless trees and every icy crag
> Tinkled like iron; while far distant hills
> Into the tumult sent an alien sound
> Of melancholy, not unnoticed while the stars
> Eastward were sparkling clear, and in the west
> The orange sky of evening died away.

How precise and graphic and distinct all this is when compared with Klopstock's hazy rapture! And the opinions of the two men about Ossian point the same moral. His " want of firm outline," to which Wordsworth objects, is precisely what attracts Klopstock. For this, and Ossianic mastery of vague emotion and feeling for sound as sound, are all qualities of his own. Herder said that his odes must be read aloud; "then," he proceeds, "they rise from the page and become a dance of syllables." This is quite true, and Klopstock too often prefers the syllable to the word, the music to the meaning; he tickles our ears with pages of "sound and fury, signifying nothing." To such an extent does he proceed in the twentieth canto of the "Messiah," that his English translator * has not ventured to render it. It contains little more than shouts of Hosannah, choruses of Hallelujah, wavings of triumphal palms. Clearly the relation here is not with the painter, but with the musician. Gervinus reminds us that seven years before Klopstock began his poem, his countryman, Handel, had composed his famous oratorio on the same subject, and with the same name. Klopstock, who loved music with his whole soul, had a peculiar affection for this piece, and regarded it as his own and his country's glory.

His own work is much liker an oratorio than an epic. It is one great ode, or rather a great collection of great odes. Klopstock is always a lyrical poet, and he is never more lyrical than in the " Messiah." If we look at it in this light we shall like it better. Indeed, much that was repugnant to the idea of an epic we may now find to be powerful and impressive. We can now understand why the fragments were so popular while the whole failed to tell; for the parts must be read as lyrics. From this point of view some

* Mrs. Collyer (or Mrs. Meeke).

of the individual passages are in their way unsurpassed. Thus the description of Adramelech's flight is lofty and sustained. Ever on the watch, he seizes the moment when the Messiah is exhausted and agonized. He swoops like a vulture from his lonely rock, and flies through the desolate valley. For an instant he pauses above a suicide who lies weltering in his blood, and whose dying blasphemies re-echo from the surrounding hills. He reaches the prostrate figure of Christ and gloats over his prey: he will overwhelm Him with mockery and scorn. At this moment the Saviour turns and casts on him the look with which He will judge the world. Instantly the fiend shrinks back; and sinks in blank amazement. He sees no longer heaven, nor earth, nor Christ. Scarce can he rally for headlong flight.

Even the debates, if we regard them as splendid pieces of lyrical invective, may obtain their meed of approbation. The best of them is the dispute in the Sanhedrim, when the perturbation of Caiaphas, the caution of Gamaliel, the charity of Nicodemus, and especially the ruthless hatred of Philo, would make a really powerful impression, were their harangues not quite so lengthy.

Many, too, of the phrases and similes have a true poetic ring. When Satan *pours* the evil dream into Judas' open ear, does it not suggest old Hamlet's tale how his brother "into the porches of his ear did pour the leperous distilment"? And the whole episode of this dream is one of Klopstock's triumphs. Satan appears, as Judas' dead father, to excite in him treasonous thoughts. He tells him that his Master neglects and despises him. He shows him the future Messianic Empire in all its splendour. Where the mountains ribbed with gold cast long shadows on the fertile vales, there shall John the beloved disciple be king. Peter shall reign over hills where vineyards are hanging, and boundless fields of waving corn. All round, in a smiling land, cities glitter in the sun, each like Jerusalem, daughter of the king; a new Jordan flows beneath stately arches, along lofty walls, and gardens gay with fruit reach down to the golden sands—these are the kingdoms of the other disciples. But far in the north lies a bleak region, wild and barren, and hideous with withered shrubs; above are drizzly clouds, below are snow and ice. "That, O Judas!" cries the fiend, "that is thine inheritance. There, companioned by birds of night, shalt thou wander alone among the aged oaks, while the other disciples smile in happy scorn."

It is in such passages as these, that afford scope for musical rhetoric, that Klopstock is at his best. It is a pity they are so scarce. They occur once or twice in the "Messiah," in the dramas hardly ever. These last effusions are indeed hopelessly dull. I have already alluded to his northern *bardiettes*. His sacred dramas are even poorer, and may be dismissed with a sentence: they are merely overgrown lyrics. The first and best of them, "Adam's Death," deals with the mystery of death as it is first seen to approach, not at the beck of a murderer, but in the common course of things, and though monotonous, does not fail to impress. These dramas, however, are chiefly famous because of the evil fashion they introduced among the poetasters of Germany. For a few years every man who could versify, Wieland among them, and many who could not, seemed to study the genealogical chapters of Scripture for the purpose of weaving tragedies about the obscurest names. In the same way, the "Messiah" called forth a swarm of epics that were no more epical and far less lyrical than itself.

Klopstock's prevailing character then is vehement high-strung enthusiasm. And it was well for reviving German literature that its first flight should be so bold and lofty. It soared at once beyond the "arrows, views, and shouts" of the profane Philistines. In his poem of the "Two Muses," Klopstock proclaims at once that no cheap triumph will suffice him. The young untried Muse of Germany disdains contest save with her victorious sister of Britain. They prepare for the race :—

> "The herald sounds; they sped with eagle flight,
> Behind them into clouds the dust was tossed :
> I looked; but when the oaks were passed, my sight
> In dimness of the dust was lost."

Whatever we may think of the contest, we must grant that Klopstock restored German art to life and. liberty. He himself revelled in this strange freedom, and abandoned himself to the guidance of his feelings. Probably this was necessary for the reformation of poetry, but it had its dangers. Klopstock's warmth of emotional raptures was wholly religious, but there were not wanting prophets of woe who foretold its issue in something very different. And they were right. It is proverbial that extremes meet. The excess of pietism swings round into an excess of frivolity. Both are the outcome of feeling and sensibility rather than of character, both look more to personal enjoyment than to a practical end. Klopstock himself was preserved from this transition by his priest-like purity and narrowness. But the logic of history made it necessary, nor is it to be considered merely a relapse. His overcharged religion and stilted diction need their supplement in an elegant style, and a gay graceful wisdom of the world. So in the fulness of days the spirit of Klopstock, who has been called the German Milton, moved and fulfilled itself, and assumed a new form in Wieland, who has been called the German Voltaire.

PRINTED BY WILLIAM CLOWES AND SONS, LIMITED,
LONDON AND BECCLES.

A LIST OF

KEGAN PAUL, TRENCH & CO.'S PUBLICATIONS.

8. 86

1, *Paternoster Square*,
London.

A LIST OF
KEGAN PAUL, TRENCH & CO.'S
PUBLICATIONS.

CONTENTS.

	PAGE		PAGE
GENERAL LITERATURE.	2	MILITARY WORKS.	35
PARCHMENT LIBRARY	20	POETRY.	36
PULPIT COMMENTARY	23	NOVELS AND TALES	42
INTERNATIONAL SCIENTIFIC		BOOKS FOR THE YOUNG	44
SERIES	32		

GENERAL LITERATURE.

A. K. H. B.—From a Quiet Place. A Volume of Sermons. Crown 8vo, 5s.

ALEXANDER, William, D.D., Bishop of Derry.—The Great Question, and other Sermons. Crown 8vo, 6s.

ALLEN, Rev. R., M.A.—Abraham: his Life, Times, and Travels, 3800 years ago. Second Edition. Post 8vo, 6s.

ALLIES, T. W., M.A.—Per Crucem ad Lucem. The Result of a Life. 2 vols. Demy 8vo, 25s.

A Life's Decision. Crown 8vo, 7s. 6d.

AMHERST, Rev. W. J.—The History of Catholic Emancipation and the Progress of the Catholic Church in the British Isles (chiefly in England) from 1771-1820. 2 vols. Demy 8vo, 24s.

AMOS, Professor Sheldon.—The History and Principles of the Civil Law of Rome. An aid to the Study of Scientific and Comparative Jurisprudence. Demy 8vo. 16s.

Ancient and Modern Britons. A Retrospect. 2 vols. Demy 8vo, 24s.

ANDERDON, Rev. W. H.—Evenings with the Saints. Crown 8vo, 5s.

ANDERSON, David.—"Scenes" in the Commons. Crown 8vo, 5s.

ARISTOTLE.—**The Nicomachean Ethics of Aristotle.** Translated by F. H. Peters, M.A. Second Edition. Crown 8vo, 6s.

ARMSTRONG, Richard A., B.A.—**Latter-Day Teachers.** Six Lectures. Small crown 8vo, 2s. 6d.

AUBERTIN, J. J.—**A Flight to Mexico.** With Seven full-page Illustrations and a Railway Map of Mexico. Crown 8vo, 7s. 6d.

Six Months in Cape Colony and Natal. With Illustrations and Map. Crown 8vo, 6s.

BADGER, George Percy, D.C.L.—**An English-Arabic Lexicon.** In which the equivalent for English Words and Idiomatic Sentences are rendered into literary and colloquial Arabic. Royal 4to, 80s.

BAGEHOT, Walter.—**The English Constitution.** New and Revised Edition. Crown 8vo, 7s. 6d.

Lombard Street. A Description of the Money Market. Eighth Edition. Crown 8vo, 7s. 6d.

Essays on Parliamentary Reform. Crown 8vo, 5s.

Some Articles on the Depreciation of Silver, and Topics connected with it. Demy 8vo, 5s.

BAGOT, Alan, C.E.—**Accidents in Mines:** their Causes and Prevention. Crown 8vo, 6s.

The Principles of Colliery Ventilation. Second Edition, greatly enlarged. Crown 8vo, 5s.

The Principles of Civil Engineering as applied to Agriculture and Estate Management. Crown 8vo, 7s. 6d.

BAKER, Sir Sherston, Bart.—**The Laws relating to Quarantine.** Crown 8vo, 12s. 6d.

BAKER, Thomas.—**A Battling Life;** chiefly in the Civil Service. An Autobiography, with Fugitive Papers on Subjects of Public Importance. Crown 8vo, 7s. 6d.

BALDWIN, Capt. J. H.—**The Large and Small Game of Bengal and the North-Western Provinces of India.** With 20 Illustrations. New and Cheaper Edition. Small 4to, 10s. 6d.

BALLIN, Ada S. and F. L.—**A Hebrew Grammar.** With Exercises selected from the Bible. Crown 8vo, 7s. 6d.

BARCLAY, Edgar.—**Mountain Life in Algeria.** With numerous Illustrations by Photogravure. Crown 4to, 16s.

BARLOW, James W.—**The Ultimatum of Pessimism.** An Ethical Study. Demy 8vo, 6s.

Short History of the Normans in South Europe. Demy 8vo, 7s. 6d.

BAUR, Ferdinand, Dr. Ph.—**A Philological Introduction to Greek and Latin for Students.** Translated and adapted from the German, by C. KEGAN PAUL, M.A., and E. D. STONE, M.A. Third Edition. Crown 8vo, 6s.

BAYLY, Capt. George.—**Sea Life Sixty Years Ago.** A Record of Adventures which led up to the Discovery of the Relics of the long-missing Expedition commanded by the Comte de la Perouse. Crown 8vo, 3s. 6d.

BELLASIS, Edward.—**The Money Jar of Plautus at the Oratory School.** An Account of the Recent Representation. With Appendix and 16 Illustrations. Small 4to, sewed, 2s.

The New Terence at Edgbaston. Being Notices of the Performances in 1880 and 1881. With Preface, Notes, and Appendix. Third Issue. Small 4to, 1s. 6d.

BENN, Alfred W.—**The Greek Philosophers.** 2 vols. Demy 8vo, 28s.

Bible Folk-Lore. A Study in Comparative Mythology. Crown 8vo, 10s. 6d.

BIRD, Charles, F.G.S.—**Higher Education in Germany and England.** Being a brief Practical Account of the Organization and Curriculum of the German Higher Schools. With critical Remarks and Suggestions with reference to those of England. Small crown 8vo, 2s. 6d.

BLECKLY, Henry.—**Socrates and the Athenians :** An Apology. Crown 8vo, 2s. 6d.

BLOOMFIELD, The Lady.—**Reminiscences of Court and Diplomatic Life.** New and Cheaper Edition. With Frontispiece. Crown 8vo, 6s.

BLUNT, The Ven. Archdeacon.—**The Divine Patriot, and other Sermons.** Preached in Scarborough and in Cannes. New and Cheaper Edition. Crown 8vo, 4s. 6d.

BLUNT, Wilfrid S.—**The Future of Islam.** Crown 8vo, 6s.

Ideas about India. Crown 8vo. Cloth, 6s.

BODDY, Alexander A.—**To Kairwân the Holy.** Scenes in Muhammedan Africa. With Route Map, and Eight Illustrations by A. F. JACASSEY. Crown 8vo, 6s.

BOSANQUET, Bernard.—**Knowledge and Reality.** A Criticism of Mr. F. H. Bradley's " Principles of Logic." Crown 8vo, 9s.

BOUVERIE-PUSEY, S. E. B.—**Permanence and Evolution.** An Inquiry into the Supposed Mutability of Animal Types. Crown 8vo, 5s.

BOWEN, H. C., M.A.—**Studies in English.** For the use of Modern Schools. Eighth Thousand. Small crown 8vo, 1s. 6d.

English Grammar for Beginners. Fcap. 8vo, 1s.

Simple English Poems. English Literature for Junior Classes. In four parts. Parts I., II., and III., 6d. each. Part IV., 1s. Complete, 3s.

BRADLEY, F. H.—The Principles of Logic. Demy 8vo, 16s.

BRIDGETT, Rev. T. E.—History of the Holy Eucharist in Great Britain. 2 vols. Demy 8vo, 18s.

BROOKE, Rev. S. A.—Life and Letters of the Late Rev. F. W. Robertson, M.A. Edited by.

   I. Uniform with Robertson's Sermons. 2 vols. With Steel Portrait. 7s. 6d.

   II. Library Edition. With Portrait. 8vo, 12s.

   III. A Popular Edition. In 1 vol., 8vo, 6s.

The Fight of Faith. Sermons preached on various occasions. Fifth Edition. Crown 8vo, 7s. 6d.

The Spirit of the Christian Life. Third Edition. Crown 8vo, 5s.

Theology in the English Poets.—Cowper, Coleridge, Wordsworth, and Burns. Fifth Edition. Post 8vo, 5s.

Christ in Modern Life. Sixteenth Edition. Crown 8vo, 5s.

Sermons. First Series. Thirteenth Edition. Crown 8vo, 5s.

Sermons. Second Series. Sixth Edition. Crown 8vo, 5s.

BROWN, Rev. J. Baldwin, B.A.—The Higher Life. Its Reality, Experience, and Destiny. Sixth Edition. Crown 8vo, 5s.

Doctrine of Annihilation in the Light of the Gospel of Love. Five Discourses. Fourth Edition. Crown 8vo, 2s. 6d.

The Christian Policy of Life. A Book for Young Men of Business. Third Edition. Crown 8vo, 3s. 6d.

BROWN, Horatio F.—Life on the Lagoons. With two Illustrations and Map. Crown 8vo, 6s.

BROWNE, H. L.—Reason and Religious Belief. Crown 8vo, 3s. 6d.

BURDETT, Henry C.—Help in Sickness—Where to Go and What to Do. Crown 8vo, 1s. 6d.

Helps to Health. The Habitation—The Nursery—The School-room and—The Person. With a Chapter on Pleasure and Health Resorts. Crown 8vo, 1s. 6d.

BURKE, The Late Very Rev. T. N.—His Life. By W. J. Fitz-patrick. 2 vols. With Portrait. Demy 8vo, 30s.

BURTON, Mrs. Richard.—The Inner Life of Syria, Palestine, and the Holy Land. Post 8vo, 6s.

CAPES, J. M.—The Church of the Apostles: an Historical Inquiry. Demy 8vo, 9s.

Carlyle and the Open Secret of His Life. By Henry Larkin. Demy 8vo, 14s.

CARPENTER, W. B., LL.D., M.D., F.R.S., etc.—The Principles of Mental Physiology. With their Applications to the Training and Discipline of the Mind, and the Study of its Morbid Conditions. Illustrated. Sixth Edition. 8vo, 12*s.*

Catholic Dictionary. Containing some Account of the Doctrine, Discipline, Rites, Ceremonies, Councils, and Religious Orders of the Catholic Church. By WILLIAM E. ADDIS and THOMAS ARNOLD, M.A. Third Edition. Demy 8vo, 21*s.*

CHEYNE, Rev. T. K.—The Prophecies of Isaiah. Translated with Critical Notes and Dissertations. 2 vols. Third Edition. Demy 8vo, 25*s.*

Circulating Capital. Being an Inquiry into the Fundamental Laws of Money. An Essay by an East India Merchant. Small crown 8vo, 6*s.*

CLAIRAUT.—Elements of Geometry. Translated by Dr. KAINES. With 145 Figures. Crown 8vo, 4*s.* 6*d.*

CLAPPERTON, Jane Hume.—Scientific Meliorism and the Evolution of Happiness. Large crown 8vo, 8*s.* 6*d.*

CLARKE, Rev. Henry James, A.K.C.—The Fundamental Science. Demy 8vo, 10*s.* 6*d.*

CLAYDEN, P. W.—Samuel Sharpe. Egyptologist and Translator of the Bible. Crown 8vo, 6*s.*

CLIFFORD, Samuel.—What Think Ye of the Christ? Crown 8vo, 6*s.*

CLODD, Edward, F.R.A.S.—The Childhood of the World: a Simple Account of Man in Early Times. Seventh Edition. Crown 8vo, 3*s.*
  A Special Edition for Schools. 1*s.*

The Childhood of Religions. Including a Simple Account of the Birth and Growth of Myths and Legends. Eighth Thousand. Crown 8vo, 5*s.*
  A Special Edition for Schools. 1*s.* 6*d.*

Jesus of Nazareth. With a brief sketch of Jewish History to the Time of His Birth. Small crown 8vo, 6*s.*

COGHLAN, J. Cole, D.D.—The Modern Pharisee and other Sermons. Edited by the Very Rev. H. H. DICKINSON, D.D., Dean of Chapel Royal, Dublin. New and Cheaper Edition. Crown 8vo, 7*s.* 6*d.*

COLE, George R. Fitz-Roy.—The Peruvians at Home. Crown 8vo, 6*s.*

COLERIDGE, Sara.—Memoir and Letters of Sara Coleridge. Edited by her Daughter. With Index. Cheap Edition. With Portrait. 7*s.* 6*d.*

Collects Exemplified. Being Illustrations from the Old and New Testaments of the Collects for the Sundays after Trinity. By the Author of "A Commentary on the Epistles and Gospels." Edited by the Rev. JOSEPH JACKSON. Crown 8vo, 5*s.*

CONNELL, A. K.—**Discontent and Danger in India.** Small crown 8vo, 3*s.* 6*d.*

The Economic Revolution of India. Crown 8vo, 4*s.* 6*d.*

COOK, Keningale, LL.D.—**The Fathers of Jesus.** A Study of the Lineage of the Christian Doctrine and Traditions. 2 vols. Demy 8vo, 28*s.*

CORY, William.—**A Guide to Modern English History.** Part I.—MDCCCXV.-MDCCCXXX. Demy 8vo, 9*s.* Part II.—MDCCCXXX.-MDCCCXXXV., 15*s.*

COTTERILL, H. B.—**An Introduction to the Study of Poetry.** Crown 8vo, 7*s.* 6*d.*

COTTON, H. J. S.—**New India, or India in Transition.** Third Edition. Crown 8vo, 4*s.* 6*d.*

COUTTS, Francis Burdett Money.—**The Training of the Instinct of Love.** With a Preface by the Rev. EDWARD THRING, M.A. Small crown 8vo, 2*s.* 6*d.*

COX, Rev. Sir George W., M.A., Bart.—**The Mythology of the Aryan Nations.** New Edition. Demy 8vo, 16*s.*

Tales of Ancient Greece. New Edition. Small crown 8vo, 6*s.*

A Manual of Mythology in the form of Question and Answer. New Edition. Fcap. 8vo, 3*s.*

An Introduction to the Science of Comparative Mythology and Folk-Lore. Second Edition. Crown 8vo. 7*s.* 6*d.*

COX, Rev. Sir G. W., M.A., Bart., and JONES, Eustace Hinton.—**Popular Romances of the Middle Ages.** Third Edition, in 1 vol. Crown 8vo, 6*s.*

COX, Rev. Samuel, D.D.—**A Commentary on the Book of Job.** With a Translation. Second Edition. Demy 8vo. 15*s.*

Salvator Mundi; or, 'Is Christ the Saviour of all Men? Tenth Edition. Crown 8vo, 5*s.*

The Larger Hope. A Sequel to "Salvator Mundi." Second Edition. 16mo, 1*s.*

The Genesis of Evil, and other Sermons, mainly expository. Third Edition. Crown 8vo, 6*s.*

Balaam. An Exposition and a Study. Crown 8vo, 5*s.*

Miracles. An Argument and a Challenge. Crown 8vo, 2*s.* 6*d.*

CRAVEN, Mrs.—**A Year's Meditations.** Crown 8vo, 6*s.*

CRAWFURD, Oswald.—**Portugal, Old and New.** With Illustrations and Maps. New and Cheaper Edition. Crown 8vo, 6*s.*

CROZIER, John Beattie, M.B.—**The Religion of the Future.** Crown 8vo, 6*s.*

CUNNINGHAM, W., B.D.—**Politics and Economics :** An Essay on the Nature of the Principles of Political Economy, together with a survey of Recent Legislation. Crown 8vo, 5*s.*

DANIELL, Clarmont.—**The Gold Treasure of India.** An Inquiry into its Amount, the Cause of its Accumulation, and the Proper Means of using it as Money. Crown 8vo, 5*s.*

Discarded Silver : a Plan for its Use as Money. Small crown, 8vo, 2*s.*

DANIEL, Gerard. **Mary Stuart : a Sketch and a Defence.** Crown 8vo, 5*s.*

DAVIDSON, Rev. Samuel, D.D., LL.D.—**Canon of the Bible :** Its Formation, History, and Fluctuations. Third and Revised Edition. Small crown 8vo, 5*s.*

The Doctrine of Last Things contained in the New Testament compared with the Notions of the Jews and the Statements of Church Creeds. Small crown 8vo, 3*s.* 6*d.*

DAWSON, Geo., M.A. **Prayers, with a Discourse on Prayer.** Edited by his Wife. First Series. Ninth Edition. Crown 8vo, 3*s.* 6*d.*

Prayers, with a Discourse on Prayer. Edited by GEORGE ST. CLAIR. Second Series. Crown 8vo, 6*s.*

Sermons on Disputed Points and Special Occasions. Edited by his Wife. Fourth Edition. Crown 8vo, 6*s.*

Sermons on Daily Life and Duty. Edited by his Wife. Fourth Edition. Crown 8vo, 6*s.*

The Authentic Gospel, and other Sermons. Edited by GEORGE ST. CLAIR, F.G.S. Third Edition. Crown 8vo, 6*s.*

Biographical Lectures. Edited by GEORGE ST. CLAIR, F.G.S. Large crown, 8vo, 7*s.* 6*d.*

DE JONCOURT, Madame Marie.—**Wholesome Cookery.** Third Edition. Crown 8vo, 3*s.* 6*d.*

Democracy in the Old World and the New. By the Author of " The Suez Canal, the Eastern Question, and Abyssinia," etc. Small crown 8vo, 2*s.* 6*d.*

DENT, H. C.—**A Year in Brazil.** With Notes on Religion, Meteorology, Natural History, etc. Maps and Illustrations. Demy 8vo, 18*s.*

Discourse on the Shedding of Blood, and The Laws of War. Demy 8vo, 2*s.* 6*d.*

DOUGLAS, Rev. Herman.—Into the Deep ; or, The Wonders of the Lord's Person. Crown 8vo, 2s. 6d.

DOWDEN, Edward, LL.D.—Shakspere : a Critical Study of his Mind and Art. Eighth Edition. Post 8vo, 12s.

Studies in Literature, 1789-1877. Third Edition. Large post 8vo, 6s.

Dulce Domum. Fcap. 8vo, 5s.

DU MONCEL, Count.—The Telephone, the Microphone, and the Phonograph. With 74 Illustrations. Third Edition. Small crown 8vo, 5s.

DURUY, Victor.—History of Rome and the Roman People. Edited by Prof. MAHAFFY. With nearly 3000 Illustrations. 4to. 6 vols. in 12 parts, 30s. each vol.

EDGEWORTH, F. Y.—Mathematical Psychics. An Essay on the Application of Mathematics to Social Science. Demy 8vo, 7s. 6d.

Educational Code of the Prussian Nation, in its Present Form. In accordance with the Decisions of the Common Provincial Law, and with those of Recent Legislation. Crown 8vo, 2s. 6d.

Education Library. Edited by PHILIP MAGNUS :—

An Introduction to the History of Educational Theories. By OSCAR BROWNING, M.A. Second Edition. 3s. 6d.

Old Greek Education. By the Rev. Prof. MAHAFFY, M.A. Second Edition. 3s. 6d.

School Management. Including a general view of the work of Education, Organization and Discipline. By JOSEPH LANDON. Fifth Edition. 6s.

EDWARDES, Major-General Sir Herbert B.—Memorials of his Life and Letters. By his Wife. With Portrait and Illustrations. 2 vols. Demy 8vo. 36s.

ELSDALE, Henry.—Studies in Tennyson's Idylls. Crown 8vo, 5s.

Emerson's (Ralph Waldo) Life. By OLIVER WENDELL HOLMES. English Copyright Edition. With Portrait. Crown 8vo, 6s.

Enoch the Prophet. The Book of. Archbishop LAURENCE'S Translation, with an Introduction by the Author of "The Evolution of Christianity." Crown 8vo, 5s.

Eranus. A Collection of Exercises in the Alcaic and Sapphic Metres. Edited by F. W. CORNISH, Assistant Master at Eton. Second Edition. Crown 8vo, 2s.

EVANS, Mark.—The Story of Our Father's Love, told to Children. Sixth and Cheaper Edition. With Four Illustrations. Fcap. 8vo, 1s. 6d.

"Fan Kwae" at Canton before Treaty Days 1825–1844.
By an old Resident. With Frontispiece. Crown 8vo, 5s.

Faith of the Unlearned, The. Authority, apart from the Sanction
of Reason, an Insufficient Basis for It. By "One Unlearned."
Crown 8vo, 6s.

FEIS, Jacob.—**Shakspere and Montaigne.** An Endeavour to
Explain the Tendency of Hamlet from Allusions in Contemporary
Works. Crown 8vo, 5s.

FLOREDICE, W. H.—**A Month among the Mere Irish.** Small
crown 8vo. Second Edition. 3s. 6d.

Frank Leward. Edited by CHARLES BAMPTON. Crown 8vo, 7s. 6d.

FULLER, Rev. Morris.—**The Lord's Day ; or, Christian Sunday.**
Its Unity, History, Philosophy, and Perpetual Obligation.
Sermons. Demy 8vo, 10s. 6d.

GARDINER, Samuel R., and J. BASS MULLINGER, M.A.—
Introduction to the Study of English History. Second
Edition. Large crown 8vo, 9s.

GARDNER, Dorsey.—**Quatre Bras, Ligny, and Waterloo.** A
Narrative of the Campaign in Belgium, 1815. With Maps and
Plans. Demy 8vo, 16s.

GELDART, E. M.—**Echoes of Truth.** Sermons, with a Short
Selection of Prayers and an Introductory Sketch, by the Rev.
C. B. UPTON. Crown 8vo, 6s.

Genesis in Advance of Present Science. A Critical Investigation
of Chapters I.–IX. By a Septuagenarian Beneficed Presbyter.
Demy 8vo. 10s. 6d.

GEORGE, Henry.—**Progress and Poverty :** An Inquiry into the
Causes of Industrial Depressions, and of Increase of Want with
Increase of Wealth. The Remedy. Fifth Library Edition.
Post 8vo, 7s. 6d. Cabinet Edition. Crown 8vo, 2s. 6d. Also a
Cheap Edition. Limp cloth, 1s. 6d. Paper covers, 1s.

    Protection, or Free Trade. An Examination of the Tariff
Question, with especial regard to the Interests of Labour. Crown
8vo, 5s.

    Social Problems. Fourth Thousand. Crown 8vo, 5s. Cheap
Edition. Paper covers, 1s.

GLANVILL, Joseph.—**Scepsis Scientifica ;** or, Confest Ignorance,
the Way to Science ; in an Essay of the Vanity of Dogmatizing
and Confident Opinion. Edited, with Introductory Essay, by
JOHN OWEN. Elzevir 8vo, printed on hand-made paper, 6s.

Glossary of Terms and Phrases. Edited by the Rev. H. PERCY
SMITH and others. Second and Cheaper Edition. Medium
8vo, 7s. 6d.

GLOVER, F., M.A.—**Exempla Latina.** A First Construing Book, with Short Notes, Lexicon, and an Introduction to the Analysis of Sentences. Second Edition. Fcap. 8vo, 2*s.*

GOLDSMID, Sir Francis Henry, Bart., Q.C., M.P.—**Memoir of.** With Portrait. Second Edition, Revised. Crown 8vo, 6*s.*

GOODENOUGH, Commodore J. G.—**Memoir of,** with Extracts from his Letters and Journals. Edited by his Widow. With Steel Engraved Portrait. Third Edition. Crown 8vo, 5*s.*

GORDON, Major-Genl. C. G.—**His Journals at Kartoum.** Printed from the original MS. With Introduction and Notes by A. EGMONT HAKE. Portrait, 2 Maps, and 30 Illustrations. Two vols., demy 8vo, 21*s.* Also a Cheap Edition in 1 vol., 6*s.*

Gordon's (General) Last Journal. A Facsimile of the last Journal received in England from GENERAL GORDON. Reproduced by Photo-lithography. Imperial 4to, £3 3*s.*

Events in his Life. From the Day of his Birth to the Day of his Death. By Sir H. W. GORDON. With Maps and Illustrations. Demy 8vo, 18*s.*

GOSSE, Edmund.—**Seventeenth Century Studies.** A Contribution to the History of English Poetry. Demy 8vo, 10*s.* 6*d.*

GOULD, Rev. S. Baring, M.A.—**Germany, Present and Past.** New and Cheaper Edition. Large crown 8vo, 7*s.* 6*d.*

GOWAN, Major Walter E.—**A. Ivanoff's Russian Grammar.** (16th Edition.) Translated, enlarged, and arranged for use of Students of the Russian Language. Demy 8vo, 6*s.*

GOWER, Lord Ronald. **My Reminiscences.** MINIATURE EDITION, printed on hand-made paper, limp parchment antique, 10*s.* 6*d.*

Last Days of Mary Antoinette. An Historical Sketch. With Portrait and Facsimiles. Fcap. 4to, 10*s.* 6*d.*

Notes of a Tour from Brindisi to Yokohama, 1883–1884. Fcap. 8vo, 2*s.* 6*d.*

GRAHAM, William, M.A.—**The Creed of Science,** Religious, Moral, and Social. Second Edition, Revised. Crown 8vo, 6*s.*

The Social Problem, in its Economic, Moral, and Political Aspects. Demy 8vo, 14*s.*

GREY, Rowland.—**In Sunny Switzerland.** A Tale of Six Weeks. Second Edition. Small crown 8vo, 5*s.*

Lindenblumen and other Stories. Small crown 8vo, 5*s.*

GRIMLEY, Rev. H. N., M.A.—**Tremadoc Sermons, chiefly on the Spiritual Body, the Unseen World, and the Divine Humanity.** Fourth Edition. Crown 8vo, 6*s.*

GUSTAFSON, Alex.—**The Foundation of Death.** Third Edition. Crown 8vo, 5*s.*

GUSTAFSON, Alex.—continued.

Some Thoughts on Moderation. Reprinted from a Paper read at the Reeve Mission Room, Manchester Square, June 8, 1885. Crown 8vo, 1s.

HADDON, Caroline.—**The Larger Life, Studies in Hinton's Ethics.** Crown 8vo, 5s.

HAECKEL, Prof. Ernst.—**The History of Creation.** Translation revised by Professor E. RAY LANKESTER, M.A., F.R.S. With Coloured Plates and Genealogical Trees of the various groups of both Plants and Animals. 2 vols. Third Edition. Post 8vo, 32s.

The History of the Evolution of Man. With numerous Illustrations. 2 vols. Post 8vo, 32s.

A Visit to Ceylon. Post 8vo, 7s. 6d.

Freedom in Science and Teaching. With a Prefatory Note by T. H. HUXLEY, F.R.S. Crown 8vo, 5s.

HALF-CROWN SERIES :—

A Lost Love. By ANNA C. OGLE [Ashford Owen].

Sister Dora : a Biography. By MARGARET LONSDALE.

True Words for Brave Men : a Book for Soldiers and Sailors. By the late CHARLES KINGSLEY.

Notes of Travel : being Extracts from the Journals of Count VON MOLTKE.

English Sonnets. Collected and Arranged by J. DENNIS.

Home Songs for Quiet Hours. By the Rev. Canon R. H. BAYNES.

Hamilton, Memoirs of Arthur, B.A., of Trinity College, Cambridge. Crown 8vo, 6s.

HARRIS, William.—**The History of the Radical Party in Parliament.** Demy 8vo, 15s.

HARROP, Robert.—**Bolingbroke.** A Political Study and Criticism. Demy 8vo, 14s.

HART, Rev. J. W. T.—**The Autobiography of Judas Iscariot.** A Character Study. Crown 8vo, 3s. 6d.

HAWEIS, Rev. H. R., M.A.—**Current Coin.** Materialism—The Devil—Crime—Drunkenness—Pauperism—Emotion—Recreation—The Sabbath. Fifth Edition. Crown 8vo, 5s.

Arrows in the Air. Fifth Edition. Crown 8vo, 5s.

Speech in Season. Fifth Edition. Crown 8vo, 5s.

Thoughts for the Times. Thirteenth Edition. Crown 8vo, 5s.

Unsectarian Family Prayers. New Edition. Fcap. 8vo, 1s. 6d.

HAWKINS, Edwards Comerford.—**Spirit and Form.** Sermons preached in the Parish Church of Leatherhead. Crown 8vo, 6*s.*

HAWTHORNE, Nathaniel.—**Works.** Complete in Twelve Volumes. Large post 8vo, 7*s.* 6*d.* each volume.

VOL. I. TWICE-TOLD TALES.
II. MOSSES FROM AN OLD MANSE.
III. THE HOUSE OF THE SEVEN GABLES, AND THE SNOW IMAGE.
IV. THE WONDERBOOK, TANGLEWOOD TALES, AND GRAND-FATHER'S CHAIR.
V. THE SCARLET LETTER, AND THE BLITHEDALE ROMANCE.
VI. THE MARBLE FAUN. [Transformation.]
VII.
VIII. } OUR OLD HOME, AND ENGLISH NOTE-BOOKS.
IX. AMERICAN NOTE-BOOKS.
X. FRENCH AND ITALIAN NOTE-BOOKS.
XI. SEPTIMIUS FELTON, THE DOLLIVER ROMANCE, FANSHAWE, AND, IN AN APPENDIX, THE ANCESTRAL FOOTSTEP.
XII. TALES AND ESSAYS, AND OTHER PAPERS, WITH A BIO-GRAPHICAL SKETCH OF HAWTHORNE.

HEATH, Francis George.—**Autumnal Leaves.** Third and cheaper Edition. Large crown 8vo, 6*s.*

Sylvan Winter. With 70 Illustrations. Large crown 8vo, 14*s.*

HENNESSY, Sir John Pope.—**Ralegh in Ireland.** With his Letters on Irish Affairs and some Contemporary Documents. Large crown 8vo, printed on hand-made paper, parchment, 10*s.* 6*d.*

HENRY, Philip.—**Diaries and Letters of.** Edited by MATTHEW HENRY LEE, M.A. Large crown 8vo, 7*s.* 6*d.*

HINTON, J.—**Life and Letters.** With an Introduction by Sir W. W. GULL, Bart., and Portrait engraved on Steel by C. H. Jeens. Fifth Edition. Crown 8vo, 8*s.* 6*d.*

Philosophy and Religion. Selections from the Manuscripts of the late James Hinton. Edited by CAROLINE HADDON. Second Edition. Crown 8vo, 5*s.*

The Law Breaker, and The Coming of the Law. Edited by MARGARET HINTON. Crown 8vo, 6*s.*

The Mystery of Pain. New Edition. Fcap. 8vo, 1*s.*

Hodson of Hodson's Horse ; or, Twelve Years of a Soldier's Life in India. Being extracts from the Letters of the late Major W. S. R. Hodson. With a Vindication from the Attack of Mr. Bosworth Smith. Edited by his brother, G. H. HODSON, M.A. Fourth Edition. Large crown 8vo, 5*s.*

HOLTHAM, E. G.—**Eight Years in Japan, 1873-1881.** Work, Travel, and Recreation. With three Maps. Large crown 8vo, 9*s.*

Homology of Economic Justice. An Essay by an East India Merchant. Small crown 8vo, 5s.

HOOPER, Mary.—**Little Dinners: How to Serve them with Elegance and Economy.** Twentieth Edition. Crown 8vo, 2s. 6d.

Cookery for Invalids, Persons of Delicate Digestion, and Children. Fifth Edition. Crown 8vo, 2s. 6d.

Every-Day Meals. Being Economical and Wholesome Recipes for Breakfast, Luncheon, and Supper. Sixth Edition. Crown 8vo, 2s. 6d.

HOPKINS, Ellice.—**Work amongst Working Men.** Sixth Edition. Crown 8vo, 3s. 6d.

HORNADAY, W. T.—**Two Years in a Jungle.** With Illustrations. Demy 8vo, 21s.

HOSPITALIER, E.—**The Modern Applications of Electricity.** Translated and Enlarged by JULIUS MAIER, Ph.D. 2 vols. Second Edition, Revised, with many additions and numerous Illustrations. Demy 8vo, 12s. 6d. each volume.

VOL. I.—Electric Generators, Electric Light.
VOL. II.—Telephone : Various Applications : Electrical Transmission of Energy.

HOWARD, Robert, M.A.—**The Church of England and other Religious Communions.** A course of Lectures delivered in the Parish Church of Clapham. Crown 8vo, 7s. 6d.

HUMPHREY, Rev. William.—**The Bible and Belief.** A Letter to a Friend. Small Crown 8vo, 2s. 6d.

HUNTER, William C.—**Bits of Old China.** Small crown 8vo, 6s.

HUNTINGFORD, Rev. E., D.C.L.—**The Apocalypse.** With a Commentary and Introductory Essay. Demy 8vo, 5s.

HUTCHINSON, H.—**Thought Symbolism, and Grammatic Illusions.** Being a Treatise on the Nature, Purpose, and Material of Speech. Crown 8vo, 2s. 6d.

HUTTON, Rev. C. F.—**Unconscious Testimony ;** or, The Silent Witness of the Hebrew to the Truth of the Historical Scriptures. Crown 8vo, 2s. 6d.

HYNDMAN, H. M.—**The Historical Basis of Socialism in England.** Large crown 8vo, 8s. 6d.

IDDESLEIGH, Earl of.—**The Pleasures, Dangers, and Uses of Desultory Reading.** Fcap. 8vo, in Whatman paper cover, 1s.

IM THURN, Everard F.—**Among the Indians of Guiana.** Being Sketches, chiefly anthropologic, from the Interior of British Guiana. With 53 Illustrations and a Map. Demy 8vo, 18s.

JACCOUD, Prof. S.—**The Curability and Treatment of Pulmonary Phthisis.** Translated and edited by MONTAGU LUBBOCK, M.D. Demy 8vo, 15s.

Jaunt in a Junk : A Ten Days' Cruise in Indian Seas. Large crown 8vo, 7s. 6d.

JENKINS, E., and RAYMOND, J.—**The Architect's Legal Handbook.** Third Edition, revised. Crown 8vo, 6s.

JENKINS, Rev. Canon R. C.—**Heraldry : English and Foreign.** With a Dictionary of Heraldic Terms and 156 Illustrations. Small crown 8vo, 3s. 6d.

JERVIS, Rev. W. Henley.—**The Gallican Church and the Revolution.** A Sequel to the History of the Church of France, from the Concordat of Bologna to the Revolution. Demy 8vo, 18s.

JOEL, L.—**A Consul's Manual and Shipowner's and Shipmaster's Practical Guide in their Transactions Abroad.** With Definitions of Nautical, Mercantile, and Legal Terms ; a Glossary of Mercantile Terms in English, French, German, Italian, and Spanish ; Tables of the Money, Weights, and Measures of the Principal Commercial Nations and their Equivalents in British Standards ; and Forms of Consular and Notarial Acts. Demy 8vo, 12s.

JOHNSTON, H. H., F.Z.S.—**The Kilima-njaro Expedition.** A Record of Scientific Exploration in Eastern Equatorial Africa, and a General Description of the Natural History, Languages, and Commerce of the Kilima-njaro District. With 6 Maps, and over 80 Illustrations by the Author. Demy 8vo, 21s.

JOYCE, P. W., LL.D., etc.—**Old Celtic Romances.** Translated from the Gaelic. Crown 8vo, 7s. 6d.

KAUFMANN, Rev. M., B.A.—**Socialism :** its Nature, its Dangers, and its Remedies considered. Crown 8vo, 7s. 6d.

Utopias ; or, Schemes of Social Improvement, from Sir Thomas More to Karl Marx. Crown 8vo, 5s.

KAY, David, F.R.G.S.—**Education and Educators.** Crown 8vo, 7s. 6d.

KAY, Joseph.—**Free Trade in Land.** Edited by his Widow. With Preface by the Right Hon. JOHN BRIGHT, M.P. Seventh Edition. Crown 8vo, 5s.

*** Also a cheaper edition, without the Appendix, but with a Revise of Recent Changes in the Land Laws of England, by the RIGHT HON. G. OSBORNE MORGAN, Q.C., M.P. Cloth, 1s. 6d. Paper covers, 1s.

KELKE, W. H. H.—**An Epitome of English Grammar for the Use of Students.** Adapted to the London Matriculation Course and Similar Examinations. Crown 8vo, 4s. 6d.

KEMPIS, Thomas à.—**Of the Imitation of Christ.** Parchment Library Edition.—Parchment or cloth, 6*s.* ; vellum, 7*s.* 6*d.* The Red Line Edition, fcap. 8vo, red edges, 2*s.* 6*d.* The Cabinet Edition, small 8vo, cloth limp, 1*s.* ; cloth boards, red edges, 1*s.* 6*d.* The Miniature Edition, red edges, 32mo, 1*s.*

   *** All the above Editions may be had in various extra bindings.

KETTLEWELL, Rev. S.—**Thomas à Kempis and the Brothers of Common Life.** With Portrait. Crown 8vo, 7*s.* 6*d.*

KIDD, Joseph, M.D.—**The Laws of Therapeutics ;** or, the Science and Art of Medicine. Second Edition. Crown 8vo, 6*s.*

KINGSFORD, Anna, M.D.—**The Perfect Way in Diet.** A Treatise advocating a Return to the Natural and Ancient Food of our Race. Second Edition. Small crown 8vo, 2*s.*

KINGSLEY, Charles, M.A.—**Letters and Memories of his Life.** Edited by his Wife. With two Steel Engraved Portraits, and Vignettes on Wood. Fifteenth Cabinet Edition. 2 vols. Crown 8vo, 12*s.*

   *** Also a People's Edition, in one volume. With Portrait. Crown 8vo, 6*s.*

All Saints' Day, and other Sermons. Edited by the Rev. W. HARRISON. Third Edition. Crown 8vo, 7*s.* 6*d.*

True Words for Brave Men. A Book for Soldiers' and Sailors' Libraries. Eleventh Edition. Crown 8vo, 2*s.* 6*d.*

KNOX, Alexander A.—**The New Playground ;** or, Wanderings in Algeria. New and Cheaper Edition. Large crown 8vo, 6*s.*

Land Concentration and Irresponsibility of Political Power, as causing the Anomaly of a Widespread State of Want by the Side of the Vast Supplies of Nature. Crown 8vo, 5*s.*

LANDON, Joseph.—**School Management ;** Including a General View of the Work of Education, Organization, and Discipline. Fifth Edition. Crown 8vo, 6*s.*

LEE, Rev. F. G., D.C.L.—**The Other World ;** or, Glimpses of the Supernatural. 2 vols. A New Edition. Crown 8vo, 15*s.*

Letters from an Unknown Friend. By the Author of "Charles Lowder." With a Preface by the Rev. W. H. CLEAVER. Fcap. 8vo, 1*s.*

Leward, Frank. Edited by CHARLES BAMPTON. Crown 8vo, 7*s.* 6*d.*

LEWIS, Edward Dillon.—**A Draft Code of Criminal Law and Procedure.** Demy 8vo, 21*s.*

Life of a Prig. By ONE. Third Edition. Fcap. 8vo, 3*s.* 6*d.*

LILLIE, Arthur, M.R.A.S.—**The Popular Life of Buddha.** Containing an Answer to the Hibbert Lectures of 1881. With Illustrations. Crown 8vo, 6*s.*

LLOYD, Walter.—The Hope of the World : An Essay on Universal Redemption. Crown 8vo, 5*s.*

LONGFELLOW, H. Wadsworth.—Life. By his Brother, SAMUEL LONGFELLOW. With Portraits and Illustrations. 2 vols. Demy 8vo, 28*s.*

LONSDALE, Margaret.—Sister Dora : a Biography. With Portrait. Cheap Edition. Small crown 8vo, 2*s.* 6*d.*

George Eliot: Thoughts upon her Life, her Books, and Herself. Second Edition. Small crown 8vo, 1*s.* 6*d.*

LOUNSBURY, Thomas R.—James Fenimore Cooper. With Portrait. Crown 8vo, 5*s.*

LOWDER, Charles.—A Biography. By the Author of " St. Teresa." New and Cheaper Edition. Crown 8vo. With Portrait. 3*s.* 6*d.*

LÜCKES, Eva C. E.—Lectures on General Nursing, delivered to the Probationers of the London Hospital Training School for Nurses. Crown 8vo, 2*s.* 6*d.*

LYALL, William Rowe, D.D.—Propædeia Prophetica ; or, The Use and Design of the Old Testament Examined. New Edition. With Notices by GEORGE C. PEARSON, M.A., Hon. Canon of Canterbury. Demy 8vo, 10*s.* 6*d.*

LYTTON, Edward Bulwer, Lord.—Life, Letters and Literary Remains. By his Son, the EARL OF LYTTON. With Portraits, Illustrations and Facsimiles. Demy 8vo. Vols. I. and II., 32*s.*

MACAULAY, G. C.—Francis Beaumont : A Critical Study. Crown 8vo, 5*s.*

MAC CALLUM, M. W.—Studies in Low German and High German Literature. Crown 8vo, 6*s.*

MACHIAVELLI, Niccolò. — Life and Times. By Prof. VILLARI. Translated by LINDA VILLARI. 4 vols. Large post 8vo, 48*s.*

MACHIAVELLI, Niccolò.—Discourses on the First Decade of Titus Livius. Translated from the Italian by NINIAN HILL THOMSON, M.A. Large crown 8vo, 12*s.*

The Prince. Translated from the Italian by N. H. T. Small crown 8vo, printed on hand-made paper, bevelled boards, 6*s.*

MACKENZIE, Alexander.—How India is Governed. Being an Account of England's Work in India. Small crown 8vo, 2*s.*

MAGNUS, Mrs.—About the Jews since Bible Times. From the Babylonian Exile till the English Exodus. Small crown 8vo, 6*s.*

MAGUIRE, Thomas.—Lectures on Philosophy. Demy 8vo, 9*s.*

MAIR, R. S., M.D., F.R.C.S.E.—The Medical Guide for Anglo-Indians. Being a Compendium of Advice to Europeans in India, relating to the Preservation and Regulation of Health. With a Supplement on the Management of Children in India. Second Edition. Crown 8vo, limp cloth, 3*s.* 6*d.*

MALDEN, Henry Elliot.—**Vienna, 1683.** The History and Consequences of the Defeat of the Turks before Vienna, September 12th, 1683, by John Sobieski, King of Poland, and Charles Leopold, Duke of Lorraine. Crown 8vo, 4*s*. 6*d*.

Many Voices. A volume of Extracts from the Religious Writers of Christendom from the First to the Sixteenth Century. With Biographical Sketches. Crown 8vo, cloth extra, red edges, 6*s*.

MARKHAM, Capt. Albert Hastings, R.N.—**The Great Frozen Sea :** A Personal Narrative of the Voyage of the *Alert* during the Arctic Expedition of 1875-6. With 6 Full-page Illustrations, 2 Maps, and 27 Woodcuts. Sixth and Cheaper Edition. Crown 8vo, 6*s*.

MARTINEAU, Gertrude.—**Outline Lessons on Morals.** Small crown 8vo, 3*s*. 6*d*.

MAUDSLEY, H., M.D.—**Body and Will.** Being an Essay concerning Will, in its Metaphysical, Physiological, and Pathological Aspects. 8vo, 12*s*.

   Natural Causes and Supernatural Seemings. Crown 8vo, 6*s*.

McGRATH, Terence.—**Pictures from Ireland.** New and Cheaper Edition. Crown 8vo, 2*s*.

MEREDITH, M.A.—**Theotokos, the Example for Woman.** Dedicated, by permission, to Lady Agnes Wood. Revised by the Venerable Archdeacon DENISON. 32mo, limp cloth, 1*s*. 6*d*.

MILLER, Edward.—**The History and Doctrines of Irvingism ;** or, The so-called Catholic and Apostolic Church. 2 vols. Large post 8vo, 25*s*.

   The Church in Relation to the State. Large crown 8vo, 7*s*. 6*d*.

MITCHELL, Lucy M.—**A History of Ancient Sculpture.** With numerous Illustrations, including 6 Plates in Phototype. Super royal 8vo, 42*s*.

MITFORD, Bertram.—**Through the Zulu Country.** Its Battlefields and its People. With Five Illustrations. Demy 8vo, 14*s*.

MOCKLER, E.—**A Grammar of the Baloochee Language,** as it is spoken in Makran (Ancient Gedrosia), in the Persia-Arabic and Roman characters. Fcap. 8vo, 5*s*.

MOLESWORTH, Rev. W. Nassau, M.A.—**History of the Church of England from 1660.** Large crown 8vo, 7*s*. 6*d*.

MORELL, J. R.—**Euclid Simplified in Method and Language.** Being a Manual of Geometry. Compiled from the most important French Works, approved by the University of Paris and the Minister of Public Instruction. Fcap. 8vo, 2*s*. 6*d*.

MORGAN, C. Lloyd.—**The Springs of Conduct.** An Essay in Evolution. Large crown 8vo, cloth, 7*s*. 6*d*.

MORRIS, *George.*—**The Duality of all Divine Truth in our Lord Jesus Christ.** For God's Self-manifestation in the Impartation of the Divine Nature to Man. Large crown 8vo, 7s. 6d.

MORSE, *E. S., Ph.D.*—**First Book of Zoology.** With numerous Illustrations. New and Cheaper Edition. Crown 8vo, 2s. 6d.

NELSON, *J. H., M.A.*—**A Prospectus of the Scientific Study of the Hindû Law.** Demy 8vo, 9s.

NEWMAN, *Cardinal.*—**Characteristics from the Writings of.** Being Selections from his various Works. Arranged with the Author's personal Approval. Seventh Edition. With Portrait. Crown 8vo, 6s.

⁎ A Portrait of Cardinal Newman, mounted for framing, can be had, 2s. 6d.

NEWMAN, *Francis William.*—**Essays on Diet.** Small crown 8vo, cloth limp, 2s.

New Truth and the Old Faith: Are they Incompatible? By a Scientific Layman. Demy 8vo, 10s. 6d.

New Social Teachings. By POLITICUS. Small crown 8vo, 5s.

NICOLS, *Arthur, F.G.S., F.R.G.S.*—**Chapters from the Physical History of the Earth:** an Introduction to Geology and Palæontology. With numerous Illustrations. Crown 8vo, 5s.

NOEL, *The Hon. Roden.*—**Essays on Poetry and Poets.** Demy 8vo, 12s.

NOPS, *Marianne.*—**Class Lessons on Euclid.** Part I. containing the First Two Books of the Elements. Crown 8vo, 2s. 6d.

Nuces: EXERCISES ON THE SYNTAX OF THE PUBLIC SCHOOL LATIN PRIMER. New Edition in Three Parts. Crown 8vo, each 1s.

⁎ The Three Parts can also be had bound together, 3s.

OATES, *Frank, F.R.G.S.*—**Matabele Land and the Victoria Falls.** A Naturalist's Wanderings in the Interior of South Africa. Edited by C. G. OATES, B.A. With numerous Illustrations and 4 Maps. Demy 8vo, 21s.

O'CONNOR, *T. P., M.P.*—**The Parnell Movement.** With a Sketch of Irish Parties from 1843. Large crown 8vo, 7s. 6d.

OGLE, *W., M.D., F.R.C.P.*—**Aristotle on the Parts of Animals.** Translated, with Introduction and Notes. Royal 8vo, 12s. 6d.

O'HAGAN, *Lord, K.P.* — **Occasional Papers and Addresses.** Large crown 8vo, 7s. 6d.

O'MEARA, *Kathleen.*—**Frederic Ozanam,** Professor of the Sorbonne: His Life and Work. Second Edition. Crown 8vo, 7s. 6d.

Henri Perreyve and his Counsels to the Sick. Small crown 8vo, 5s.

One and a Half in Norway. A Chronicle of Small Beer. By Either and Both. Small crown 8vo, 3s. 6*d.*

O'NEIL, the late Rev. Lord.—**Sermons.** With Memoir and Portrait. Crown 8vo, 6*s.*

Essays and Addresses. Crown 8vo, 5*s.*

Only Passport to Heaven, The. By One who has it. Small crown 8vo, 1*s.* 6*d.*

OSBORNE, Rev. W. A.—**The Revised Version of the New Testament.** A Critical Commentary, with Notes upon the Text. Crown 8vo, 5*s.*

OTTLEY, H. Bickersteth.—**The Great Dilemma.** Christ His Own Witness or His Own Accuser. Six Lectures. Second Edition. Crown 8vo, 3*s.* 6*d.*

Our Public Schools—Eton, Harrow, Winchester, Rugby, Westminster, Marlborough, The Charterhouse. Crown 8vo, 6*s.*

OWEN, F. M.—**John Keats :** a Study. Crown 8vo, 6*s.*

Across the Hills. Small crown 8vo, 1*s.* 6*d.*

OWEN, Rev. Robert, B.D.—**Sanctorale Catholicum ;** or, Book of Saints. With Notes, Critical, Exegetical, and Historical. Demy 8vo, 18*s.*

OXONIENSIS.—**Romanism, Protestantism, Anglicanism.** Being a Layman's View of some questions of the Day. Together with Remarks on Dr. Littledale's "Plain Reasons against joining the Church of Rome." Crown 8vo, 3*s.* 6*d.*

PALMER, the late William.—**Notes of a Visit to Russia in 1840-1841.** Selected and arranged by JOHN H. CARDINAL NEWMAN, with Portrait. Crown 8vo, 8*s.* 6*d.*

Early Christian Symbolism. A Series of Compositions from Fresco Paintings, Glasses, and Sculptured Sarcophagi. Edited by the Rev. Provost NORTHCOTE, D.D., and the Rev. Canon BROWNLOW, M.A. With Coloured Plates, folio, 42*s.*, or with Plain Plates, folio, 25*s.*

Parchment Library. Choicely Printed on hand-made paper, limp parchment antique or cloth, 6*s.* ; vellum, 7*s.* 6*d.* each volume.

The Poetical Works of John Milton. 2 vols.

Letters and Journals of Jonathan Swift. Selected and edited, with a Commentary and Notes, by STANLEY LANE POOLE.

De Quincey's Confessions of an English Opium Eater. Reprinted from the First Edition. Edited by RICHARD GARNETT.

The Gospel according to Matthew, Mark, and Luke.

Parchment Library—*continued.*

Selections from the Prose Writings of Jonathan Swift. With a Preface and Notes by STANLEY LANE-POOLE and Portrait.

English Sacred Lyrics.

Sir Joshua Reynolds's Discourses. Edited by EDMUND GOSSE.

Selections from Milton's Prose Writings. Edited by ERNEST MYERS.

The Book of Psalms. Translated by the Rev. T. K. CHEYNE, M.A.

The Vicar of Wakefield. With Preface and Notes by AUSTIN DOBSON.

English Comic Dramatists. Edited by OSWALD CRAWFURD.

English Lyrics.

The Sonnets of John Milton. Edited by MARK PATTISON. With Portrait after Vertue.

French Lyrics. Selected and Annotated by GEORGE SAINTS-BURY. With a Miniature Frontispiece designed and etched by H. G. Glindoni.

Fables by Mr. John Gay. With Memoir by AUSTIN DOBSON, and an Etched Portrait from an unfinished Oil Sketch by Sir Godfrey Kneller.

Select Letters of Percy Bysshe Shelley. Edited, with an Introduction, by RICHARD GARNETT.

The Christian Year. Thoughts in Verse for the Sundays and Holy Days throughout the Year. With Miniature Portrait of the Rev. J. Keble, after a Drawing by G. Richmond, R.A.

Shakspere's Works. Complete in Twelve Volumes.

Eighteenth Century Essays. Selected and Edited by AUSTIN DOBSON. With a Miniature Frontispiece by R. Caldecott.

Q. Horati Flacci Opera. Edited by F. A. CORNISH, Assistant Master at Eton. With a Frontispiece after a design by L. Alma Tadema, etched by Leopold Lowenstam.

Edgar Allan Poe's Poems. With an Essay on his Poetry by ANDREW LANG, and a Frontispiece by Linley Sambourne.

Shakspere's Sonnets. Edited by EDWARD DOWDEN. With a Frontispiece etched by Leopold Lowenstam, after the Death Mask.

English Odes. Selected by EDMUND GOSSE. With Frontispiece on India paper by Hamo Thornycroft, A.R.A.

Parchment Library—*continued.*

Of the Imitation of Christ. By THOMAS À KEMPIS. A revised Translation. With Frontispiece on India paper, from a Design by W. B. Richmond.

Poems: Selected from PERCY BYSSHE SHELLEY. Dedicated to Lady Shelley. With a Preface by RICHARD GARNETT and a Miniature Frontispiece.

PARSLOE, Joseph.—Our Railways. Sketches, Historical and Descriptive. With Practical Information as to Fares and Rates, etc., and a Chapter on Railway Reform. Crown 8vo, 6*s.*

PASCAL, Blaise.—The Thoughts of. Translated from the Text of Auguste Molinier, by C. KEGAN PAUL. Large crown 8vo, with Frontispiece, printed on hand-made paper, parchment antique, or cloth, 12*s.*; vellum, 15*s.*

PAUL, Alexander.—Short Parliaments. A History of the National Demand for frequent General Elections. Small crown 8vo, 3*s.* 6*d.*

PAUL, C. Kegan.—Biographical Sketches. Printed on hand-made paper, bound in buckram. Second Edition. Crown 8vo, 7*s.* 6*d.*

PEARSON, Rev. S.—Week-day Living. A Book for Young Men and Women. Second Edition. Crown 8vo, 5*s.*

PENRICE, Major J.—Arabic and English Dictionary of the Koran. 4to, 21*s.*

PESCHEL, Dr. Oscar.—The Races of Man and their Geographical Distribution. Second Edition. Large crown 8vo, 9*s.*

PHIPSON, E.—The Animal Lore of Shakspeare's Time. Including Quadrupeds, Birds, Reptiles, Fish and Insects. Large post 8vo, 9*s.*

PIDGEON, D.—An Engineer's Holiday; or, Notes of a Round Trip from Long. 0° to 0°. New and Cheaper Edition. Large crown 8vo, 7*s.* 6*d.*

Old World Questions and New World Answers. Second Edition. Large crown 8vo, 7*s.* 6*d.*

Plain Thoughts for Men. Eight Lectures delivered at Forester's Hall, Clerkenwell, during the London Mission, 1884. Crown 8vo, cloth, 1*s.* 6*d*; paper covers, 1*s.*

POE, Edgar Allan.—Works of. With an Introduction and a Memoir by RICHARD HENRY STODDARD. In 6 vols. With Frontispieces and Vignettes. Large crown 8vo, 6*s.* each.

POPE, J. Buckingham. — Railway Rates and Radical Rule. Trade Questions as Election Tests. Crown 8vo, 2*s.* 6*d.*

PRICE, Prof. Bonamy. — Chapters on Practical Political Economy. Being the Substance of Lectures delivered before the University of Oxford. New and Cheaper Edition. Crown 8vo, 5*s.*

Pulpit Commentary, The. (Old Testament Series.) Edited by the Rev. J. S. EXELL, M.A., and the Rev. Canon H. D. M. SPENCE.

> **Genesis.** By the Rev. T. WHITELAW, M.A. With Homilies by the Very Rev. J. F. MONTGOMERY, D.D., Rev. Prof. R. A. REDFORD, M.A., LL.B., Rev. F. HASTINGS, Rev. W. ROBERTS, M.A. An Introduction to the Study of the Old Testament by the Venerable Archdeacon FARRAR, D.D., F.R.S.; and Introductions to the Pentateuch by the Right Rev. H. COTTERILL, D.D., and Rev. T. WHITELAW, M.A. Eighth Edition. 1 vol., 15s.

> **Exodus.** By the Rev. Canon RAWLINSON. With Homilies by Rev. J. ORR, Rev. D. YOUNG, B.A., Rev. C. A. GOODHART, Rev. J. URQUHART, and the Rev. H. T. ROBJOHNS. Fourth Edition. 2 vols., 18s.

> **Leviticus.** By the Rev. Prebendary MEYRICK, M.A. With Introductions by the Rev. R. COLLINS, Rev. Professor A. CAVE, and Homilies by Rev. Prof. REDFORD, LL.B., Rev. J. A. MACDONALD, Rev. W. CLARKSON, B.A., Rev. S. R. ALDRIDGE, LL.B., and Rev. McCHEYNE EDGAR. Fourth Edition. 15s.

> **Numbers.** By the Rev. R. WINTERBOTHAM, LL.B. With Homilies by the Rev. Professor W. BINNIE, D.D., Rev. E. S. PROUT, M.A., Rev. D. YOUNG, Rev. J. WAITE, and an Introduction by the Rev. THOMAS WHITELAW, M.A. Fourth Edition. 15s.

> **Deuteronomy.** By the Rev. W. L. ALEXANDER, D.D. With Homilies by Rev. C. CLEMANCE, D.D., Rev. J. ORR, B.D., Rev. R. M. EDGAR, M.A., Rev. D. DAVIES, M.A. Fourth edition. 15s.

> **Joshua.** By Rev. J. J. LIAS, M.A. With Homilies by Rev. S. R. ALDRIDGE, LL.B., Rev. R. GLOVER, REV. E. DE PRESSENSÉ, D.D., Rev. J. WAITE, B.A., Rev. W. F. ADENEY, M.A.; and an Introduction by the Rev. A. PLUMMER, M.A. Fifth Edition. 12s. 6d.

> **Judges and Ruth.** By the Bishop of Bath and Wells, and Rev. J. MORISON, D.D. With Homilies by Rev. A. F. MUIR, M.A., Rev. W. F. ADENEY, M.A., Rev. W. M. STATHAM, and Rev. Professor J. THOMSON, M.A. Fifth Edition. 10s. 6d.

> **1 Samuel.** By the Very Rev. R. P. SMITH, D.D. With Homilies by Rev. DONALD FRASER, D.D., Rev. Prof. CHAPMAN, and Rev. B. DALE. Sixth Edition. 15s.

> **1 Kings.** By the Rev. JOSEPH HAMMOND, LL.B. With Homilies by the Rev. E. DE PRESSENSÉ, D.D., Rev. J. WAITE, B.A., Rev. A. ROWLAND, LL.B., Rev. J. A. MACDONALD, and Rev. J. URQUHART. Fourth Edition. 15s.

Pulpit Commentary, The—*continued.*

1 Chronicles. By the Rev. Prof. P. C. BARKER, M.A., LL.B. With Homilies by Rev. Prof. J. R. THOMSON, M.A., Rev. R. TUCK, B.A., Rev. W. CLARKSON, B.A., Rev. F. WHITFIELD, M.A., and Rev. RICHARD GLOVER. 15*s.*

Ezra, Nehemiah, and Esther. By Rev. Canon G. RAWLINSON, M.A. With Homilies by Rev. Prof. J. R. THOMSON, M.A., Rev. Prof. R. A. REDFORD, LL.B., M.A., Rev. W. S. LEWIS, M.A., Rev. J. A. MACDONALD, Rev. A. MACKENNAL, B.A., Rev. W. CLARKSON, B.A., Rev. F. HASTINGS, Rev. W. DINWIDDIE, LL.B., Rev. Prof. ROWLANDS, B.A., Rev. G. WOOD, B.A., Rev. Prof. P. C. BARKER, M.A., LL.B., and the Rev. J. S. EXELL, M.A. Sixth Edition. 1 vol., 12*s.* 6*d.*

Jeremiah. (Vol. I.) By the Rev. T. K. CHEYNE, M.A. With Homilies by the Rev. W. F. ADENEY, M.A., Rev. A. F. MUIR, M.A., Rev. S. CONWAY, B.A., Rev. J. WAITE, B.A., and Rev. D. YOUNG, B.A. Second Edition. 15*s.*

Jeremiah (Vol. II.) and Lamentations. By Rev. T. K. CHEYNE, M.A. With Homilies by Rev. Prof. J. R. THOMSON, M.A., Rev. W. F. ADENEY, M.A., Rev. A. F. MUIR, M.A., Rev. S. CONWAY, B.A., Rev. D. YOUNG, B.A. 15*s.*

Pulpit Commentary, The. (New Testament Series.)

St. Mark. By Very Rev. E. BICKERSTETH, D.D., Dean of Lichfield. With Homilies by Rev. Prof. THOMSON, M.A., Rev. Prof. GIVEN, M.A., Rev. Prof. JOHNSON, M.A., Rev. A. ROWLAND, B.A., LL.B., Rev. A. MUIR, and Rev. R. GREEN. Fifth Edition. 2 vols., 21*s.*

The Acts of the Apostles. By the Bishop of Bath and Wells. With Homilies by Rev. Prof. P. C. BARKER, M.A., LL.B., Rev. Prof. E. JOHNSON, M.A., Rev. Prof. R. A. REDFORD, M.A., Rev. R. TUCK, B.A., Rev. W. CLARKSON, B.A. Third Edition. 2 vols., 21*s.*

I. Corinthians. By the Ven. Archdeacon FARRAR, D.D. With Homilies by Rev. Ex-Chancellor LIPSCOMB, LL.D., Rev. DAVID THOMAS, D.D., Rev. D. FRASER, D.D., Rev. Prof. J. R. THOMSON, M.A., Rev. J. WAITE, B.A., Rev. R. TUCK, B.A., Rev. E. HURNDALL, M.A., and Rev. H. BREMNER, B.D. Third Edition. Price 15*s.*

II. Corinthians and Galatians. By the Ven. Archdeacon FARRAR, D.D., and Rev. Preb. E. HUXTABLE. With Homilies by Rev. Ex-Chancellor LIPSCOMB, LL.D., Rev. DAVID THOMAS, D.D., Rev. DONALD FRASER, D.D., Rev. R. TUCK, B.A., Rev. E. HURNDALL, M.A., Rev. Prof. J. R. THOMSON, M.A., Rev. R. FINLAYSON, B.A., Rev. W. F. ADENEY, M.A., Rev. R. M. EDGAR, M.A., and Rev. T. CROSKERRY, D.D. Price 21*s.*

Pulpit Commentary, The. (New Testament Series.)—*continued.*

Ephesians, Phillipians, and Colossians. By the Rev. Prof. W. G. BLAIKIE, D.D., Rev. B. C. CAFFIN, M.A., and Rev. G. G. FINDLAY, B.A. With Homilies by Rev. D. THOMAS, D.D., Rev. R. M. EDGAR, M.A., Rev. R. FINLAYSON, B.A., Rev. W. F. ADENEY, M.A., Rev. Prof. T. CROSKERRY, D.D., Rev. E. S. PROUT, M.A., Rev. Canon VERNON HUTTON, and Rev. U. R. THOMAS, D.D. Price 21*s.*

Hebrews and James. By the Rev. J. BARNBY, D.D., and Rev. Prebendary E. C. S. GIBSON, M.A. With Homiletics by the Rev. C. JERDAN, M.A., LL.B., and Rev. Prebendary E. C. S. GIBSON. And Homilies by the Rev. W. JONES, Rev. C. NEW, Rev. D. YOUNG, B.A., Rev. J. S. BRIGHT, Rev. T. F. LOCKYER, B.A., and Rev. C. JERDAN, M.A., LL.B. Price 15*s.*

PUNCHARD, E. G., D.D.—**Christ of Contention.** Three Essays. Fcap. 8vo, 2*s.*

PUSEY, Dr.—**Sermons for the Church's Seasons from Advent to Trinity.** Selected from the Published Sermons of the late EDWARD BOUVERIE PUSEY, D.D. Crown 8vo, 5*s.*

RANKE, Leopold von.—**Universal History.** The oldest Historical Group of Nations and the Greeks. Edited by G. W. PROTHERO. Demy 8vo, 16*s.*

RENDELL, J. M.—**Concise Handbook of the Island of Madeira.** With Plan of Funchal and Map of the Island. Fcap. 8vo, 1*s.* 6*d.*

REYNOLDS, Rev. J. W.—**The Supernatural in Nature.** A Verification by Free Use of Science. Third Edition, Revised and Enlarged. Demy 8vo, 14*s.*

The Mystery of Miracles. Third and Enlarged Edition. Crown 8vo, 6*s.*

The Mystery of the Universe; Our Common Faith. Demy 8vo, 14*s.*

RIBOT, Prof. Th.—**Heredity:** A Psychological Study on its Phenomena, its Laws, its Causes, and its Consequences. Second Edition. Large crown 8vo, 9*s.*

RIMMER, William, M.D.—**Art Anatomy.** A Portfolio of 81 Plates. Folio, 70*s.*, nett.

ROBERTSON, The late Rev. F. W., M.A.—**Life and Letters of.** Edited by the Rev. STOPFORD BROOKE, M.A.

 I. Two vols., uniform with the Sermons. With Steel Portrait. Crown 8vo, 7*s.* 6*d.*
 II. Library Edition, in Demy 8vo, with Portrait. 12*s.*
 III. A Popular Edition, in 1 vol. Crown 8vo, 6*s.*

Sermons. Four Series. Small crown 8vo, 3*s.* 6*d.* each.

The Human Race, and other Sermons. Preached at Cheltenham, Oxford, and Brighton. New and Cheaper Edition. Small crown 8vo, 3*s.* 6*d.*

ROBERTSON, The late Rev. F. W., M.A.—continued.

Notes on Genesis. New and Cheaper Edition. Small crown 8vo, 3*s.* 6*d.*

Expository Lectures on St. Paul's Epistles to the Corinthians. A New Edition. Small crown 8vo, 5*s.*

Lectures and Addresses, with other Literary Remains. A New Edition. Small crown 8vo, 5*s.*

An Analysis of Tennyson's " In Memoriam." (Dedicated by Permission to the Poet-Laureate.) Fcap. 8vo, 2*s.*

The Education of the Human Race. Translated from the German of GOTTHOLD EPHRAIM LESSING. Fcap. 8vo, 2*s.* 6*d.*

The above Works can also be had, bound in half morocco.
*** A Portrait of the late Rev. F. W. Robertson, mounted for framing, can be had, 2*s.* 6*d.*

*ROMANES, G. J.—***Mental Evolution in Animals.** With a Posthumous Essay on Instinct by CHARLES DARWIN, F.R.S. Demy 8vo, 12*s.*

ROOSEVELT, Theodore. **Hunting Trips of a Ranchman.** Sketches of Sport on the Northern Cattle Plains. With 26 Illustrations. Royal 8vo, 18*s.*

Rosmini's Origin of Ideas. Translated from the Fifth Italian Edition of the Nuovo Saggio *Sull' origine delle idee.* 3 vols. Demy 8vo, cloth, 16*s.* each.

Rosmini's Psychology. 3 vols. Demy 8vo. [Vols. I. and II. now ready, 16*s.* each.

Rosmini's Philosophical System. Translated, with a Sketch of the Author's Life, Bibliography, Introduction, and Notes by THOMAS DAVIDSON. Demy 8vo, 16*s.*

*RULE, 'Martin, M.A.—***The Life and Times of St. Anselm, Archbishop of Canterbury and Primate of the Britains.** 2 vols. Demy 8vo, 32*s.*

*SAMUEL, Sydney M.—***Jewish Life in the East.** Small crown 8vo, 3*s.* 6*d.*

*SARTORIUS, Ernestine.—***Three Months in the Soudan.** With 11 Full-page Illustrations. Demy 8vo, 14*s.*

*SAYCE, Rev. Archibald Henry.—***Introduction to the Science of Language.** 2 vols. Second Edition. Large post 8vo, 21*s.*

*SCOONES, W. Baptiste.—***Four Centuries of English Letters:** A Selection of 350 Letters by 150 Writers, from the Period of the Paston Letters to the Present Time. Third Edition. Large crown 8vo, 6*s.*

*SEE, Prof. Germain.—***Bacillary Phthisis of the Lungs.** Translated and edited for English Practitioners by WILLIAM HENRY WEDDELL, M.R.C.S. Demy 8vo, 10*s.* 6*d.*

Shakspere's Works. The Avon Edition, 12 vols., fcap. 8vo, cloth, 18*s.* ; in cloth box, 21*s.* ; bound in 6 vols., cloth, 15*s.*

SHILLITO, Rev. Joseph.—**Womanhood :** its Duties, Temptations, and Privileges. A Book for Young Women. Third Edition. Crown 8vo, 3*s.* 6*d.*

SIDNEY, Algernon.—**A Review.** By GERTRUDE M. IRELAND BLACKBURNE. Crown 8vo, 6*s.*

Sister Augustine, Superior of the Sisters of Charity at the St. Johannis Hospital at Bonn. Authorised Translation by HANS THARAU, from the German "Memorials of AMALIE VON LASAULX." Cheap Edition. Large crown 8vo, 4*s.* 6*d.*

SKINNER, James.—**A Memoir.** By the Author of "Charles Lowder." With a Preface by the Rev. Canon CARTER, and Portrait. Large crown, 7*s.* 6*d.*

   *** Also a cheap Edition. With Portrait. Crown 8vo, 3*s.* 6*d.*

SMITH, Edward, M.D., LL.B., F.R.S.—**Tubercular Consumption in its Early and Remediable Stages.** Second Edition. Crown 8vo, 6*s.*

SMITH, Sir W. Cusack, Bart.—**Our War Ships.** A Naval Essay. Crown 8vo, 5*s.*

Spanish Mystics. By the Editor of " Many Voices." Crown 8vo, 5*s.*

Specimens of English Prose Style from Malory to Macaulay. Selected and Annotated, with an Introductory Essay, by GEORGE SAINTSBURY. Large crown 8vo, printed on handmade paper, parchment antique or cloth, 12*s.* ; vellum, 15*s.*

SPEDDING, James.—**Reviews and Discussions, Literary, Political, and Historical not relating to Bacon.** Demy 8vo, 12*s.* 6*d.*

   Evenings with a Reviewer ; or, Macaulay and Bacon. With a Prefatory Notice by G. S. VENABLES, Q.C. 2 vols. Demy 8vo, 18*s.*

STAPFER, Paul.—**Shakespeare and Classical Antiquity :** Greek and Latin Antiquity as presented in Shakespeare's Plays. Translated by EMILY J. CAREY. Large post 8vo, 12*s.*

STATHAM, F. Reginald.—**Free Thought and Truth Thought.** A Contribution to an Existing Argument. Crown 8vo, 6*s.*

STEVENSON, Rev. W. F.—**Hymns for the Church and Home.** Selected and Edited by the Rev. W. FLEMING STEVENSON.

      The Hymn Book consists of Three Parts :—I. For Public Worship.—II. For Family and Private Worship.—III. For Children. SMALL EDITION. Cloth limp, 10*d.* ; cloth boards, 1*s.* LARGE TYPE EDITION. Cloth limp, 1*s.* 3*d.* ; cloth boards, 1*s.* 6*d.*

Stray Papers on Education, and Scenes from School Life. By B. H. Second Edition. Small crown 8vo, 3*s.* 6*d.*

STREATFEILD, Rev. G. S., M.A.—**Lincolnshire and the Danes.** Large crown 8vo, 7*s.* 6*d.*

STRECKER-WISLICENUS.—**Organic Chemistry.** Translated and Edited, with Extensive Additions, by W. R. HODGKINSON, Ph.D., and A. J. GREENAWAY, F.I.C. Second and cheaper Edition. Demy 8vo, 12*s*. 6*d*.

Suakin, 1885 ; being a Sketch of the Campaign of this year. By an Officer who was there. Second Edition. Crown 8vo, 2*s*. 6*d*.

SULLY, James, M.A.—**Pessimism :** a History and a Criticism. Second Edition. Demy 8vo, 14*s*.

Sunshine and Sea. A Yachting Visit to the Channel Islands and Coast of Brittany. With Frontispiece from a Photograph and 24 Illustrations. Crown 8vo, 6*s*.

SWEDENBORG, Eman.—**De Cultu et Amore Dei ubi Agitur de Telluris ortu, Paradiso et Vivario, tum de Primogeniti Seu Adami Nativitate Infantia, et Amore.** Crown 8vo, 6*s*.

   On the Worship and Love of God. Treating of the Birth of the Earth, Paradise, and the Abode of Living Creatures. Translated from the original Latin. Crown 8vo, 7*s*. 6*d*.

   Prodromus Philosophiæ Ratiocinantis de Infinito, et Causa Finali Creationis : deque Mechanismo Operationis Animæ et Corporis. Edidit THOMAS MURRAY GORMAN, M.A. Crown 8vo, 7*s*. 6*d*.

TACITUS.—**The Agricola.** A Translation. Small crown 8vo, 2*s*. 6*d*.

TAYLOR, Rev. Isaac.—**The Alphabet.** An Account of the Origin and Development of Letters. With numerous Tables and Facsimiles. 2 vols. Demy 8vo, 36*s*.

TAYLOR, Jeremy.—**The Marriage Ring.** With Preface, Notes, and Appendices. Edited by FRANCIS BURDETT MONEY COUTTS. Small crown 8vo, 2*s*. 6*d*.

TAYLOR, Sedley. — **Profit Sharing between Capital and Labour.** To which is added a Memorandum on the Industrial Partnership at the Whitwood Collieries, by ARCHIBALD and HENRY BRIGGS, with remarks by SEDLEY TAYLOR. Crown 8vo, 2*s*. 6*d*.

"They Might Have Been Together Till the Last." An Essay on Marriage, and the position of Women in England. Small crown 8vo, 2*s*.

Thirty Thousand Thoughts. Edited by the Rev. CANON SPENCE, Rev. J. S. EXELL, and Rev. CHARLES NEIL. 6 vols. Super royal 8vo.

               [Vols. I.–IV. now ready, 16*s*. each.

THOM, J. Hamilton.—**Laws of Life after the Mind of Christ.** Two Series. Crown 8vo, 7*s*. 6*d*. each.

THOMPSON, Sir H.—**Diet in Relation to Age and Activity.** Fcap. 8vo, cloth, 1*s*. 6*d*. ; Paper covers, 1*s*.

TIPPLE, Rev. S. A.—Sunday Mornings at Norwood. Prayers and Sermons. Crown 8vo, 6s.

TODHUNTER, Dr. J.—A Study of Shelley. Crown 8vo, 7s.

TOLSTOI, Count Leo.—Christ's Christianity. Translated from the Russian. Large crown 8vo, 7s. 6d.

TRANT, William.—Trade Unions: Their Origin, Objects, and Efficacy. Small crown 8vo, 1s. 6d.; paper covers, 1s.

TREMENHEERE, Hugh Seymour, C.B.—A Manual of the Principles of Government, as set forth by the Authorities of Ancient and Modern Times. New and Enlarged Edition. Crown 8vo, 3s. 6d. Cheap Edition, limp cloth, 1s.

TRENCH, The late R. C., Archbishop.—Notes on the Parables of Our Lord. Fourteenth Edition. 8vo, 12s.

Notes on the Miracles of Our Lord. Twelfth Edition. 8vo, 12s.

Studies in the Gospels. Fifth Edition, Revised. 8vo, 10s. 6d.

Brief Thoughts and Meditations on Some Passages in Holy Scripture. Third Edition. Crown 8vo, 3s. 6d.

Synonyms of the New Testament. Ninth Edition, Enlarged. 8vo, 12s.

Selected Sermons. Crown 8vo, 6s.

On the Authorized Version of the New Testament. Second Edition. 8vo, 7s.

Commentary on the Epistles to the Seven Churches in Asia. Fourth Edition, Revised. 8vo, 8s. 6d.

The Sermon on the Mount. An Exposition drawn from the Writings of St. Augustine, with an Essay on his Merits as an Interpreter of Holy Scripture. Fourth Edition, Enlarged. 8vo, 10s. 6d.

Shipwrecks of Faith. Three Sermons preached before the University of Cambridge in May, 1867. Fcap. 8vo, 2s. 6d.

Lectures on Mediæval Church History. Being the Substance of Lectures delivered at Queen's College, London. Second Edition. 8vo, 12s.

English, Past and Present. Thirteenth Edition, Revised and Improved. Fcap. 8vo, 5s.

On the Study of Words. Nineteenth Edition, Revised. Fcap. 8vo, 5s.

Select Glossary of English Words Used Formerly in Senses Different from the Present. Fifth Edition, Revised and Enlarged. Fcap. 8vo, 5s.

Proverbs and Their Lessons. Seventh Edition, Enlarged. Fcap. 8vo, 4s.

Poems. Collected and Arranged anew. Ninth Edition. Fcap. 8vo, 7s. 6d.

TRENCH, The late R. C., Archbishop.—continued.

Poems. Library Edition. 2 vols. Small crown 8vo, 10s.

Sacred Latin Poetry. Chiefly Lyrical, Selected and Arranged for Use. Third Edition, Corrected and Improved. Fcap. 8vo, 7s.

A Household Book of English Poetry. Selected and Arranged, with Notes. Fourth Edition, Revised. Extra fcap. 8vo, 5s. 6d.

An Essay on the Life and Genius of Calderon. With Translations from his "Life's a Dream" and "Great Theatre of the World." Second Edition, Revised and Improved. Extra fcap. 8vo, 5s. 6d.

Gustavus Adolphus in Germany, and other Lectures on the Thirty Years' War. Second Edition, Enlarged. Fcap. 8vo, 4s.

Plutarch : his Life, his Lives, and his Morals. Second Edition, Enlarged. Fcap. 8vo, 3s. 6d.

Remains of the late Mrs. Richard Trench. Being Selections from her Journals, Letters, and other Papers. New and Cheaper Issue. With Portrait. 8vo, 6s.

TUKE, Daniel Hack, M.D., F.R.C.P.—Chapters in the History of the Insane in the British Isles. With Four Illustrations. Large crown 8vo, 12s.

TWINING, Louisa.—Workhouse Visiting and Management during Twenty-Five Years. Small crown 8vo, 2s.

TYLER, J.—The Mystery of Being : or, What Do We Know ? Small crown 8vo, 3s. 6d.

VAUGHAN, H. Halford.—New Readings and Renderings of Shakespeare's Tragedies. 3 vols. Demy 8vo, 12s. 6d. each.

VILLARI, Professor.—Niccolò Machiavelli and his Times. Translated by LINDA VILLARI. 4 vols. Large post 8vo, 48s.

VILLIERS, The Right Hon. C. P.—Free Trade Speeches of. With Political Memoir. Edited by a Member of the Cobden Club. 2 vols. With Portrait. Demy 8vo, 25s.

   **** People's Edition. 1 vol. Crown 8vo, limp cloth, 2s. 6d.

VOGT, Lieut.-Col. Hermann.—The Egyptian War of 1882. A translation. With Map and Plans. Large crown 8vo, 6s.

VOLCKXSOM, E. W. v.—Catechism of Elementary Modern Chemistry. Small crown 8vo, 3s.

WALLER, Rev. C. B.—The Apocalypse, reviewed under the Light of the Doctrine of the Unfolding Ages, and the Restitution of All Things. Demy 8vo, 12s.

The Bible Record of Creation viewed in its Letter and Spirit. Two Sermons preached at St. Paul's Church, Woodford Bridge. Crown 8vo, 1s. 6d.

WALPOLE, Chas. George.—**A Short History of Ireland from the Earliest Times to the Union with Great Britain.** With 5 Maps and Appendices. Second Edition. Crown 8vo, 6*s*.

WARD, William George, Ph.D.—**Essays on the Philosophy of Theism.** Edited, with an Introduction, by WILFRID WARD. 2 vols. Demy 8vo, 21*s*.

WARD, Wilfrid.—**The Wish to Believe.** A Discussion Concerning the Temper of Mind in which a reasonable Man should undertake Religious Inquiry. Small crown 8vo, 5*s*.

WARTER, J. W.—**An Old Shropshire Oak.** 2 vols. Demy 8vo, 28*s*.

WEDDERBURN, Sir David, Bart., M.P.—**Life of.** Compiled from his Journals and Writings by his sister, Mrs. E. H. PERCIVAL. With etched Portrait, and facsimiles of Pencil Sketches. Demy 8vo, 14*s*.

WEDMORE, Frederick.—**The Masters of Genre Painting.** With Sixteen Illustrations. Post 8vo, 7*s*. 6*d*.

WHITE, R. E.—**Recollections of Woolwich during the Crimean War and Indian Mutiny, and of the Ordnance and War Departments;** together with complete Lists of Past and Present Officials of the Royal Arsenal, etc. Crown 8vo, 2*s*. 6*d*.

WHITNEY, Prof. William Dwight.—**Essentials of English Grammar,** for the Use of Schools. Second Edition. Crown 8vo, 3*s*. 6*d*.

WHITWORTH, George Clifford.—**An Anglo-Indian Dictionary:** a Glossary of Indian Terms used in English, and of such English or other Non-Indian Terms as have obtained special meanings in India. Demy 8vo, cloth, 12*s*.

WILLIAMS, Rowland, D.D.—**Psalms, Litanies, Counsels, and Collects for Devout Persons.** Edited by his Widow. New and Popular Edition. Crown 8vo, 3*s*. 6*d*.

Stray Thoughts from the Note Books of the late Rowland Williams, D.D. Edited by his Widow. Crown 8vo, 3*s*. 6*d*.

WILSON, Lieut.-Col. C. T.—**The Duke of Berwick, Marshal of France, 1702-1734.** Demy 8vo, 15*s*.

WILSON, Mrs. R. F.—**The Christian Brothers.** Their Origin and Work. With a Sketch of the Life of their Founder, the Ven. JEAN BAPTISTE, de la Salle. Crown 8vo, 6*s*.

WOLTMANN, Dr. Alfred, and WOERMANN, Dr. Karl.—**History of Painting.** With numerous Illustrations. Vol. I. Painting in Antiquity and the Middle Ages. Medium 8vo, 28*s*., bevelled boards, gilt leaves, 30*s*. Vol. II. The Painting of the Renascence.

YOUMANS, Eliza A.—**First Book of Botany.** Designed to Cultivate the Observing Powers of Children. With 300 Engravings. New and Cheaper Edition. Crown 8vo, 2*s.* 6*d.*

YOUMANS, Edward L., M.D.—**A Class Book of Chemistry,** on the Basis of the New System. With 200 Illustrations. Crown 8vo, 5*s.*

THE INTERNATIONAL SCIENTIFIC SERIES.

I. **Forms of Water:** a Familiar Exposition of the Origin and Phenomena of Glaciers. By J. Tyndall, LL.D., F.R.S. With 25 Illustrations. Ninth Edition. 5*s.*

II. **Physics and Politics;** or, Thoughts on the Application of the Principles of "Natural Selection" and "Inheritance" to Political Society. By Walter Bagehot. Seventh Edition. 4*s.*

III. **Foods.** By Edward Smith, M.D., LL.B., F.R.S. With numerous Illustrations. Eighth Edition. 5*s.*

IV. **Mind and Body:** the Theories of their Relation. By Alexander Bain, LL.D. With Four Illustrations. Seventh Edition. 4*s.*

V. **The Study of Sociology.** By Herbert Spencer. Twelfth Edition. 5*s.*

VI. **On the Conservation of Energy.** By Balfour Stewart, M.A., LL.D., F.R.S. With 14 Illustrations. Sixth Edition. 5*s.*

VII. **Animal Locomotion;** or Walking, Swimming, and Flying. By J. B. Pettigrew, M.D., F.R.S., etc. With 130 Illustrations. Third Edition. 5*s.*

VIII. **Responsibility in Mental Disease.** By Henry Maudsley, M.D. Fourth Edition. 5*s.*

IX. **The New Chemistry.** By Professor J. P. Cooke. With 31 Illustrations. Eighth Edition, remodelled and enlarged. 5*s.*

X. **The Science of Law.** By Professor Sheldon Amos. Sixth Edition. 5*s.*

XI. **Animal Mechanism:** a Treatise on Terrestrial and Aerial Locomotion. By Professor E. J. Marey. With 117 Illustrations. Third Edition. 5*s.*

XII. **The Doctrine of Descent and Darwinism.** By Professor Oscar Schmidt. With 26 Illustrations. Sixth Edition. 5*s.*

XIII. **The History of the Conflict between Religion and Science.** By J. W. Draper, M.D., LL.D. Nineteenth Edition. 5*s.*

XIV. **Fungi:** their Nature, Influences, Uses, etc. By M. C. Cooke, M.D., LL.D. Edited by the Rev. M. J. Berkeley, M.A., F.L.S. With numerous Illustrations. Third Edition. 5*s.*

XV. **The Chemical Effects of Light and Photography.** By Dr. Hermann Vogel. With 100 Illustrations. Fourth Edition. 5*s.*

XVI. **The Life and Growth of Language.** By Professor William Dwight Whitney. Fifth Edition. 5*s.*

XVII. **Money and the Mechanism of Exchange.** By W. Stanley Jevons, M.A., F.R.S. Seventh Edition. 5*s.*

XVIII. **The Nature of Light.** With a General Account of Physical Optics. ·By Dr. Eugene Lommel. With 188 Illustrations and a Table of Spectra in Chromo-lithography. Third Edition. 5*s.*

XIX. **Animal Parasites and Messmates.** By P. J. Van Beneden. With 83 Illustrations. Third Edition. 5*s.*

XX. **Fermentation.** By Professor Schützenberger. With 28 Illustrations. Fourth Edition. 5*s.*

XXI. **The Five Senses of Man.** By Professor Bernstein. With 91 Illustrations. Fifth Edition. 5*s.*

XXII. **The Theory of Sound in its Relation to Music.** By Professor Pietro Blaserna. With numerous Illustrations. Third Edition. 5*s.*

XXIII. **Studies in Spectrum Analysis.** By J. Norman Lockyer, F.R.S. With six photographic Illustrations of Spectra, and numerous engravings on Wood. Third Edition. 6*s.* 6*d.*

XXIV. **A History of the Growth of the Steam Engine.** By Professor R. H. Thurston. With numerous Illustrations. Third Edition. 6*s.* 6*d.*

XXV. **Education as a Science.** By Alexander Bain, LL.D. Fifth Edition. 5*s.*

XXVI. **The Human Species.** By Professor A. de Quatrefages. Third Edition. 5*s.*

XXVII. **Modern Chromatics.** With Applications to Art and Industry. By Ogden N. Rood. With 130 original Illustrations. Second Edition. 5*s.*

XXVIII. **The Crayfish :** an Introduction to the Study of Zoology. By Professor T. H. Huxley. With 82 Illustrations. Fourth Edition. 5*s.*

XXIX. **The Brain as an Organ of Mind.** By H. Charlton Bastian, M.D. With numerous Illustrations. Third Edition. 5*s.*

XXX. **The Atomic Theory.** By Prof. Wurtz. Translated by G. Cleminshaw, F.C.S. Fourth Edition. 5*s.*

XXXI. **The Natural Conditions of Existence as they affect Animal Life.** By Karl Semper. With 2 Maps and 106 Woodcuts. Third Edition. 5*s.*

XXXII. **General Physiology of Muscles and Nerves.** By Prof. J. Rosenthal. Third Edition. With Illustrations. 5*s.*

D

XXXIII. **Sight** : an Exposition of the Principles of Monocular and Binocular Vision. By Joseph le Conte, LL.D. Second Edition. With 132 Illustrations. 5*s.*

XXXIV. **Illusions** : a Psychological Study. By James Sully. Second Edition. 5*s.*

XXXV. **Volcanoes : what they are and what they teach.** By Professor J. W. Judd, F.R.S. With 92 Illustrations on Wood. Third Edition. 5*s.*

XXXVI. **Suicide** : an Essay on Comparative Moral Statistics. By Prof. H. Morselli. Second Edition. With Diagrams. 5*s.*

XXXVII. **The Brain and its Functions.** By J. Luys. With Illustrations. Second Edition. 5*s.*

XXXVIII. **Myth and Science** : an Essay. By Tito Vignoli. Second Edition. 5*s.*

XXXIX. **The Sun.** By Professor Young. With Illustrations. Second Edition. 5*s.*

XL. **Ants, Bees, and Wasps** : a Record of Observations on the Habits of the Social Hymenoptera. By Sir John Lubbock, Bart., M.P. With 5 Chromo-lithographic Illustrations. Eighth Edition. 5*s.*

XLI. **Animal Intelligence.** By G. J. Romanes, LL.D., F.R.S. Third Edition. 5*s.*

XLII. **The Concepts and Theories of Modern Physics.** By J. B. Stallo. Third Edition. 5*s.*

XLIII. **Diseases of the Memory** ; An Essay in the Positive Psychology. By Prof. Th. Ribot. Second Edition. 5*s.*

XLIV. **Man before Metals.** By N. Joly, with 148 Illustrations. Third Edition. 5*s.*

XLV. **The Science of Politics.** By Prof. Sheldon Amos. Third Edition. 5*s.*

XLVI. **Elementary Meteorology.** By Robert H. Scott. Third Edition. With Numerous Illustrations. 5*s.*

XLVII. **The Organs of Speech and their Application in the Formation of Articulate Sounds.** By Georg Hermann Von Meyer. With 47 Woodcuts. 5*s.*

XLVIII. **Fallacies.** A View of Logic from the Practical Side. By Alfred Sidgwick. 5*s.*

XLIX. **Origin of Cultivated Plants.** By Alphonse de Candolle. 5*s.*

L. **Jelly-Fish, Star-Fish, and Sea-Urchins.** Being a Research on Primitive Nervous Systems. By G. J. Romanes. With Illustrations. 5*s.*

LI. **The Common Sense of the Exact Sciences.** By the late William Kingdon Clifford. Second Edition. With 100 Figures. 5*s.*

LII. **Physical Expression: Its Modes and Principles.** By Francis Warner, M.D., F.R.C.P. With 50 Illustrations. 5*s.*

LIII. **Anthropoid Apes.** By Robert Hartmann. With 63 Illustrations. 5*s.*

LIV. **The Mammalia in their Relation to Primeval Times.** By Oscar Schmidt. With 51 Woodcuts. 5*s.*

LV. **Comparative Literature.** By H. Macaulay Posnett, LL.D. 5*s.*

LVI. **Earthquakes and other Earth Movements.** By Prof. John Milne. With 38 Figures. 5*s.*

LVII. **Microbes, Ferments, and Moulds.** By E. L. Trouessart. With 107 Illustrations. 5*s.*

MILITARY WORKS.

BRACKENBURY, Col. C. B., R.A.—**Military Handbooks for Regimental Officers.**

I. **Military Sketching and Reconnaissance.** By Col. F. J. Hutchison and Major H. G. MacGregor. Fourth Edition. With 15 Plates. Small crown 8vo, 4*s.*

II. **The Elements of Modern Tactics Practically applied to English Formations.** By Lieut.-Col. Wilkinson Shaw. Fifth Edition. With 25 Plates and Maps. Small crown 8vo, 9*s.*

III. **Field Artillery.** Its Equipment, Organization and Tactics. By Major Sisson C. Pratt, R.A. With 12 Plates. Second Edition. Small crown 8vo, 6*s.*

IV. **The Elements of Military Administration.** First Part: Permanent System of Administration. By Major J. W. Buxton. Small crown 8vo. 7*s.* 6*d.*

V. **Military Law: Its Procedure and Practice.** By Major Sisson C. Pratt, R.A. Second Edition. Small crown 8vo, 4*s.* 6*d.*

VI. **Cavalry in Modern War.** By Col. F. Chenevix Trench. Small crown 8vo, 6*s.*

VII. **Field Works.** Their Technical Construction and Tactical Application. By the Editor, Col. C. B. Brackenbury, R.A. Small crown 8vo.

BRENT, Brig.-Gen. J. L.—**Mobilizable Fortifications and their Controlling Influence in War.** Crown 8vo, 5*s.*

BROOKE, Major, C. K.—**A System of Field Training.** Small crown 8vo, cloth limp, 2*s.*

CLERY, C., Lieut.-Col.—**Minor Tactics.** With 26 Maps and Plans. Seventh Edition, Revised. Crown 8vo, 9*s.*

COLVILE, Lieut.-Col. C. F.—**Military Tribunals.** Sewed, 2*s. 6d.*

CRAUFURD, Capt. H. J.—**Suggestions for the Military Training of a Company of Infantry.** Crown 8vo, 1*s. 6d.*

HAMILTON, Capt. Ian, A.D.C.—**The Fighting of the Future.** 1*s.*

HARRISON, Col. R.—**The Officer's Memorandum Book for Peace and War.** Fourth Edition, Revised throughout. Oblong 32mo, red basil, with pencil, 3*s. 6d.*

Notes on Cavalry Tactics, Organisation, etc. By a Cavalry Officer. With Diagrams. Demy 8vo, 12*s.*

PARR, Capt. H. Hallam, C.M.G.—**The Dress, Horses, and Equipment of Infantry and Staff Officers.** Crown 8vo, 1*s.*

SCHAW, Col. H.—**The Defence and Attack of Positions and Localities.** Third Edition, Revised and Corrected. Crown 8vo, 3*s. 6d.*

STONE, Capt. F. Gleadowe, R.A.—**Tactical Studies from the Franco-German War of 1870–71.** With 22 Lithographic Sketches and Maps. Demy 8vo, 30*s.*

WILKINSON, H. Spenser, Capt. 20th Lancashire R.V.—**Citizen Soldiers.** Essays towards the Improvement of the Volunteer Force. Crown 8vo, 2*s. 6d.*

POETRY.

ADAM OF ST. VICTOR.—**The Liturgical Poetry of Adam of St. Victor.** From the text of GAUTIER. With Translations into English in the Original Metres, and Short Explanatory Notes, by DIGBY S. WRANGHAM, M.A. 3 vols. Crown 8vo, printed on hand-made paper, boards, 21*s.*

AUCHMUTY, A. C.—**Poems of English Heroism :** From Brunanburh to Lucknow ; from Athelstan to Albert. Small crown 8vo, 1*s. 6d.*

BARNES, William.—**Poems of Rural Life, in the Dorset Dialect.** New Edition, complete in one vol. Crown 8vo, 8*s. 6d.*

BAYNES, Rev. Canon H. R.—**Home Songs for Quiet Hours.** Fourth and Cheaper Edition. Fcap. 8vo, cloth, 2*s. 6d.*

BEVINGTON, L. S.—**Key Notes.** Small crown 8vo, 5*s.*

BLUNT, Wilfrid Scawen.—**The Wind and the Whirlwind.** Demy 8vo, 1*s. 6d.*

BLUNT, Wilfred Scawen—continued.
> The Love Sonnets of Proteus. Fifth Edition, 18mo. Cloth extra, gilt top, 5*s.*

BOWEN, H. C., M.A.—Simple English Poems. English Literature for Junior Classes. In Four Parts. Parts I., II., and III., 6*d.* each, and Part IV., 1*s.* Complete, 3*s.*

BRYANT, W. C.—Poems. Cheap Edition, with Frontispiece. Small crown 8vo, 3*s.* 6*d.*

Calderon's Dramas: the Wonder-Working Magician — Life is a Dream—the Purgatory of St. Patrick. Translated by DENIS FLORENCE MACCARTHY. Post 8vo, 10*s.*

Camoens Lusiads. — Portuguese Text, with Translation by J. J. AUBERTIN. Second Edition. 2 vols. Crown 8vo, 12*s.*

CAMPBELL, Lewis.—Sophocles. The Seven Plays in English Verse. Crown 8vo, 7*s.* 6*d.*

CERVANTES.—Journey to Parnassus. Spanish Text, with Translation into English Tercets, Preface, and Illustrative Notes, by JAMES Y. GIBSON. Crown 8vo, 12*s.*

> Numantia: a Tragedy. Translated from the Spanish, with Introduction and Notes, by JAMES Y. GIBSON. Crown 8vo, printed on hand-made paper, 5*s.*

CHAVANNES, Mary Charlotte. — A Few Translations from Victor Hugo and other Poets. Small crown 8vo, 2*s.* 6*d.*

CHRISTIE, A. J.—The End of Man. With 4 Autotype Illustrations. 4to, 10*s.* 6*d.*

Chronicles of Christopher Columbus. A Poem in 12 Cantos. By M. D. C. Crown 8vo, 7*s.* 6*d.*

CLARKE, Mary Cowden.—Honey from the Weed. Verses. Crown 8vo, 7*s.*

COXHEAD, Ethel.—Birds and Babies. Imp. 16mo. With 33 Illustrations. Gilt, 2*s.* 6*d.*

DE BERANGER.—A Selection from his Songs. In English Verse. By WILLIAM TOYNBEE. Small crown 8vo, 2*s.* 6*d.*

DENNIS, J.—English Sonnets. Collected and Arranged by. Small crown 8vo, 2*s.* 6*d.*

DE VERE, Aubrey.—Poetical Works.
> I. THE SEARCH AFTER PROSERPINE, etc. 6*s.*
> II. THE LEGENDS OF ST. PATRICK, etc. 6*s.*
> III. ALEXANDER THE GREAT, etc. 6*s.*

> The Foray of Queen Meave, and other Legends of Ireland's Heroic Age. Small crown 8vo, 5*s.*

> Legends of the Saxon Saints. Small crown 8vo, 6*s.*

D 3

DOBSON, Austin.—Old World Idylls and other Verses. Sixth Edition. Elzevir 8vo, gilt top, 6*s*.

> **At the Sign of the Lyre.** Fourth Edition. Elzevir 8vo, gilt top, 6*s*.

DOMETT, Alfred.—**Ranolf and Amohia.** A Dream of Two Lives. New Edition, Revised. 2 vols. Crown 8vo, 12*s*.

Dorothy : a Country Story in Elegiac Verse. With Preface. Demy 8vo, 5*s*.

DOWDEN, Edward, LL.D.—**Shakspere's Sonnets.** With Introduction and Notes. Large post 8vo, 7*s*. 6*d*.

Dulce Cor : being the Poems of Ford Berêton. With Two Illustrations. Crown 8vo, 6*s*.

DUTT, Toru.—**A Sheaf Gleaned in French Fields.** New Edition. Demy 8vo, 10*s*. 6*d*.

> **Ancient Ballads and Legends of Hindustan.** With an Introductory Memoir by EDMUND GOSSE. Second Edition, 18mo. Cloth extra, gilt top, 5*s*.

EDWARDS, Miss Betham.—**Poems.** Small crown 8vo, 3*s*. 6*d*.

ELDRYTH, Maud.—**Margaret,** and other Poems. Small crown 8vo, 3*s*. 6*d*.

> **All Soul's Eve,** "**No God,**" and other Poems. Fcap. 8vo, 3*s*. 6*d*.

ELLIOTT, Ebenezer, The Corn Law Rhymer.—**Poems.** Edited by his son, the Rev. EDWIN ELLIOTT, of St. John's, Antigua. 2 vols. Crown 8vo, 18*s*.

English Verse. Edited by W. J. LINTON and R. H. STODDARD. 5 vols. Crown 8vo, cloth, 5*s*. each.
> I.   CHAUCER TO BURNS.
> II. TRANSLATIONS.
> III. LYRICS OF THE NINETEENTH CENTURY.
> IV. DRAMATIC SCENES AND CHARACTERS.
> V.   BALLADS AND ROMANCES.

ENIS.—**Gathered Leaves.** Small crown 8vo, 3*s*. 6*d*.

EVANS, Anne.—**Poems and Music.** With Memorial Preface by ANN THACKERAY RITCHIE. Large crown 8vo, 7*s*.

GOODCHILD, John A.—**Somnia Medici.** Two series. Small crown 8vo, 5*s*. each.

GOSSE, Edmund W.—**New Poems.** Crown 8vo, 7*s*. 6*d*.

> **Firdausi in Exile,** and other Poems. Elzevir 8vo, gilt top, 6*s*.

GRINDROD, Charles.—**Plays from English History.** Crown 8vo, 7*s*. 6*d*.

> **The Stranger's Story,** and his Poem, The Lament of Love : An Episode of the Malvern Hills. Small crown 8vo, 2*s*. 6*d*.

GURNEY, Rev. Alfred.—The Vision of the Eucharist, and other Poems. Crown 8vo, 5*s*.

A Christmas Faggot. Small crown 8vo, 5*s*.

HENRY, Daniel, Junr.—Under a Fool's Cap. Songs. Crown 8vo, cloth, bevelled boards, 5*s*.

HEYWOOD, J. C.—Herodias, a Dramatic Poem. New Edition, Revised. Small crown 8vo, 5*s*.

Antonius. A Dramatic Poem. New Edition, Revised. Small crown 8vo, 5*s*.

HICKEY, E. H.—A Sculptor, and other Poems. Small crown 8vo, 5*s*.

HOLE, W. G.—Procris, and other Poems. Fcap. 8vo, 3*s*. 6*d*.

KEATS, John.—Poetical Works. Edited by W. T. ARNOLD. Large crown 8vo, choicely printed on hand-made paper, with Portrait in *eau-forte*. Parchment or cloth, 12*s*. ; vellum, 15*s*.

KING, Mrs. Hamilton.—The Disciples. Eighth Edition, and Notes. Small crown 8vo, 5*s*.

A Book of Dreams. Crown 8vo, 3*s*. 6*d*.

KNOX, The Hon. Mrs. O. N.—Four Pictures from a Life, and other Poems. Small crown 8vo, 3*s*. 6*d*.

LANG, A.—XXXII Ballades in Blue China. Elzevir 8vo, 5*s*.

Rhymes à la Mode. With Frontispiece by E. A. Abbey. Elzevir 8vo, cloth extra, gilt top, 5*s*.

LAWSON, Right Hon. Mr. Justice.—Hymni Usitati Latine Redditi : with other Verses. Small 8vo, parchment, 5*s*.

Lessing's Nathan the Wise. Translated by EUSTACE K. CORBETT. Crown 8vo, 6*s*.

Life Thoughts. Small crown 8vo, 2*s*. 6*d*.

Living English Poets MDCCCLXXXII. With Frontispiece by Walter Crane. Second Edition. Large crown 8vo. Printed on hand-made paper. Parchment or cloth, 12*s*. ; vellum, 15*s*.

LOCKER, F.—London Lyrics. Tenth Edition. With Portrait, Elzevir 8vo. Cloth extra, gilt top, 5*s*.

Love in Idleness. A Volume of Poems. With an Etching by W. B. Scott. Small crown 8vo, 5*s*.

LUMSDEN, Lieut.-Col. H. W.—Beowulf : an Old English Poem. Translated into Modern Rhymes. Second and Revised Edition. Small crown 8vo, 5*s*.

LYSAGHT, Sidney Royse.—A Modern Ideal. A Dramatic Poem. Small crown 8vo, 5*s*.

MACGREGOR, Duncan.—Clouds and Sunlight. Poems. Small crown 8vo, 5*s*.

MAGNUSSON, Eirikr, M.A., and *PALMER, E. H., M.A.*—Johan Ludvig Runeberg's Lyrical Songs, Idylls, and Epigrams. Fcap. 8vo, 5*s*.

MAKCLOUD, Even.—Ballads of the Western Highlands and Islands of Scotland. Small crown 8vo, 3*s*. 6*d*.

MC'NAUGHTON, J. H.—Onnalinda. A Romance. Small crown 8vo, 7*s*. 6*d*.

MEREDITH, Owen [*The Earl of Lytton*].—Lucile. New Edition. With 32 Illustrations. 16mo, 3*s*. 6*d*. Cloth extra, gilt edges, 4*s*. 6*d*.

MORRIS, Lewis.—Poetical Works of. New and Cheaper Editions, with Portrait. Complete in 3 vols., 5*s*. each.
> Vol. I. contains "Songs of Two Worlds." Eleventh Edition.
> Vol. II. contains "The Epic of Hades." Twentieth Edition.
> Vol. III. contains "Gwen" and "The Ode of Life." Sixth Edition.

The Epic of Hades. With 16 Autotype Illustrations, after the Drawings of the late George R. Chapman. 4to, cloth extra, gilt leaves, 21*s*.

The Epic of Hades. Presentation Edition. 4to, cloth extra, gilt leaves, 10*s*. 6*d*.

Songs Unsung. Fifth Edition. Fcap. 8vo, 5*s*.

The Lewis Morris Birthday Book. Edited by S. S. COPEMAN, with Frontispiece after a Design by the late George R. Chapman. 32mo, cloth extra, gilt edges, 2*s*.; cloth limp, 1*s*. 6*d*.

MORSHEAD, E. D. A.—The House of Atreus. Being the Agamemnon, Libation-Bearers, and Furies of Æschylus. Translated into English Verse. Crown 8vo, 7*s*.

The Suppliant Maidens of Æschylus. Crown 8vo, 3*s*. 6*d*.

MOZLEY, J. Rickards.—The Romance of Dennell. A Poem in Five Cantos. Crown 8vo, 7*s*. 6*d*.

MULHOLLAND, Rosa.—Vagrant Verses. Small crown 8vo, 5*s*.

NOEL, The Hon. Roden.—A 'Little Child's Monument. Third Edition. Small crown 8vo, 3*s*. 6*d*.

The House of Ravensburg. New Edition. Small crown 8vo, 6*s*.

The Red Flag, and other Poems. New Edition. Small crown 8vo, 6*s*.

Songs of the Heights and Deeps. Crown 8vo, 6*s*.

OBBARD, Constance Mary.—Burley Bells. Small crown 8vo, 3*s*. 6*d*.

O'HAGAN, John.—The Song of Roland. Translated into English Verse. New and Cheaper Edition. Crown 8vo, 5*s*.

PFEIFFER, Emily.—The Rhyme of the Lady of the Rock, and How it Grew. Second Edition. Small crown 8vo, 3*s*. 6*d*.

PFEIFFER, Emily—continued.
>Gerard's Monument, and other Poems. Second Edition. Crown 8vo, 6s.
>Under the Aspens: Lyrical and Dramatic. With Portrait. Crown 8vo, 6s.

PIATT, J. J.—Idyls and Lyrics of the Ohio Valley. Crown 8vo, 5s.

PIATT, Sarah M. B.—A Voyage to the Fortunate Isles, and other Poems. 1 vol. Small crown 8vo, gilt top, 5s.
>In Primrose Time. A New Irish Garland. Small crown 8vo, 2s. 6d.

Rare Poems of the 16th and 17th Centuries. Edited W. J. LINTON. Crown 8vo, 5s.

RHOADES, James.—The Georgics of Virgil. Translated into English Verse. Small crown 8vo, 5s.
>Poems. Small crown 8vo, 4s. 6d.

ROBINSON, A. Mary F.—A Handful of Honeysuckle. Fcap. 8vo, 3s. 6d.
>The Crowned Hippolytus. Translated from Euripides. With New Poems. Small crown 8vo, 5s.

ROUS, Lieut.-Col.—Conradin. Small crown 8vo, 2s.

SANDYS, R. H.—Egeus, and other Poems. Small crown 8vo, 3s. 6d.

SCHILLER, Friedrich.—Wallenstein. A Drama. Done in English Verse, by J. A. W. HUNTER, M.A. Crown 8vo, 7s. 6d.

SCOTT, E. J. L.—The Eclogues of Virgil.—Translated into English Verse. Small crown 8vo, 3s. 6d.

SCOTT, George F. E.—Theodora and other Poems. Small crown 8vo, 3s. 6d.

SEYMOUR, F. H. A.—Rienzi. A Play in Five Acts. Small crown 8vo, 5s.

Shakspere's Works. The Avon Edition, 12 vols., fcap. 8vo, cloth, 18s.; and in box, 21s.; bound in 6 vols., cloth, 15s.

SHERBROOKE, Viscount.—Poems of a Life. Second Edition. Small crown 8vo, 2s. 6d.

SMITH, J. W. Gilbart.—The Loves of Vandyck. A Tale of Genoa. Small crown 8vo, 2s. 6d.
>The Log o' the "Norseman." Small crown 8vo, 5s.

Songs of Coming Day. Small crown 8vo, 3s. 6d.

Sophocles: The Seven Plays in English Verse. Translated by LEWIS CAMPBELL. Crown 8vo, 7s. 6d.

SPICER, Henry.—Haska: a Drama in Three Acts (as represented at the Theatre Royal, Drury Lane, March 10th, 1877). Third Edition. Crown 8vo, 3s. 6d.
>Uriel Acosta, in Three Acts. From the German of Gatzkow. Small crown 8vo, 2s. 6d.

SYMONDS, John Addington.—Vagabunduli Libellus.   Crown 8vo, 6s.

Tasso's Jerusalem Delivered.   Translated by Sir JOHN KINGSTON JAMES, Bart.   Two Volumes.   Printed on hand-made paper, parchment, bevelled boards.   Large crown 8vo, 21s.

TAYLOR, Sir H.—Works.   Complete in Five Volumes.   Crown 8vo, 30s.
>   Philip Van Artevelde.   Fcap. 8vo, 3s. 6d.
>   The Virgin Widow, etc.   Fcap. 8vo, 3s. 6d.
>   The Statesman.   Fcap. 8vo, 3s. 6d.

TAYLOR, Augustus.—Poems.   Fcap. 8vo, 5s.

TAYLOR, Margaret Scott.—"Boys Together," and other Poems.   Small crown 8vo, 6s.

TODHUNTER, Dr. J.—Laurella, and other Poems.   Crown 8vo, 6s. 6d.
>   Forest Songs.   Small crown 8vo, 3s. 6d.
>   The True Tragedy of Rienzi : a Drama.   3s. 6d.
>   Alcestis : a Dramatic Poem.   Extra fcap. 8vo, 5s.
>   Helena in Troas.   Small crown 8vo, 2s. 6d.

TYLER, M. C.—Anne Boleyn.   A Tragedy in Six Acts.   Second Edition.   Small crown 8vo, 2s. 6d.

TYNAN, Katherine.—Louise de la Valliere, and other Poems.   Small crown 8vo, 3s. 6d.

WEBSTER, Augusta.—In a Day : a Drama.   Small crown 8vo, 2s. 6d.
>   Disguises : a Drama.   Small crown 8vo, 5s.

Wet Days.   By a Farmer.   Small crown 8vo, 6s.

WOOD, Rev. F. H.—Echoes of the Night, and other Poems.   Small crown 8vo, 3s. 6d.

Wordsworth Birthday Book, The.   Edited by ADELAIDE and VIOLET WORDSWORTH.   32mo, limp cloth, 1s. 6d. ; cloth extra, 2s.

YOUNGMAN, Thomas George.—Poems.   Small crown 8vo, 5s.

YOUNGS, Ella Sharpe.—Paphus, and other Poems.   Small crown 8vo, 3s. 6d.
>   A Heart's Life, Sarpedon, and other Poems.   Small crown 8vo, 3s. 6d.

NOVELS AND TALES.

"All But : " a Chronicle of Laxenford Life.   By PEN OLIVER, F.R.C.S.   With 20 Illustrations.   Second Edition.   Crown 8vo, 6s.

BANKS, Mrs. G. L.—God's Providence House.   New Edition.   Crown 8vo, 3s. 6d.

CHICHELE, Mary.—Doing and Undoing.   A Story.   Crown 8vo, 4s. 6d.

Danish Parsonage.   By an Angler.   Crown 8vo, 6s.

HUNTER, Hay.—The Crime of Christmas Day. A Tale of the
Latin Quarter. By the Author of "My Ducats and my
Daughter." 1*s*.

HUNTER, Hay, and WHYTE, Walter.—My Ducats and My
Daughter. New and Cheaper Edition. With Frontispiece.
Crown 8vo, 6*s*.

Hurst and Hanger. A History in Two Parts. 3 vols. 31*s*. 6*d*.

INGELOW, Jean.—Off the Skelligs : a Novel. With Frontispiece.
Second Edition. Crown 8vo, 6*s*.

JENKINS, Edward.—A Secret of Two Lives. Crown 8vo, 2*s*. 6*d*.

KIELLAND, Alexander L.—Garman and Worse. A Norwegian
Novel. Authorized Translation, by W. W. Kettlewell. Crown
8vo, 6*s*.

MACDONALD, G.—Donal Grant. A Novel. Second Edition.
With Frontispiece. Crown 8vo, 6*s*.

   Castle Warlock. A Novel. Second Edition. With Frontispiece. Crown 8vo, 6*s*.

   Malcolm. With Portrait of the Author engraved on Steel.
Seventh Edition. Crown 8vo, 6*s*.

   The Marquis of Lossie. Sixth Edition. With Frontispiece.
Crown 8vo, 6*s*.

   St. George and St. Michael. Fifth Edition. With Frontispiece. Crown 8vo, 6*s*.

   What's Mine's Mine. Second Edition. With Frontispiece.
Crown 8vo, 6*s*.

   Annals of a Quiet Neighbourhood. Fifth Edition. With
Frontispiece. Crown 8vo, 6*s*.

   The Seaboard Parish : a Sequel to "Annals of a Quiet Neighbourhood." Fourth Edition. With Frontispiece. Crown 8vo, 6*s*.

   Wilfred Cumbermede. An Autobiographical Story. Fourth
Edition. With Frontispiece. Crown 8vo, 6*s*.

MALET, Lucas.—Colonel Enderby's Wife. A Novel. New and
Cheaper Edition. With Frontispiece. Crown 8vo, 6*s*.

MULHOLLAND, Rosa.—Marcella Grace. An Irish Novel. Crown
8vo.

PALGRAVE, W. Gifford.—Hermann Agha : an Eastern Narrative.
Third Edition. Crown 8vo, 6*s*.

SHAW, Flora L.—Castle Blair : a Story of Youthful Days. New and
Cheaper Edition. Crown 8vo, 3*s*. 6*d*.

STRETTON, Hesba.—Through a Needle's Eye : a Story. New
and Cheaper Edition, with Frontispiece. Crown 8vo, 6*s*.

TAYLOR, Col. Meadows, C.S.I., M.R.I.A.—Seeta : a Novel. With
Frontispiece. Crown 8vo, 6*s*.

   Tippoo Sultaun : a Tale of the Mysore War. With Frontispiece.
Crown 8vo, 6*s*.

   Ralph Darnell. With Frontispiece. Crown 8vo, 6*s*.

   A Noble Queen. With Frontispiece. Crown 8vo, 6*s*.

   The Confessions of a Thug. With Frontispiece. Crown 8vo, 6*s*.

   Tara : a Mahratta Tale. With Frontispiece. Crown 8vo, 6*s*.

   Within Sound of the Sea. With Frontispiece. Crown 8vo, 6*s*.

BOOKS FOR THE YOUNG.

Brave Men's Footsteps. A Book of Example and Anecdote for Young People. By the Editor of "Men who have Risen." With 4 Illustrations by C. Doyle. Eighth Edition. Crown 8vo, 3s. 6d.

COXHEAD, Ethel.—**Birds and Babies.** Imp. 16mo. With 33 Illustrations. Cloth gilt, 2s. 6d.

DAVIES, G. Christopher.—**Rambles and Adventures of our School Field Club.** With 4 Illustrations. New and Cheaper Edition. Crown 8vo, 3s. 6d.

EDMONDS, Herbert.—**Well Spent Lives:** a Series of Modern Biographies. New and Cheaper Edition. Crown 8vo, 3s. 6d.

EVANS, Mark.—**The Story of our Father's Love,** told to Children. Sixth and Cheaper Edition of Theology for Children. With 4 Illustrations. Fcap. 8vo, 1s. 6d.

JOHNSON, Virginia W.—**The Catskill Fairies.** Illustrated by Alfred Fredericks. 5s.

MAC KENNA, S. J.—**Plucky Fellows.** A Book for Boys. With 6 Illustrations. Fifth Edition. Crown 8vo, 3s. 6d.

REANEY, Mrs. G. S.—**Waking and Working;** or, From Girlhood to Womanhood. New and Cheaper Edition. With a Frontispiece. Crown 8vo, 3s. 6d.

    Blessing and Blessed: a Sketch of Girl Life. New and Cheaper Edition. Crown 8vo, 3s. 6d.

    Rose Gurney's Discovery. A Story for Girls. Dedicated to their Mothers. Crown 8vo, 3s. 6d.

    English Girls: Their Place and Power. With Preface by the Rev. R. W. Dale. Fourth Edition. Fcap. 8vo, 2s. 6d.

    Just Anyone, and other Stories. Three Illustrations. Royal 16mo, 1s. 6d.

    Sunbeam Willie, and other Stories. Three Illustrations. Royal 16mo, 1s. 6d.

    Sunshine Jenny, and other Stories. Three Illustrations. Royal 16mo, 1s. 6d.

STOCKTON, Frank R.—**A Jolly Fellowship.** With 20 Illustrations. Crown 8vo, 5s.

STORR, Francis, and TURNER, Hawes.—**Canterbury Chimes;** or, Chaucer Tales re-told to Children. With 6 Illustrations from the Ellesmere Manuscript. Third Edition. Fcap. 8vo, 3s. 6d.

STRETTON, Hesba.—**David Lloyd's Last Will.** With 4 Illustrations. New Edition. Royal 16mo, 2s. 6d.

WHITAKER, Florence.—**Christy's Inheritance.** A London Story. Illustrated. Royal 16mo, 1s. 6d.